Global Community

Global Community

*The Role of International Organizations
in the Making of the Contemporary World*

Akira Iriye

UNIVERSITY OF CALIFORNIA PRESS

Berkeley   Los Angeles   London

To Lucy Marie

University of California Press
Berkeley and Los Angeles, California

University of California Press, Ltd.
London, England

© 2002 by the Regents of the University of California

Originally presented as the Jefferson Memorial Lectures at
Berkeley

Library of Congress Cataloging-in-Publication Data

Iriye, Akira.
    Global community : the role of international
organizations in the contemporary world / Akira Iriye.
        p.   cm.
    Includes bibliographical references and index.
    ISBN 0–520–23127–9 (cloth : alk. paper). —
    1. Non-governmental organizations.   I. Title.

JZ4841 .I75   2002
327'.06 — dc21   2001004247

Manufactured in the United States of America
10   09   08   07   06   05   04   03   02   01
10 9 8 7 6 5 4 3 2 1

The paper used in this publication is both acid-free and
totally chlorine-free (TCF). It meets the minimum
requirements of ANSI/NISO Z39.48–1992 (R 1997)
(*Permanence of Paper*). ⊖

CONTENTS

PREFACE

I am grateful to the University of California, Berkeley, for the invitation it graciously extended to me to deliver the Thomas Jefferson Memorial Lecture in the spring of 2000. The invitation gave me the impetus to complete this manuscript; my lecture was based on one of the chapters.

I must admit that the world I describe in the book, the world in which international organizations play an important role in establishing connections among different parts of the globe, is not exactly a Jeffersonian one. Thomas Jefferson's world, both in reality and in his vision, was very different, where only a handful of international organizations existed — and, we could add, only a small number of independent nations as well. How he would view the contemporary international situation and the role of the United States in it is an interesting question. But I am not attempting to answer it. My aim here is to trace the historical evolution of international organizations, both governmental and nongovernmental, since the nineteenth century, in particular during the last fifty years, and to show how they have contributed to the making of the contemporary world. That world, it seems to me, is an arena for an increasingly complex interplay of states and nonstate actors, including multinational corporations, religious organizations, regional communities, transnational private associations, and even stateless persons. It is in many ways a chaotic world, but at the same time many of these actors are making efforts to establish interconnections among nations and peoples so as to develop a sense of global community. Forces encouraging global inter-connectedness on one hand and local identities on the other exist simultaneously, but if universalism and localism can come together to contribute to the development of a stable world order, international organizations will play an important role in the process, for many of them express the aspirations of people everywhere for peace, justice, and interdependence.

In that very broad sense, international organizations may exemplify some Jeffersonian principles. Thomas Jefferson's ideas about foreign affairs are often characterized as isolationist, eschewing international complications and giving priority to the cultivation of the American pastoral utopia. Yet he was never a parochial thinker. Not only did the Declaration of Independence that he authored address the aspirations of the whole of humanity, to such an extent that many countries have copied it in their own struggles for freedom, but his personal writings were sprinkled with references to "the opinion of the world," "the reason and freedom of the globe," and other concepts that are also the guiding principles of many international organizations. For they are founded on the assumption that there are such things as world public opinion and common human values, and they see themselves as manifestations of this global consciousness. When Jefferson insisted that "between society and society the same moral duties exist" as between individuals, he was anticipating the philosophy of the international organizations that would be founded precisely on the same idea.[1] How to connect the United States with the rest of the world was as keen an issue in Jefferson's age as it is today, and it would not be too far-fetched to argue that he would have preferred international connections to be made out of shared interests and values, as those organizations do, and not out of self-centered ambitions and dogmas. In United States foreign affairs today, among the most crucial questions are first, whether there exist international norms that guide the conduct of nations, and second, what role the nation should play in the development and implementation of those norms. With regard to both questions, it behooves us to recall the Jeffersonian tradition as well as the manifold activities by international organizations.

It has taken many years to complete this small volume. It does something I have not attempted systematically before: to focus on nonstate actors in a study of international relations. I have written about formal affairs among certain states and about transnational cultural relations in general. But this is my first attempt at examining international organizations as an integral part of modern world history. The presentation is necessarily impressionistic; I have been arbitrary in choosing a small number of examples from hundreds of thousands of organizations, many of which have published their own histories and have made available through the Internet descriptions of their current activities. I have not tried to summarize such information, even with respect to the few organizations that I do mention. My purpose has been not to catalogue international organizations but rather to try to understand their role in the making of the world today. Since this is essentially my first plunge into new territory, I have relied on the work of the pioneering scholars in this field, as well as the advice of professional colleagues with whom I have been privileged to exchange ideas. As always, I have been a beneficiary of contributions by my current and former students. Frank Ninkovich in particular has been a most valuable critic of my ideas, and Robert David Johnson has saved me from a number of errors at the final stages of the manuscript's preparation. Hugh McNeil and Lee Hampton have been tireless and conscientious research assistants at the beginning and at the end of this project, respectively. For providing me with Japanese material on nongovernmental organizations, I am grateful to Professor Gen'ichi Saitō of Kokushikan University. For the errors of fact or judgment that I am sure still remain in the book, I alone am responsible. I am eager to hear comments and criticisms from readers, as I hope to continue studying the subject as part of a reexamination of the history of the modern world.

Introduction

This book seeks to examine the roles that international organizations play in modern world affairs. There are three principal reasons for undertaking this task. First, there is the obvious fact that international organizations have steadily grown in number and in the scope and variety of their activities since the late nineteenth century, to such an extent that the contemporary world would be incomprehensible without taking them into consideration. Second, most writings on modern world affairs, especially by historians, have nevertheless almost entirely ignored this fact. This scholarly void somehow must be filled. And finally, a focus on international organizations, rather than nations and states, as units of analysis provides a fresh perspective on the evolution of international relations and enables us to reconceptualize modern world history. For example, the phenomenon known as globalization might be better understood if we examined the ways in which international organizations have for decades been seeking to establish transnational connections, politically, economically, and culturally.

Roughly speaking, there are two types of international organizations: intergovernmental organizations and international nongovernmental organizations. The former category consists of institutions that come into existence through formal agreements among nations and represent their respective governments. The United Nations is the best-known example, but several thousands of them exist today. The latter, in contrast, refers to associations that are established by private individuals and groups. According to the Economic and Social Council of the United Nations, any international organization that is not established by an agreement among governments is an international nongovernmental organization.[1] This, however, is too broad a definition, and in this study a nongovernmental organization will be more narrowly construed as a voluntary nonstate, nonprofit, nonreligious, and nonmilitary association. The voluntary nature of these organizations — that is, their openness to all those who wish to join — distinguishes them from others that are restricted to certain categories of people, whether nationality, gender, religion, class, region, or any other division. Business enterprises in most countries are, of course, nongovernmental organizations, but their profit-seeking nature distinguishes them fundamentally from the rest. Churches, synagogues, cemeteries, and other religious bodies are also mostly nongovernmental institutions, but for the sake of analysis, this book will mention them only when their activities are secular, such as humanitarian relief and cultural exchange, rather than confessional or evangelical. The distinction is a tenuous one, but to include a discussion of religious institutions would make the study of nongovernmental organizations, at this stage of scholarship, unmanageable. Last, it seems to make sense to exclude the consideration of terrorist societies and other armed gangs; a nongovernmental organization by definition will not have its own military force, given that, in theory at least, the state is supposed to monopolize arms and "violence." In reality, there are nonstate, indeed antistate, groups with their own arms that engage in violent activities. Although the relationship between such groups and unarmed organizations is a serious question in some parts of the world, this book will touch on the issue only in a few instances, focusing instead on activities by nonmilitary organizations.[2] Thus rather narrowly defined, international nongovernmental organizations constitute only a part of nonstate actors. Even so, there are almost thirty thousand of them today, and one purpose of this book will be to trace their evolution over time.[3]

It would be neither feasible nor meaningful to try to be comprehensive or to generalize about the activities of thousands of international organizations, intergovernmental or nongovernmental. Instead I focus on six types of organizations: those dealing with humanitarian relief, cultural exchange, peace and disarmament, developmental assistance, human rights, and environmentalism.

The choice of these six categories is arbitrary, for many other organized activities exist in the world, as well as alternative ways of categorizing them. Harold Jacobson divides international organizations into three broad types: those concerned with security and peace, with trade and other economic affairs, and with "social welfare and human rights."[4] Evan Luard classifies international organizations by the functions they perform, such as sea transport, energy, and development; altogether Luard lists fifteen different types of functions.[5] Lyman Cromwell White's seminal work on international nongovernmental organizations enumerates twelve fields of activity such organizations are engaged in, ranging from "communications, transport, and travel" to "pursuit of peace."[6] A recent book by Lester M. Salaman and Helmut K. Anheier on nonprofit organizations suggests twelve "major activity groups": culture and recreation; education and research; health; social services; environment; development and housing; law, advocacy, and politics; philanthropic intermediaries and voluntarism promotion; international activities; religion; business and professional associations and unions; and groups "not elsewhere classified." These categories define domestic nongovernmental organizations except for "international activities," which involve cross-national functions and efforts. Within this category Salaman and Anheier include seven types of activities and organizations: exchange/friendship/cultural programs; development assistance associations; international disaster and relief organizations; international human rights and peace organizations; multipurpose international organizations; support and service organizations; auxiliaries, councils, standard setting and governance organizations; and international organizations not elsewhere classified.[7]

These are all useful classificatory schemes. Since, however, this book's main goal is not to be comprehensive but to illustrate the roles that international organizations play in shaping the contemporary world, I focus on those organizations whose activities in the six areas mentioned earlier seem to have made a significant difference in international affairs. However limited in scope, an examination of some of these organizations' agendas and activities seems worthwhile, if only because historians have not paid them the attention they deserve.

Scholars have written volumes on the history of the contemporary world, or more specifically of modern international relations, but few such volumes seem to contain more than a passing reference, if at all, to international organizations.[8] This lack of scholarly attention by historians is puzzling, given that political scientists have carefully studied international organizations since at least the 1970s.[9] Such scholars have produced important surveys and case studies of international organizations, and some writers have incorporated these studies into international relations theory. At the same time, however, the bulk of the political science literature remains nonhistorical. Most writings by nonhistorians on international organizations tend to focus on very recent developments or current phenomena. Even when discussing some episodes from the past, political scientists appear to be more interested in drawing policy-relevant conclusions from them than in placing them in a historical context. While all such work is valuable, historians may have a different perspective and wish for a more systematic examination of the historical development of international organizations, their activities, and their possible impact on world affairs. In this book I attempt to provide such an examination.

One basic and obvious reason why historians of international relations have not been paying sufficient attention to international organizations is their preoccupation with state-centered activities: political, diplomatic, military, and economic. States and their activities constitute geopolitical "realities," and historians have been examining these realities as they have changed over time through interstate interactions and clashes. Writers have focused on such themes as "diplomacy," "the rise and fall of the great powers," "the causes of wars," and "the origins of the First (or the Second) World War," to cite a few examples from books with these titles.[10] So long as one continues to be fascinated by these topics — and of course they remain legitimate objects of scholarly inquiry — it will be easy to neglect international organizations, dismissing them as irrelevant to the diplomatic and military dramas being played out by the states. The same thing may be said of those works that have focused on the economic aspect of international affairs. Apart from a few that present the movement of goods, capital, and labor as worldwide phenomena, most studies by historians seem to retain their national frameworks, examining foreign economic policies of various countries or exploring trade, banking, and other issues among them.[11]

A fundamental assumption seems to underlie the study of international relations through an examination of diplomacy (political and economic) and war: international affairs are seen as a sum of activities of nations as they try to safeguard their respective interests and enhance their power positions in the world while engaging in negotiations and preparing for possible clashes of interest. This is a conflictual (or "anarchical") view of the world, whether conflict is seen as latent or real.[12] In such an anarchical situation, international organizations will be of no importance except as means for promoting national interests. But these organizations will make a difference if one construes world affairs in a different way. If, for instance, one is to explore possibilities for world order rather than anarchy, one will have to take the activities of international organizations more seriously, simply because the majority of these organizations are by definition oriented toward seeking international order, cooperation, and interdependence. Of course, sovereign states may also cooperate with one another to establish some sort of international system, and historians have written volumes on "the Westphalian system," "the Vienna system," "the Versailles system," "the Yalta system," and the like.[13] These systems could be so defined as to exclude any participant except states. But that would be a narrow view of the international system and ignore the fact that international organizations have existed side by side with the states for over a century and have contributed to the making of the contemporary world.

It is true that state-centered approaches to the study of war and diplomacy have begun to be challenged by historians who stress the social, ideological, and cultural bases of a country's foreign affairs and conceptualize international relations as intercultural relations.[14] Excellent monographs have been published on the effect of social relations (involving issues of gender, class, and ethnicity), ideology, and culture (such as historical memory) on foreign policy.[15] While these studies elaborate how such nonstate, nongeopolitical factors have affected the processes of foreign policy decision making, others have examined nonstate, nonofficial dealings across national boundaries, such as missionary activities and cultural exchange programs.[16] All these writings have enriched our understanding of international relations by broadening the scope of inquiry beyond the state. Nevertheless, most of them still take nations as units of analysis; their inquiry may go beyond the formal governmental apparatus and embrace society and individuals, but they assume that social and cultural phenomena, just like diplomatic and military affairs, are comprehensible within a national framework. International organizations have, therefore, little room in such analyses. The world consisting of societies and cultures may be different from one made up of sovereign states, but it is still a world with national and territorial boundaries.

International organizations, on the other hand, assume that there is yet another world, one that is produced by forces that cut across national frontiers. These forces create networks of shared interests and concerns that go beyond national interests and concerns. The transnational migration of people and the deterioration of the natural environment are but two of the most obvious examples. These are transnational phenomena to be addressed as much by intergovernmental organizations and nongovernmental organizations as by independent states. And to the extent that international organizations effectively reflect transnational concerns and in turn strengthen the sense of global, human interdependence, they may be said to be creating an alternative world, one that is not identical with the sum of sovereign states and nations.

The emergence of such a world has been noticed by an increasing number of observers, who have given it various names: "the society world" (to distinguish it from the world of nation-states), "international society," "transnational civil society," and "the global public."[17] These terms describe a global arena in which individuals and organizations other than sovereign states come together and engage in activities separate from those pursued by national governments. That is why terms such as "global civil society" and "transnational civil society" have gained in popularity.[18] "Civil society" is a term that has been long in use to describe domestic nonstate actors, including business enterprises and religious organizations as well as private associations, and it may be difficult to postulate an exact analogue to it in the global context, where there is no super-entity corresponding to the state apparatus. Nevertheless, "international civil society," like "the society world" and similar terms, suggests the existence of a world community that is not interchangeable with the world consisting of independent nations. International organizations may be viewed as one among the many ingredients of transnational civil society, one of many forces that have linked different parts of the world. These forces are, in that sense, more properly called "global," or even "human," than "international." International history may have been in existence only since the seventeenth century, but global history has had a longer life, and human history a longer one yet.

Thus conceived, the study of international organizations may be viewed as one way of examining the phenomenon known as globalization. The scholarly literature on globalization is rapidly growing.[19] A number of sociologists and anthropologists, as well as political scientists and economists (although as yet very few historians), have undertaken to explore the evolution and contemporary characteristics of what has been called "the new realities that mark the last decades of the [twentieth] century."[20] The transformation of human life brought about by global economic and technological linkages has been closely examined, as have the fierce local loyalties and identities that have arisen in opposition to globalizing tendencies.[21] Few studies of globalization, however, have paid attention to the roles that international organizations have played in promoting globalization, in seeking to steer it in a desirable direction, or, though more rarely, resisting aspects of the globalizing force. I hope that the discussion in this book will serve to clarify the relationship between international organizations and globalization.

I have chosen to call this book *Global Community* as a way of describing the role of international organizations in a world that has been increasingly globalizing or becoming globalized. (That the word "globalize" may be used both as a transitive and an intransitive verb is interesting and is a useful reminder that globalization is at once an inexorable material development and a conscious human process.) However, "global community" is not meant to be synonymous with "globalization"; the following chapters do not discuss crucial features of globalization such as technological innovations and the expansion of international financial transactions.[22] Rather, the term suggests the building of transnational networks that are based upon a global consciousness, the idea that there is a wider world over and above separate states and national societies, and that individuals and groups, no matter where they are, share certain interests and concerns in that wider world. This consciousness has to be given some institutional form if it is to become effective — hence the role of international organizations. By examining their history, we shall gain an understanding of one aspect of the phenomenon of globalization and of the historical process that has created transnational, global, and human forces and movements defining the world today.

CHAPTER I

The Origins
of Global Community

How did the global community, both as an idea and as a reality, emerge and develop? This question may be examined in many ways, but one possible approach would be to look at the creation, growth, and activities of international organizations, both governmental and nongovernmental. The number and functioning of these organizations may be taken as a good measure of the degree of "globality" at a given moment in time, a circumstance that contributes to establishing transnational connections and to shaping a world community existing in conjunction with the international order made up of nations. In this and the following chapters, I examine how intergovernmental and international nongovernmental organizations have interacted with each other and with the existing states, in the process transforming the nature of international relations.

For both intergovernmental organizations and international nongovernmental organizations to emerge, nations and peoples had to be strongly aware that they shared certain interests and objectives across national boundaries and that they could best solve their many problems by pooling their resources and effecting transnational cooperation, rather than through individual countries' unilateral efforts. Such a view, such global consciousness, may be termed *internationalism*, the idea that nations and peoples should cooperate instead of preoccupying themselves with their respective national interests or pursuing uncoordinated approaches to promote them. A characteristic of nineteenth- and twentieth-century history was that internationalism grew in strength, as exemplified by the increasing number of nonstate organizations, even as states and nations developed as important definers of people's lives and of world affairs.

Internationalism in the sense of cooperation among states and among governments had always existed, of course, in the shape of alliances, treaties, and agreements. Most of these, however, were temporary measures to ensure the security and interests of the parties involved and did not necessarily presage the construction of a global community with shared concerns and objectives. Through treaties and agreements, the nations of the world periodically sought to establish an international system, however fragile and temporary it might prove, but much more would be involved if they were to organize a global community, what Hedley Bull terms an "international society."[1] Such a community would arise only if nations and their people recognized that some issues affected them equally and that to cope with them, institutions had to be created to establish common rules and to protect their shared interests. This sort of internationalism was reflected, for instance, in various conventions the nations of the world entered into during the nineteenth century to standardize weights and measures, to adopt uniform postal and telegraphic rates, and to cope with the danger of communicable diseases.[2] Some of these conventions led to the establishment of international organizations such as the Universal Postal Union, the International Telegraph Union, and the International Sanitary Council.[3]

These institutions were among the earliest intergovernmental organizations. It is a measure of the maturing of international relations during the nineteenth century that according to one count, their number increased from just one at the beginning of the century to eleven by 1900.[4] The institution that is usually viewed as the first modern intergovernmental organization, the Central Commission for the Navigation of the Rhine, established at the Congress of Vienna in 1815, was limited to participation by central European (mostly German) states, whereas a Superior Council of Health founded in 1838 in Constantinople to deal with the spread of communicable diseases included both Ottoman and European delegates.[5] That inclusiveness was becoming the trend; increasingly, international organizations came to involve members from other parts of the globe in addition to those from Europe.[6] Together with such parallel developments as the codification of international law, the establishment of international courts of arbitration, and the convening of international conferences to discuss ways to prevent war, these organizations attested to awareness that nations existed not simply to provide for the security and interests of their citizens but also to promote the well-being of all of them collectively, and that in the modern world more could be gained through international cooperation than through unilateral action.

It was against the background of these developments that international nongovernmental organizations began to be created in the second half of the nineteenth century. Although a small number — one survey mentions five — of such organizations may have existed prior to 1850, most studies agree that it was in the last decades of the century that many more (numbering about ten every year during the 1890s, for instance) were established.[7] It is not difficult to understand why. For one thing, technological developments, such as the locomotive, the steamship, the telegraph, and the telephone, were bringing peoples of the world into ever closer contact. While such proximity periodically produced friction and conflict, it also gave rise to global consciousness, the idea that efforts should be made to ensure peaceful interactions among peoples of the world through transnational initiatives.

The growth of these initiatives is an important theme in international history at the opening of the twentieth century. Most accounts of that history still tend to be presented in the framework of "the road to war" or "the origins of the World War," as though nothing else mattered. Apart from the fact that there were many roads to the war that erupted in 1914, things might have developed in such a way that one would not even be talking about a road to war. Alternatives to war, and paths to peace, also existed, thanks to the efforts by individuals and organizations that were dedicated to peace. International organizations, particularly of the nongovernmental variety, played a crucial role in this story.

The growth of international nongovernmental organizations was also greatly facilitated by the development of worldwide networks of goods, capital, and labor at the end of the nineteenth century, and at the beginning of the twentieth, the phenomenon known as economic globalization. The relationship between economic growth and the development of such organizations is clear. As more wealth was generated, corporations and individuals were able to finance various private initiatives, best exemplified by the philanthropic organizations that made their appearance in the United States. International nongovernmental organizations could be funded by these foundations as well as by individual donors. Without a flourishing world economy at the beginning of the century, those organizations might have been much slower to develop.

It might be tempting to go a step further and assert, as some do, that nongovernmental organizations were agents of global capitalism, that they promoted the interests of European and American capitalists by forging closer links among distant lands and by spreading certain uniform (i.e., Western) rules and standards of behavior. But that would be ignoring the fact that nongovernmental organizations, at least of the kind that this book describes, were nonprofit bodies engaged in activities that were sometimes at odds with the interests of global capitalism. Globalization contained many elements: technological, economic, organizational, intellectual, artistic, and psychological. To pick just two of these elements and establish a causal connection between them would be a gross oversimplification. Globalization as a state of mind (global consciousness) was always a key ingredient of international organizations, and that cannot be equated with capitalist acquisitiveness.

In an ideological sense, however, capitalism and nongovernmental institutions may be said to have had something in common. Liberalism, the body of thought that emphasized individual rights, initiatives, and freedoms against state authority, provided an ideological underpinning both for entrepreneurs and for philanthropists, both for traders and for organizers of humanitarian endeavors. While liberal ideology had emerged earlier, against eighteenth-century absolutism and mercantilism, it gained new significance toward the end of the nineteenth century, the period that witnessed the emergence of modern states such as Germany, Italy, Russia, and Japan that joined the more established nation-states in Western Europe to constitute the civilized world. (The United States became a modern state after the Civil War.) Precisely because the tendency of these states was to strengthen central governmental authority, there were forces that sought to preserve the autonomy of business activities or to protect the rights of citizens, and quite often such forces fortified themselves through establishing contact across national boundaries. The growth of international nongovernmental organizations was one clear manifestation of this phenomenon.[8] Liberalism in the age of global capitalism was becoming internationalized.

This does not mean, however, that from the beginning international nongovernmental organizations were conceived as antagonistic to state agencies. Most such organizations in fact worked closely with governments. Perhaps the most conspicuous example was the International Red Cross. At first, it was more an intergovernmental than a nongovernmental organization. As is well known, the impetus for its founding came from a Swiss doctor, Jean Henry Dunant, whose *Un souvenir de Solferino* (1862), an account of what he had witnessed at the Battle of Solferino (1859) between Sardinia and France on one side and Austria on the other, appealed to his government to convene an international congress for improving the treatment of the war-wounded.[9] By the time the Swiss government organized such a conference in 1864, a Red Cross had been established in Geneva through private efforts, and similar organizations had begun to appear elsewhere. The governments that were represented at the conference signed a treaty, endorsing the activities of these Red Cross societies, which now formed the International Red Cross with its headquarters in the Swiss city.

The initiative that the Swiss government took, and the fact that an international treaty ratified the establishment of the International Red Cross, suggest that even such a nongovernmental humanitarian agency was intimately connected to existing national governments. This could complicate the operation of such a body. For instance, in 1906, when the Swiss government convened another international conference to consider revision of the 1864 treaty to bring it up-to-date, the Japanese government was adamant that Korea not be invited. Although the Korean government had ratified the original convention, in 1905 Japan had established its protectorate over Korea, and Tokyo now insisted that Japan would henceforth handle Korea's diplomatic affairs. Switzerland relented, and the Korean Red Cross came under the jurisdiction of the Red Cross of Japan. Even the fate of an international nongovernmental organization dedicated to humanitarian assistance could thus be affected by power politics.[10] Besides, national Red Cross societies tended to be "integrated into the plans of both armies and their medical authorities," as John F. Hutchinson notes.[11] The line between the state apparatus and a nonstate organization was never clear-cut.

The same thing may be said of international nongovernmental organizations in the field of cultural and intellectual exchange. The late nineteenth century saw the creation of many such organizations aiming at the exchange of scientists, artists, musicians, and others across national boundaries, thereby establishing what today would be called "epistemic communities" — groups of individuals sharing ideas and interests. But the state was never remote from those undertakings. To cite a typical example, when a world congress of historians was planned for 1898 to be held in Amsterdam, invitations were sent out in the name of the Dutch government and communicated to foreign governments through their ambassadors and ministers in The Hague. Various countries' political leaders were listed on the program as honorary chairmen.[12] In most instances, a foreign government in receipt of the invitation transmitted it to an appropriate agency, such as the ministry of education, and the latter in turn contacted universities, academic societies, and individuals to inform them of the opportunity. Some governments selected scholars to attend The Hague gathering and funded their travels. Similar episodes could be duplicated in the gatherings of geographers, artists, musicians, and others that became more and more numerous in the period preceding the World War.

Likewise, in sanitation and health care, a number of international conferences were held and organizations established around the beginning of the century, such as the Pan-American Sanitary Bureau and the International Central Bureau for the Campaign against Tuberculosis, both founded in 1902. These were international nongovernmental organizations but were closely connected with national medical and health care societies, which in turn were under state supervision in many ways. Thus nongovernmental organizations were never completely independent of national governments. The two often cooperated, and it may be argued that without the support and encouragement of the states, many of the incipient organizations might not have been able to function at all.

Nevertheless, the existence and growth of those organizations, as well as of the international gatherings they sponsored, were not simply another aspect of international relations defined by the interaction of sovereign states. The activities of the nongovernmental organizations, as well as of intergovernmental organizations, were adding a new element to world affairs. This can be seen particularly well in some organizations that functioned quite independently of governmental agencies. For instance, the Esperanto movement grew rapidly at the beginning of the century: there were three Esperanto clubs in 1890, twenty-six in 1900, and eighteen hundred by 1914. Neither these clubs nor the Universal Esperanto Association, created in 1908 as the first international organization of Esperantists, was connected to governmental agencies but instead sought to promote international peace and understanding through cross-national communication.[13]

Another significant development, the growth of international women's organizations, was also independent of state authorities. As Leila J. Rupp has noted, it was toward the end of the nineteenth century that women's associations in the United States and Europe — those "in trades, professions and reforms, as well as . . . those advocating political rights," according to the initial letter of invitation — recognized the need to come together to form an international body. The International Council of Women was established in 1888, followed by a number of similar organizations that, at least in principle, included as members women "of whatever race, nativity, or creed."[14]

As a third example, we may consider the International Olympic Committee, established in 1894 in Lausanne as "the supreme authority" over the holding of the Olympic games. First held in 1896 (as a revival of the sporting event that had taken place in ancient Greece), the games were initially a rather casual and informal affair in which athletes from a small number of countries, mostly European, participated. The concept of sport, as distinguished from games and gymnastic exercises, was a product of late–nineteenth century Western society where people began to have leisure and resources to devote to athletic competition.[15] And there was unquestionably a nationalistic basis to the encouragement of physical strength: to prepare a nation's youth for war. As Kristin Hoganson suggests, nations were stressing manliness as a way to survive in the modern world, and sport was one way to cultivate it.[16] But the key in our context is that the International Olympic Committee from its inception was a nongovernmental organization that made up its own rules about the Olympics, including their location and timing as well as the qualifications of the competing athletes. These rules were to be applied to all countries, and as more and more of them came to participate, the Committee grew into a major international organization that established universal standards quite independent of national governmental authorities.

At the beginning of the century, various religious organizations began to engage in international activities that were social and cultural. Of course, these activities were religious in the broadest sense, but they were not just extensions of the traditional proselytizing efforts but reflected an awareness of the importance of establishing close links with various parts of the world at a time when the globe was becoming smaller. The World's YWCA, founded in 1894 to coordinate activities by national Young Women's Christian Associations, defined one of its objectives as the fostering of "Christian principles of social and international conduct by encouraging the development of a right public conscience such as shall strengthen all those forces which are working for the promotion of peace and better understanding between classes, nations, and races."[17] Such language suggests that religious organizations were becoming interested in international social issues, not just in purely evangelical work. Just as the Social Gospel movement was making headway in the United States domestically in an effort to turn the attention of Christians to the consequences of rapid industrialization and urbanization, internationalization of Christianity was taking place, in which secular endeavors in fields such as education, medicine, and social welfare became objects of the new organizations. In this sense, they fall within our definition of international nongovernmental organizations.

The growth of international organizations, both intergovernmental and nongovernmental, became so conspicuous that in 1910, some of their leaders came together in Brussels to found a center for international organizations: Office Central des Associations Internationales. It was intended as the headquarters for those organizations, a clear indication that they had become too numerous to be ignored. As the editors of *La vie internationale*, the organ of the Office Central, declared in its first issue (1912), the movement of ideas, events, and organizations had come to constitute "international life," penetrating all activities of people, who were no longer confined to their villages, provinces, or countries, and was enveloping "the entire terrestrial globe."[18] The Brussels center, though it functioned more as a clearinghouse of information than as an advocate of particular agendas, showed that the "entire globe" was indeed being covered with ideas and forces that found their expression in international organizations.

Globalization, as a state of mind and as an institutional expression, was dawning. Indeed, some economists argue that global markets and capital transfers were even more extensive in the years before the Great War than today.[19] This was also the time when imperialism — one state's control over other states, lands, and people — became truly global, covering all corners of the earth. Whether the imperialistic states were "the most powerful agents of globalization," as some scholars argue, economic globalization and territorial imperialism undoubtedly reinforced each other.[20] Improvements in transportation and communications technology facilitated the governance of distant lands, while overseas colonies and spheres of influence created networks of interdependencies. In the age of imperialism, aspects of modern civilization, exemplified by hospital facilities, hygienic programs, sewage systems, schools, roads, and the like, began to spread throughout the world, as did the consciousness of human diversity.

Imperialism, however, did not generate internationalism, the sense of global community in which all nations and people shared certain interests and commitments. That had to come from international organizations. The awareness that the constantly increasing number of such organizations reflected the coming of a new age — that of global interdependence — was perhaps best expressed by Leonard Woolf, whose *International Government* (1916) was a remarkable statement of institutional internationalism, not least because it was written and published during the European war. Despite the tragic conflict, Woolf was convinced that "in every department of life the beginnings, and more than the beginnings, of International Government already exist." By "International Government" he did not mean a world government but the conventions, committees, and organizations that nations had set up to serve international interests. According to him, the "recognition of international interests, and that national interests are international interests, and *vice versa*, was the great social discovery of the last 100 years."[21]

Against this background, the coming of war in Europe in 1914 must be seen not merely as yet another story in the drama of power politics, or as some inevitable development proceeding along a predetermined "road to war," but also as an instance when forces of globalization came to serve destructive purposes of nations, rather than being steered in a constructive direction. It had been the task of international organizations to ensure that this latter path would be followed, but in the end it was not. Globalizing forces and global consciousness, which had emerged before 1914, proved inadequate to overcome parochial interests and ambitions of states and peoples. Whatever the intensity of the new global awareness, or however large the number of international organizations, these were powerless to prevent the nations from behaving traditionally, in pursuit of their national interests and concerns. With a few exceptions — perhaps the most notable was the Women's International League for Peace and Freedom, which convened a congress of women in The Hague in the middle of the war — both intergovernmental organizations and international nongovernmental organizations stopped functioning during the war, and many domestic nongovernmental organizations devoted their energies to the war effort. (The Red Cross societies of the belligerent nations worked closely with their armed forces to care for the wounded.)

Nevertheless, the war, which became global with the participation of Japan, China, the United States, and other extra-European states, affected globalization in complex ways. At one level, all the combatants developed weapons (aircraft, submarines, tanks, and larger and faster warships) that could traverse distances much more quickly than ever before. These were used for destructive purposes, but the technology was bound to be utilized for peaceful ends once the conflict stopped. Economically, the World War disrupted patterns of international trade and shipping, especially in Europe, but elsewhere the movements of goods and capital continued, and some countries began to undertake industrialization. As for global consciousness, the war may have strengthened it, even amid the unprecedented mass slaughter. As Leon Trotsky noted in 1917, the war seemed to raise "to new heights the feeling of 'universality,' of awareness of the indissoluble tie between the fate of an individual and the fate of all mankind."[22] Even more important, the Great War never wholly discredited or discouraged internationalist movements. Actually, to an observer such as Woolf, the conflict was "just a little sagging to one side, to violence and stupidity and barbarism," but the fact that international institutions had been created long before the war would ensure that "in ten or fifteen or twenty years' time there will be a sagging to the other side, to what we dimly recognize as progress and civilization."[23]

The task after the war, then, was to continue globalization but to steer it in a more peaceful, constructive direction. And the key, it seemed to Woolf and numerous others, lay in rejuvenating and strengthening international organizations. The renewed faith in the power of international organization was clearly expressed by Mary P. Follett, an American political scientist, who wrote shortly after the United States entered the war against Germany that "the contribution of America to the Great War will be told as America's taking her stand squarely and responsibly on the position that national particularism was in 1917 dead." Nations, she noted, "have fought for national rights," but these "are as obsolete as the individual rights of the last century." What Follett was suggesting was that interdependence of individuals and of nations had become a feature of contemporary life. The war, because it was a product of a contrary (and therefore obsolete) force, was certain to reinforce the commitment to "organized cooperation" in international affairs. This was so because all "interests," "destinies," and "movements" were becoming "internationalized."[24]

In such a perspective, the growth of international organizations in the aftermath of the Great War was not so much a reaction against the brutal and senseless fighting as a resumption of an earlier trend that had been momentarily suspended. According to one source, the number of intergovernmental organizations declined from thirteen before the war to nine in 1920, but during the following ten years, it increased to thirty-one. Even more impressive was that there were more international nongovernmental organizations in 1920 than in 1910: 214 compared with

135. By 1930 the number had reached 375, almost triple the figure on the eve of the war.[25]

Among the new intergovernmental organizations, the League of Nations was the most dramatic example, an embodiment of the prevailing "group psychology," according to Follett.[26] Organization was taken to be the key to postwar international (and national) affairs, so the League was the most conspicuous institutional expression of "the community of nations." It was an international organization with global interests, concerning itself not just with security matters but also with labor, health, cultural, and other issues throughout the world. For these larger tasks, the League established a number of affiliate organizations such as the International Labor Organization and the League of Nations Health Organization, many of which would continue to function throughout the postwar decades until they would become part of the United Nations after the Second World War.

Some of these bodies were not new creations but postwar incarnations of earlier organizations. For instance, the League of Nations Health Organization expanded on the work of a prewar entity, the Office International d'Hygiène Publique, which had been founded in Paris in 1907 to oversee the quarantining of ships and ports affected with plague and cholera.[27] And some of the prewar activities that the International Bureau for the Suppression of Traffic in Women and Children (established in 1899) and other organizations carried out became part of the agenda for the newly established International Labor Organization.[28] One of the most interesting affiliates of the League was the International Committee on Intellectual Cooperation, established in 1922 to promote cultural and intellectual exchanges among nations. This body was envisaged as a committee of intellectuals from all over the world who would represent "a small group of men and women" in each country "who have the means of influencing opinion," as a British spokesman said.[29] Such thinking was hardly new. Before the war, as noted earlier, a number of epistemic communities had come into existence to bring together intellectuals and artists from various parts of the world. In the aftermath of the war, they were more determined than ever to help create a global community transcending national egoisms and interests. A sister organization, the International Institute for Intellectual Cooperation, was set up in Paris in 1926 with initial financial support from the French government. Many other countries from Europe, Latin America, the Middle East, and Asia contributed funds to the institute and created their own national committees on intellectual cooperation. The membership in both organizations of so many countries was typical of postwar internationalism. As was suggested by the fact that the League of Nations started with thirty-two member countries, more than half of which were outside Europe, international organizations now were far more global in scope than before the war.

The same thing can be said of the new intergovernmental organizations that came into being in the aftermath of the Great War. To bodies that had long been in existence, such as the International Telegraph Union and the Universal Postal Union, were now added organizations that reflected the technological changes that were further narrowing temporal and spatial distances among nations: air navigation, long-distance telephones, radio transmission, and the like. The war heralded the coming of the age of the airplane, and the widespread prediction was that peacetime air travel would provide an increasingly important mode of transportation. Already at the Paris peace conference, several nations were able to agree upon a draft "convention for the regulation of aerial navigation," and after its ratification the International Commission for Air Navigation was set up. At this stage, this commission did not internationalize air travel regulations; the 1919 treaty specified that "every Power has complete and exclusive sovereignty over the air space above its territory."[30] Nevertheless, the creation of the International Commission was important, as it worked assiduously throughout the postwar years to establish a uniform air code for all countries. The Commission's efforts would bear fruit during the waning years of the Second World War, when a Chicago conference of 1944 would produce a much-strengthened system for regulating air navigation. In the meantime, long-distance telephone systems had vastly improved during the European war, and after the conflict an international body, the International Consultative Committee for Long-Distance Telephony, was created as the principal body that would recommend the establishment and maintenance of international telephone cables and would conduct joint experiments for technological improvement.[31]

Also at this time, the question of allocating radio frequencies among nations arose. The radiotelegraph had proved vitally important during the war, and the need for expanding and regulating frequencies was well recognized by the victorious powers, which tried to set up an international commission to deal with these matters as soon as the conflict was over. The idea was to assign certain frequencies to each country for radio broadcasting, an ambitious attempt even in the prevailing atmosphere of postwar internationalism. No worldwide governmental agreement was reached at this time, but a nongovernmental organization, the International Broadcasting Union, was established in 1925 as a voluntary institution to make suggestions, some of which were to become the bases for official agreements.[32]

As this last example shows, the relationship between national governments and international organizations, and between intergovernmental and nongovernmental organizations, was already becoming complex. Yet all these organizations tried earnestly in the postwar years to work together to solve problems that faced the whole world. That may be one way of characterizing international relations during the 1920s. Whatever the tensions created among states by such issues as German reparations, inter-Allied debt to the United States, or Soviet propaganda — themes that are stressed in most accounts of the decade — internationalism was being fostered through international organizations working cooperatively among themselves and with state agencies.

To be sure, a lack of cooperation sometimes plagued their work. John F. Hutchinson's recent study of the International Relief Union, created in 1927, offers a good example.[33] Representatives of forty-three countries met in Geneva to establish this organization, which was dedicated to the relief of victims of natural disasters, especially earthquakes. The inspiration came from Giovanni Ciraolo, president of the Italian Red Cross, who naturally expected that the International Committee of the Red Cross would support the initiative. But another international Red Cross organization, the League of Red Cross Societies, had come into existence in 1919, and an often acrimonious rivalry existed between these two organizations. Some national Red Cross societies stood aloof or actively opposed Ciraolo's internationalist agenda. As a result, despite the lofty language that heralded the founding of the organization, it accomplished little in international disaster relief. Such a story suggests that institutional rivalry and personal jealousies were just as conspicuous among international organizations as within governmental institutions. Despite such frustrations, however, the number of international organizations never stopped growing, and they continued to engage in an increasing variety of activities during the decades after the war.

More successful instances of collaboration among different types of organizations may be seen in air navigation and shipping. The previously mentioned International Commission for Air Navigation, an intergovernmental body, was paralleled by the establishment of a nongovernmental organization, the International Air Traffic Association, to study and propose standardization of international traffic rates, timetables, and other services.[34] The Association frequently met to discuss these issues, and its recommendations were then submitted to the Commission for its approval and adoption by nations. In international shipping, the League of Nations was instrumental in promoting agreements on maritime labor, safety, and commerce, but in this work the world body was assisted by the nongovernmental International Shipping Conference, created in 1921.[35]

Nature conservation was also beginning to attract the attention of international, not just national, organizations at this time. "International protection of nature" had been attempted a few times before the war, but the founding of the League of Nations made it possible for private organizations as well as some concerned states to work through the world organization to arrive at specific agreements on conservation of wildlife. Most notably, the League, various national committees, and governments cooperated to produce a convention in 1930 to prohibit killing certain kinds of whales.[36] One of the most enduring of nongovernmental organizations concerned with nature conservancy, the International Council for Bird Preservation, was established in 1922 in London through the initiative of an American ornithologist, T. Gilbert Pearson, a major figure behind the founding of the National Audubon Society.[37]

In the meantime, irrespective of intergovernmental conferences and agreements, international nongovernmental organizations were pursuing their own agendas, enriching the world arena with networks of interdependence. Cultural and social internationalism best describes their activities, since they were all founded on the assumption that cultural and social questions knew no national boundaries and that they required an international framework for solution. A few examples illustrate the impressive variety of their activities. Several nongovernmental organizations were established right after the war to deal with cross-national educational issues. Promoting exchanges among teachers, students, and philosophers of education of different countries appeared to be one important way to prevent another calamitous war in which young men of school and university age had suffered the bulk of casualties. Thus in the immediate aftermath of the war, the International Confederation of Students was organized in Brussels to "create bonds of esteem and friendship between students throughout the world," the International Federation of University Women in London to "promote understanding and friendship between university women in all countries," and the World Association for Adult Education, also in London, to promote "continuing education" among workers, prisoners, and many others.[38] A large number of scientists, mathematicians, and geographers, on their part, created an International Research Council in 1919 in London to "coordinate international efforts in the different branches of science and its applications."[39] Several of their members were to play important roles in the creation of the International Council of Scientific Unions, organized in 1931 to bring together the world's scientific community.[40] Virtually all of these organizations were initiated by Europeans and had their headquarters in European cities, obviously reflecting the sense of urgency felt in the wake of the war to promote mutual cooperation and understanding. From the beginning, however, these associations included members from other parts of the world, and their periodic conferences typically attracted participants from the Middle East, Asia, the Pacific, North America, and Latin America.

Comparable in importance to educational institutions were the new service organizations, which, together with those established before the war, focused on international relief work. In 1919, for instance, the Save the Children Fund was established in Britain, which became the Save the Children International Union in the following year, to coordinate efforts at providing help to starving children in various parts of the world. The Union's philosophy was unmistakably internationalist; as one of its statements declared, "In relief of suffering neither national nor political distinctions are to be taken to account."[41] Also in 1920, a French pacifist, Pierre Ceresole, founded Service Civil International, to organize work camps in France and other countries to help with community development and to diffuse wartime hostilities.[42] A pacifist organization in the United States, the American Friends Service Committee, had been established in 1917 to engage in nonmilitary service during the war, and after the conflict ended, it continued to engage in international relief and educational activities. Although more "a national organization having international activity" than an international nongovernmental organization, it worked closely with Quaker societies throughout the world. More international, perhaps, was the European Central Bureau for Interchurch Relief, established in 1922 as a result of a meeting of American and Swiss church members in Copenhagen. They continued the efforts that various Christian organizations began right after the war to help rebuild churches destroyed during the fighting.[43] By the end of the decade, postwar relief programs had given way to a new emphasis on social work, to develop welfare policies and programs in various countries. But it was widely recognized that this, too, was an item that called for cross-national cooperation, and in 1928 the first "international conference on social work" was held in Paris, in which nearly twenty-five hundred delegates from thirty-four countries participated.[44]

One of the most interesting nongovernmental organizations at that time was the Institute of Pacific Relations, first launched in Honolulu through the initiative of YMCA-linked Christian leaders to bring together "men and women deeply interested in the Pacific area, who meet and work not as representatives of their governments, or of any other organization, but as individuals." From the beginning, the international and nongovernmental nature of the organization was apparent. In preparation for its founding, in 1923 the YMCA in Honolulu created an executive committee consisting of American, Chinese, and Japanese residents of Hawaii, and an international advisory body with members from Australia, Canada, China, Japan, Korea, New Zealand, the Philippines, and the United States.[45] Moreover, despite the YMCA initiative, by the time the Institute was formally created in 1925, it had become less a religious than a secular organization committed to a cross-national exchange of ideas on a broad range of issues such as interracial relations and security in the Pacific. These countries established their own national committees of the Institute of Pacific Relations, analogous to the national committees on intellectual cooperation and similarly promoting the cause of internationalism. As Frank Atherton, one of the Honolulu leaders, stated at the opening meeting of the Institute, "each nation has its contribution to make to the family of nations and each should take an active and constructive part in working out that plan which shall be for the welfare of all."[46]

That the Institute's members, especially those from China and Japan, were not always mindful of "the welfare of all" but began to engage in often acrimonious debate, especially after the organization was moved to New York in 1927, does not detract from the historic significance of this multinational experiment. After all, this was the first international nongovernmental organization devoted to continuing dialogue on Asian and

Pacific affairs—what would come to be called "track two" dialogue many decades later, bringing officials (participating in an unofficial capacity) and public opinion leaders from several countries together for an intensive discussion of bilateral and multilateral issues. Delegates from China, Japan, and the United States continued to participate in the conferences organized by the Institute of Pacific Relations throughout the 1930s, thereby setting an important precedent for future track two endeavors.

The number of international nongovernmental organizations grew so rapidly that in 1929, when the League of Nations published the *Handbook of International Organisations* listing 478 international organizations, over 90 percent of them were private.[47] (A supplement to this publication was issued in 1932, listing 82 additional organizations, almost all of which were nongovernmental.) Lyman Cromwell White, the pioneering student of international nongovernmental organizations, noted in a study published in 1933 that most of these organizations in existence at that time fell into the categories of "humanitarianism, religion and morals, arts and sciences, and labor."[48] John Boli and George M. Thomas, among the leading scholars of the subject today, have pointed out that most international nongovernmental organizations before the Second World War were of a "universal" as opposed to a "regional" type, open to membership from all over the world.[49] This is very significant because internationalism had been primarily a European and North American phenomenon before the Great War. It was now becoming much more global, drawing members from the Middle East, Africa, Asia, and Latin America and concerned with humanitarian, religious, cross-cultural, and labor issues all over the world.

The objection may be made that the term "universal" had limited connotations at that time; not only did a large part of the globe remain colonies of the imperial powers, but the Soviet Union often adamantly refused to participate in international organizations, considering them bourgeois institutions serving the interests of capitalists. The colonial population and the Soviet Union were tied together through the

Communist International, or the Comintern, established in 1919 to dedicate itself to propaganda and political work to overthrow imperialism. The Third International was not exactly a nongovernmental organization, and it shared little with other international organizations. It was bitterly opposed by the Labor and Socialist International, founded in 1923 as the true successor to the earlier Second International. The extremely contentious relationship between the two Internationals, however, should not obscure the fact that organizing across national (and imperial) boundaries was now a universal phenomenon, going beyond the prewar activities that had been much narrower in scope and membership. Indeed, both socialists and communists were avid international organizers, bringing together workers, artists, and intellectuals for festivals and conferences. Among the most notable were the Socialist Workers' Sport International and the International Association of Worker-Peasant Organizations of Physical Culture (Sportintern), attracting athletes from all parts of the world under socialist and communist auspices, respectively. They were workers' counterparts to the bourgeois Olympics, but as noted later, the line between the two became increasingly tenuous. The belief that sport as well as art, scholarship, medicine, social welfare, and all other spheres for which there were international organizations were really transnational endeavors remained strong.

International women's organizations illustrate this point, of which there were three major ones in the postwar decade: the International Council of Women, the International Alliance of Women, and the Women's International League for Peace and Freedom. Whereas prior to 1919 their memberships had been almost wholly European and North American, during the 1920s women in Latin America, the Middle East, and Asia created their national sections and joined the international bodies. For instance, before the war China had been the only non-Western country whose women participated in the activities of the International Alliance of Women in promoting the cause of women's suffrage, but in the wake of the peace they were joined by women from such countries as Argentina, Brazil, Egypt, India, Jamaica, Japan, Syria, and Turkey.[50] The Alliance, together with the Women's International League for Peace and Freedom, whose membership also expanded to include individuals from Haiti, Japan, and Mexico, successfully lobbied the League of Nations to include a woman on its Mandates Commission, arguing that in countries "inhabited by races of different colours, the relations between the men of the governing race, and the women of the other are a source of difficulty and often an actual hindrance to good understanding."[51]

There were other examples of the successful mobilization of international women's organizational pressure, to which the League of Nations was particularly sensitive. Of course, instances of failure, or of disagreement among women, were just as numerous, especially on such contentious issues as birth control and eugenics. But even in those cases, problems were frequently discussed at international gatherings, both governmental and nongovernmental. The number of international conferences on population control, for instance, increased from seven during 1901–1910 (also during 1910–1920) to nineteen between 1921 and 1930.[52] That at these gatherings some abhorrent (in today's perspective) policies, such as sterilization of the "feeble-minded," were debated does not detract from the fact that so many issues of the day were becoming objects of worldwide concern and that international organizations provided the institutional setting for their discussion, if not always for their satisfactory solution.

The significance of international organizations did not dissipate even during the 1930s when the world moved headlong toward another war. Because we know the calamitous history of international relations during that decade that eventuated in the Second World War, it is tempting to say that all the efforts and activities that the international organizations carried out were of little or no importance. Would it not be possible to write a history of these turbulent years without paying the slightest attention to such organizations? What difference did they make anyway?

The answer to both questions depends on what is meant by "difference." If we are looking at international relations as interstate geopolitical affairs, obviously the international organizations, both governmental and nongovernmental, were powerless to stand in the way of the seemingly inexorable march of events leading to another war in Europe in 1939 or to prevent Japanese aggression in Asia and the Pacific, culminating in the global war of 1941–1945. Does this mean that international organizations were irrelevant, that they were a waste of nations' and private associations' attention and resources that might have been better allocated to prepare for the impending world crisis?

That would be the conclusion only if we put everything in international relations during the 1920s and the 1930s in the context of "the road to war" or "the origins of the Second World War." If these were the only frameworks for understanding this history, then the international organizations must be seen as having been naïve exercises in idealism at best, or misguided attempts to divert nations' and citizens' attention to irrelevant pursuits at worst. But to deny the existence and activities of these organizations is to prioritize one interpretation of the history of that era and ignore everything else. After all, there was not just one "road to war," and there could have been "roads to peace." To talk about the "origins of the Second World War" is to assume that there was to be a second world war, as if everything must be comprehended according to its place in the "origins." Obviously, international organizations occupied no significant place in the origins, except insofar as they failed to prevent such an eventuality. (The Comintern was one organization that did try, in the mid-1930s, to coalesce forces throughout the world opposed to fascist aggression. But it was much more a national than an international body, expressing the interests and objectives of the Soviet Union, and its activities, therefore, were more part of the story of interstate affairs than of international organizations.) Perhaps the existing international organizations could have tried harder to keep the nations of the world at peace with one another. But if that were the only criterion for judging whether to pay attention to organizations and individuals, then very few of them would ever become objects of historical inquiry.

If, on the other hand, we are looking for clues to other developments, one of which was surely the survival of internationalism, we shall have to give international organizations their due even during the 1930s. Indeed, precisely because of the world economic crisis and totalitarian aggressions, the need was greater than ever for international efforts to alleviate the suffering of people who were victimized by these developments. The best-known example is the World Jewish Congress, organized in 1936 to try to protect the rights of Jews in Germany and other countries. But it was not alone. The diary of Victor Klemperer, the German scholar of French literature who suffered under the Nazi regime, is filled with references to various organizations that offered assistance to persecuted Jews. In May 1935, for instance, he wrote identical letters soliciting help from the Notgemeinschaft deutscher Wissenschaftler im Ausland (Association of German Scientists Abroad) in Zurich, the Academic Assistance Council in London, and the Emergency Committee in Aid of German Scholars in New York.[53] These were all nongovernmental organizations that were involved in international rescue missions. During the Spanish Civil War, the Save the Children International Fund, originally established in 1920 to help young victims of the war in Europe and the Middle East, sent relief workers to both sides in the conflict to alleviate the suffering of children. The same organization held an international conference on African children in June 1931, and two years later it adopted a resolution deploring the growing tendency of the time toward reembracing nationalism.[54]

It was not just in emergency situations, however, that international organizations became active during the decade. Their roles were not limited to the relief of victims of war, civil war, or totalitarianism but were notable in another important development of the 1930s: national unification and strengthening in many parts of the world. Even the totalitarian dictatorships may be seen as having been examples (albeit extreme) of the tendency on the part of so many countries to become unified and strong states. National unification or reunification was a widely observed phenomenon at that time. For instance, the New Deal in the United States can be fitted into this theme; as Michael Sherry has argued, economic reconstruction and social reform were means for reunifying and strengthening the nation.[55] China is another example; it was not simply in response to Japanese aggression that efforts were made to reform its financial institutions and to centralize its banking system. These were part of the national reconstruction that had begun in the late 1920s and continued with greater urgency during the 1930s because of the Depression. Likewise, Mexico under Lázaro Cárdenas developed economic and social reforms, what historians have called a "cultural revolution," through close cooperation among the state, labor unions, teacher organizations, and many others.[56] Similar efforts were carried out in Turkey under Mustafa Kemal, where hundreds of "people's homes" and "people's rooms" were established to spread nationalist, populist, and secularist ideas.[57] In Spain two visions of nationhood came into violent conflict, resulting in the establishment of General Francisco Franco's dictatorship. Elsewhere, in countries that were gaining independence, such as Iraq and Egypt, the military tended to come to control national politics. They, too, were trying to develop themselves as strong, unified nations.

If, therefore, nation building or national reconstruction was an important theme of the decade that has been obscured by the more dramatic phenomena of totalitarianism and war, then international organizations would have to be evaluated according to what roles they played in that story. At a time when states were focusing on their domestic unity and military strengthening, did international organizations try to preserve the spirit of cross-national cooperation? Or did internationalism succumb to forces of renewed nationalism, not just of the totalitarian variety but virtually in all states? These questions cannot be answered without more monographic study. In its absence, all that can be mentioned here is the undeniable fact that international organizations did not disappear but remained active, even growing in number. The

League of Nations was a "failure" only with regard to its inability to stop Japanese aggression in China or the Italian conquest of Ethiopia. This did not mean, however, that the world organization stopped functioning. Its International Labor Organization, Committee on Intellectual Cooperation, and Health Organization continued to carry on their tasks.

As just one example, the Committee on Intellectual Cooperation and its affiliate body, the International Institute for Intellectual Cooperation in Paris, never let up their efforts to organize exchange programs, conferences, art fairs, and the like. Japan, which had withdrawn from the League, stayed in this committee and continued to participate in its activities till 1940.[58] The United States and Mexico, and over thirty countries from Europe, the Middle East, and Asia were still, on the eve of the war, represented in the organization. As for international nongovernmental organizations, Lyman Cromwell White's useful survey, published after the war, lists many of them that were active as of 1938. Most had been established earlier and continued to carry on their tasks during the 1930s. For instance, the International Migration Service, organized in 1925 to "render service through cooperative effort" to migrants, had, by 1938, set up branches in Germany, the United States, and many other countries. The World Federation of Education Associations, founded in 1923 in Washington, continued to hold biennial conferences; it was convened in Tokyo in 1937, and even in the summer of 1939, when the scheduled gathering in Rio de Janeiro had to be canceled because of the European crisis, over seven hundred non-European members undertook a cruise to various countries in the Caribbean and South America to engage in workshops and seminars.[59] In the meantime, new organizations were being established. In 1930, for example, the International Association of Children's Court Judges was created in Brussels to provide an opportunity for children's judges from various countries to come together to seek an international solution to juvenile delinquency, child welfare, and other matters. The Florence Nightingale International Foundation was founded in London in 1934 under the auspices of the League of Red Cross Societies and the International Council of Nurses for training nurses throughout the world.[60] These instances suggest that international efforts did not abate even in a decade characterized by nation-centered agendas and exclusionary orientations on the part of so many countries in the world.

Perhaps the most interesting instance of an international organization trying to promote friendly relations among states during the decade of fierce nationalism was the work of the International Olympic Committee that organized the Olympic games in Los Angeles in 1932 and in Berlin four years later. Despite the Depression, and despite the aggressive behavior of Japan, Italy, and Germany, the International Olympic Committee maintained its independence and imposed its standards and rules upon all participating nations, including these countries. The Berlin Olympics were particularly notable because they showed that despite Nazi racism, athletes of all races and countries competed under the same rules. As Barbara Keys's study shows, "sport internationalism" prevailed over totalitarianism and self-centered nationalism, albeit for a brief moment, in 1936.[61] Klemperer's diary records that the Nazis sought to draw the lesson from the games that "only hard training gets results," but this was, after all, a universally valid idea. While the diarist was disgusted with the Olympics, viewing them as "an entirely political enterprise," he also noted that at least during the duration of the games, "Jew-baiting, bellicose sentiments, everything offensive has disappeared from the papers."[62] To that extent, the Olympics demonstrated the effectiveness of an international nongovernmental organization in creating a world pursuing its own rules and internationalist agendas. That the goodwill generated in Berlin lasted only for a few weeks did not prevent the International Olympic Committee from planning for future games. Although the coming of the war made it impossible to hold the games as planned, national Olympic committees as well as amateur sport federations continued to function during these years. Indeed, the International Amateur Athletic Federation, originally established in Sweden in 1912, increased its membership from forty-eight in 1930 to fifty-one in 1938, and the Soviet Union tried very hard to join the organization, though it was not admitted until after the war.[63]

Such instances suggest that the internationalist spirit never disappeared in the 1930s. Indeed, precisely because many countries were redefining themselves along nationalistic lines, forsaking international cooperation for the pursuit of national interests and military power, internationalism, were it to survive, had to depend more than ever before on the activities of international nongovernmental organizations.[64] Writing just after the Second World War, Lyman Cromwell White noted that while during the 1930s, "nationalism gained over internationalism," these organizations remained active; "not a single organization which had attained any importance before the depression failed to survive." Some increased their membership. White cites the example of the International Federation of Trade Unions, which added to the number of its national units during the 1930s even as German trade unions withdrew.[65] International organizations, both governmental and nongovernmental, represented the conscience of the world when individual states were destroying the peace and seeking to divide the globe into self-contained empires, or else focusing on national unification and strengthening. In a period when globalization of economic and political affairs, which had begun to resume its course after the war, was being challenged by what appeared to be global militarism and anarchy, global consciousness was kept alive by the heroic efforts of nonstate actors that preserved the vision of one world.

CHAPTER 2

The New Internationalism

Shortly before Germany's spring offensive began in 1940, Leonard Woolf was reflecting on the meaning of the war and its possible consequences. He had been one of the first writers to stress the theme of global interdependence and, in particular, to note the growing importance of international organizations. He retained his faith in these organizations in the aftermath of the First World War, but as totalitarianism arose and began waging aggressive wars during the 1930s, he grew less and less optimistic about world trends. As another war began in Europe, he was convinced, despite his continued pacifist leanings, that the German offensive must be resisted and that ultimately Britain and its allies would be successful. But he was far less sanguine than he had been during the First World War that the war's end would lead to a saner, more peaceful world. As suggested by the title he gave to the volume of his autobiography that dealt with the prewar and war years, *Downhill All the Way* (1962), Woolf was not sure if humanity was capable of drawing the right lessons from these tragedies; instead, he saw nations and peoples repeating the same mistakes again and again. Unless they took some drastic measures to reverse the trend — and Woolf was not optimistic that they would — more wars would take place in the future. He concluded, "if, when this war is over, we continue to live under the threat of yet another war . . . the black-out of civilised life will be permanent."[1]

His pessimism seemed to prove justified when, no sooner than the war ended, the victorious powers began to engage in a new conflict: the Cold War. It was as if the world never knew peace, even of short duration comparable to the several years after the First World War. Somehow the Second World War seemed to inexorably lead to the Cold War, threatening "yet another war." In retrospect, however, "the black-out of civilised life" did not quite come about. International tensions and national upheavals would take place, but somehow civilization would survive. How did it do so?

Many explanations are possible, including the widespread view that the very Cold War, because it produced a nuclear arms race, served to restrain the powers from waging another world war that would have annihilated the whole world. This is the "long peace" thesis; the argument is that no third world war occurred because nuclear weapons provided a "balance of terror" that was more effective than traditional balances of power in preventing the nations from starting a war that could end up destroying all of them.[2] But the avoidance of a total war is not the same thing as the survival of civilization. "Civilised life" whose permanent "black-out" Woolf envisaged must be built not simply on the absence of war but on cooperative human endeavors, on the willingness of people to work together to create and preserve an environment conducive to promoting their material and spiritual welfare. The British writer was not optimistic that such a development would take place if the threat of war continued to hang over the whole world.

He proved wrong. In the aftermath of the Second World War, a burst of activity occurred in many parts of the world as if to belie his pessimism. Indeed, even during the war, quiet efforts had begun to be made to ensure the survival of civilized life. As one example, within less than a year after Japan's attack on Pearl Harbor brought the United States into war, representatives of several private organizations met in New York to consider coordinating their activities to plan for postwar international relief and rehabilitation. They emphasized the role of private service organizations in undertaking such programs, but they were also encouraged in their planning by the federal government, which established the Office of Foreign Relief and Rehabilitation Operations in November 1942. From these beginnings there emerged in 1943 the American Council of Voluntary Agencies for Foreign Service.[3]

The story of international relief is certainly one of the most heartening in postwar history, but we shall not even notice it if we focus on the origins and development of the Cold War when discussing international affairs during the several years after 1945. Besides relief and reconstruction, we can point to many other themes that have no place in a Cold War–centered perspective but that were as significant, if not more so, than the geopolitical drama of U.S.-U.S.S.R. confrontation. For instance, the democratization of Germany and Japan was a major theme in world history right after the war, as was the economic affluence in the United States that heralded the coming of a "consumer revolution."[4] In international relations, perhaps no development was more critical to the future shape of the world than the steps already being taken to create a European community. Equally important was the determination of the United States to push vigorously for an open system of trade by lowering its own tariffs and negotiating for the return of economic multilateralism.[5] Outside Europe and North America, a key theme in the early postwar years was the struggle for liberation from colonial rule that was bringing into question the basic framework of regional governance in Southeast and South Asia as well as the Middle East and North Africa.

These developments had their origins long before the onset of the Cold War and would have taken place even in the absence of the geopolitical conflict. Whether they would have taken different shape in the absence of the U.S.-U.S.S.R. competition for power is an interesting counterfactual question. Forces of democratization, consumerism, economic integration, or colonial liberation might have produced a different kind of civilization in the absence of the Cold War. In reality, the United States and its allies did promote these objectives — though not always consistently or enthusiastically—during the Cold War, but to dismiss them as merely instruments for, or aspects of, Cold War policy would be to privilege one phenomenon in postwar international relations over the others. The argument could even be made that the Cold War was the means for the attainment of these goals, but that immediately raises the question of why it was necessary to prepare for nuclear war and possible annihilation of humankind in order to construct an interdependent world. Fundamentally, we must recognize that the Cold War kept the globe divided, as can be seen in such concepts as "the Iron Curtain," "containment," and "the socialist bloc" that informed Western policy and strategy toward the Soviet Union, whereas democratization, economic multilateralism, and other developments continued the process of global interconnectedness. The objection may be raised that the growing awareness of "the extreme dangers to mankind" inherent in the superpowers' nuclear confrontation was itself a global phenomenon.[6] Even nuclear fear may thus have played a role in the further growth of globalization after the war, but such global awareness alone, without these other developments, would not have steered the world in a constructive direction or ensured the survival of civilization.

That the U.S.-Soviet rivalry was only one of many urgent issues confronting the postwar world was clearly recognized at a conference on United States foreign policy sponsored by the Brookings Institution and held at Dartmouth College in August 1947. A document presented at the gathering mentioned "the atmosphere of uneasiness and insecurity which pervades the world" and pointed to three factors that contributed to such a situation: absence of major peace settlements, economic dislocation and distress, and political maladjustment and social ferment. The latter two problems had little to do with the Cold War as such, although the international crisis atmosphere undoubtedly made their solution all the more complex. But the paper also noted, in a hopeful vein, that "sufficient machinery of international action and adjustment exists, if the nations are willing to employ it, to provide the basis for a clear agreement on objectives in an area of a compelling common interest."[7]

It was to cope with all these issues — absence of major peace settlements, economic dislocation, and social ferment — that international organizations, old and new, dedicated their energies in the immediate aftermath of the war. They would explore international solutions to these problems to counter the "growing tendency to think of the world as already irrevocably divided into two parts that must inevitably clash," in the words of the Brookings seminar paper.[8]

The idea of "one world" had existed for a long time, but it had gained fresh significance during the war. In a celebrated essay published in the spring of 1941, Henry Luce had written, "our world . . . is one world, fundamentally indivisible."[9] He believed that American capital, technology, philanthropy, and idealism had striven for such a world and would continue to do so once the war was over. Even during the world conflict, Wendell Willkie, the Republican Party's candidate for president in 1940, promoted the vision by publishing an enormously popular book, *One World*, in 1943.[10] Even though in the aftermath of the war, the Allies split into two contending blocs, both sides diverting their resources and energies to preparing for, and waging, Cold War, the ideal of an indivisible world never disappeared. But the ideal had to be translated into action, and this was the challenge the international organizations willingly undertook. They had, after all, been engaged in precisely that task, and although their activities had not been successful at preventing aggressions and atrocities, the tragic events of the 1930s and the war years had not discouraged them. On the contrary, the very tragedies, because they were truly global in scale, convinced the proponents of international organizations everywhere that if another calamitous war were to be avoided, they would have to redouble their efforts. As they saw it, the war had established connections among different parts of the world that had hitherto remained apart, and even while a full-scale carnage of unprecedented nature had gone on, the awareness of global interconnectedness appeared to have grown. Such awareness could be mobilized to provide the basis for postwar internationalism, a determination to strengthen movements and institutions that would reunify the world.

This determination was clearly stated in the preamble of the charter of the United Nations, adopted at a meeting of delegates from fifty nations in San Francisco in the waning months of the war. "We, the peoples of the United Nations," the preamble began, referring to the Allies in the war, determined

> to save succeeding generations from the scourge of war . . . [to] reaffirm faith in fundamental human rights . . . [to] promote social progress and better standards of life in larger freedom . . . [to] practice tolerance and live together in peace with one another as good neighbors . . . [to] employ international machinery for the promotion of the economic and social advancement of all people, have resolved to combine efforts to accomplish these aims.

Although the document was signed by representatives of the governments constituting the wartime alliance, it is remarkable that both in the preamble and in chapter 1, article 1, of the United Nations charter, "peoples" are referred to as often as "nations." Typical is the statement in this article that one of the objectives of the new world organization is the development of "friendly relations among nations based on respect for the principle of equal rights and self-determination of peoples." In contrast to the League of Nations, whose covenant never once mentioned "peoples," there was now greater emphasis on "peoples" whose well-being was to be considered a matter for international concern and solution. Although states and governments would be the primary agencies for defining economic policies or implementing social programs, ultimately the rights and interests of "peoples" would have to be safeguarded through cooperative international action.

Given such a perspective, it is not surprising that from the beginning there was recognition that nongovernmental organizations would have to play an important role in the functioning of the United Nations, which formally came into existence in October 1945. Indeed, many nongovernmental organizations, mostly from the United States but a few from elsewhere, sent their representatives to San Francisco to attend the conference that laid the groundwork for the establishment of the United Nations. Those from as many as forty-two nongovernmental organizations were actually invited to serve as advisers to the official U.S. delegation. These, and many others, would resume their tasks that the war had interrupted, and in the meantime new organizations would be created. In a United Nations survey conducted in January 1951, altogether 188 international nongovernmental organizations had been officially recognized by the world organization. Of these, 64 had been established during and after the war.[11] Each of the 188 bodies was affiliated with an agency of the United Nations so that between intergovernmental organizations and international nongovernmental organizations, a close partnership was developing — a partnership that would cover the globe with networks of shared interests and concerns. This surely was a major challenge to the geopolitics of the emerging Cold War that was threatening to divide the world.

For instance, the Economic and Social Council of the United Nations, established for "the promotion of the economic and social advancement of all people," worked closely with such church-affiliated nongovernmental organizations as the Catholic International Union for Social Service, the Commission of the Churches on International Affairs, the Consultative Council of Jewish Organizations, and the Friends' World Committee for Consultation. The International Labor Organization, formerly part of the League of Nations, now became a special agency of the United Nations, charged with the task of enhancing "social progress and better standards of life in larger freedom," and attached to itself a host of newly established organizations such as the Inter-American Confederation of Workers, the International Confederation of Free Trade Unions, and the International Federation of Agricultural Producers. In the realm of public health, an international health conference held in Geneva in 1946, in which sixty-nine countries were represented, led to the founding of the World Health Organization as another United Nations specialized agency. It took over the tasks hitherto performed by the Office International d'Hygiène Publique and absorbed several older groups, meanwhile working in close cooperation with various nongovernmental organizations, including the International Association for the Prevention of Blindness, the International Committee of the Red Cross, and the International Council of Nurses, as well as the recently created World Federation for Mental Health and the World Medical Association.

No nongovernmental organization was affiliated with the Security Council, which concerned itself with global security matters and was soon to become an arena for bitter exchanges between the United States and its allies on one side and the Soviet Union and other socialist countries on the other. This animosity, of course, is the familiar story of the Cold War. However, most of the Soviet-bloc nations as well as the rest of the world joined the other agencies of the United Nations as well as the international nongovernmental organizations attached to them. At these agencies, the measure of consultation and cooperation among the nations belonging to the two camps in the emerging Cold War was far greater than at Security Council meetings. To ignore this fact, which is illustrated later through some examples, is to distort the history of the immediate postwar years.

In those days, no international organization better exemplified the renewed faith in worldwide cooperation than the United Nations Educational, Scientific, and Cultural Organization (UNESCO). It resumed the tasks that the League's Intellectual Cooperation Organization had carried out so valiantly even during the dark years of the 1930s, an indication that the idea of cross-national cultural communication and exchange as a key to stable world order had never disappeared during the war. In the aftermath of the war, however, there was a determination to broaden the scope of cultural internationalism, to cover wider circles of people, and to engage in a greater variety of activities than the Intellectual Cooperation Organization and its affiliates. Alfred Zimmern, one of the most energetic exponents of cultural cooperation between the wars, ruefully confided after the Second World War that despite all the efforts through the League of Nations to promote exchange programs, "the cause of intellectual freedom . . . suffered a setback such as had not been experienced in the West for many centuries." The reason, he noted, was that these programs had been preoccupied "with the tools of the intellectual and artistic life rather than with the nature of that life itself."[12] What he meant was that intellectuals and artists would now have to concern themselves with much more than an ethereal pursuit of truth and beauty; they would have to broaden the scope of their activities and embrace the mass of people as well as civilizations other than that of the West. Despite such self-criticism, however, Zimmern and his fellow cultural international- ists remained committed to the vision that had bound them together for over twenty years, and they now redoubled their efforts so that this time they would bear fruit.

One obvious way of doing so was to stress the importance of educa- tion. Educational exchange had constituted an important part of prewar cultural internationalism, and a number of international associations had been established after the First World War to bring teachers and stu- dents from various countries together. Obviously, such programs had not prevented the global conflagration, but far from being discouraged, the internationalists believed they now had an opportunity to reeducate the whole world through networks of cooperation and mutual under- standing. First it would be necessary to eradicate the chauvinistic and racialist educational system that the Nazis had created, producing a gen- eration that blindly followed the leader and the state. The same was true of Italy, Japan, and other totalitarian states. That was why the occupa- tion authorities in the former Axis countries laid so much stress on democratizing educational systems, school curricula, and teacher train- ing. But that was not all. The widely shared belief was that the future of the world would be determined by the kind of education young children, teenagers, and adolescents would receive even in the victorious coun- tries. Coming after the generation that fought the war, the next genera- tion would in time have to assume the task of preserving the peace and freedom in all countries. As Ambassador John G. Winant stated in a

1944 memorandum addressed to Foreign Secretary Anthony Eden, "the future of the world depends upon what happens to the youth of this generation," and therefore international cooperation in education was of utmost importance in reestablishing world order.[13] Education was becoming an issue of international concern.

Such were the forces behind the founding of UNESCO. While in the beginning the United Nations' Economic and Social Council was charged with "economic, social, cultural, educational, health, and related matters," many considered such a list of its functions too wide-ranging and succeeded in pushing for a separate organization specifically for international educational and cultural affairs. As a consequence, UNESCO started in 1946 with the initial membership of thirty nations. Each member state established its own national commission, analogous to the prewar national committee on intellectual cooperation. Thus in the United States, a national commission for UNESCO was appointed, including such prominent figures as Archibald MacLeish, the poet and former head of the Library of Congress, and William Benton, a businessman who served as assistant secretary of state for cultural affairs. The establishment of the U.S. national commission predated the passage of Public Law 584, which created what would soon come to be known as the Fulbright program for student and scholarly exchanges. The two shared a commitment to international understanding through study abroad, and indeed many individuals served both on the national commission and on the Board of Foreign Study, created in 1947 to oversee the Fulbright exchanges. This program was formally launched in 1948, when students and scholars were exchanged between the United States, on one hand, and China, Burma, and the Philippines on the other.[14]

Those were years filled with hopes that education did make a difference in building an interdependent world community and that internationalism must be the key to education. Fortified by the vision, not only states and intergovernmental organizations but also nongovernmental organizations devoted considerable portions of their resources to resuming and expanding educational exchanges. Already by 1951 such nongovernmental organizations as the International Association for the Exchange of Students for Technical Experience, the International Association of University Professors and Lecturers, the International Economic Association, and the International Federation for Organizations for School Correspondence and Exchanges had been established and were carrying out their projects with the support of UNESCO.

Not surprisingly, exchange programs were promoted most vigorously by private foundations and educational institutions of the United States, where it was much easier than in other countries to resume such activities as soon as the war ended. Typical was the Rockefeller Foundation's funding of the Salzburg Seminar in American Studies that began in 1947.[15] F. O. Matthieson, the Harvard professor of American literature who played a leading role in the founding and operation of the Salzburg Seminar, noted in a welcoming speech that only by bringing "man . . . into communication with man" would culture flourish and international understanding be promoted.[16] Somewhat more modest, but no less reflective of the trend, was the American Field Service. First established in 1914 to send American volunteers to France to serve the wounded in the battlefield, its mission was redefined after the Second World War as the promotion of mutual understanding through student exchanges. Already in 1947, the Field Service sponsored the visit of fifty-one high school students from ten European countries.[17] In the meantime, the Institute of Pacific Relations, which had not held a plenary meeting after 1942, convened its ninth conference in January 1945 to discuss "wartime and post-war cooperation of the United Nations in the Pacific and the Far East," and its tenth in September 1947 on the theme of "problems of economic reconstruction in the Far East." Here, too, "education and technology" were among the topics discussed, along with "agricultural improvement," "industrial development," and "international economic problems."[18]

Some international organizations promoted worldwide exchanges of information. For instance, in 1947 a Washington conference of directors of meteorological institutions of various countries was held, resulting in the founding of the World Meteorological Organization to serve as the headquarters for the exchange of weather information in all parts of the globe. (The Soviet Union provided Siberian meteorological data to other countries as a matter of course.) The International Civil Aviation Organization, whose initial founding went back to the 1944 Chicago conference of aviation officials, likewise served as a channel of communication on the world's geographical and climactic conditions along civil air routes. In 1946 Moscow hosted a conference of sixty-six technical experts and administrators on international telecommunication. They were heirs to the organizations that had been created long before the war to regulate cross-national telephone and telegraph communication, but after the Second World War there was virtually universal recognition that much like aviation, distances among nations would continue to narrow thanks to the spread of, and improvements in, telecommunications technology. The conference resulted in the establishment of an International Frequency Registration Board that served as the clearinghouse of information regarding radio frequencies.[19] All these instances suggest that the exchange of information, broadly put, was among the items on which a great deal of cooperation existed among nations in the immediate aftermath of the war.

Any history of that period would have to take note of these developments, not just the more dramatic episodes of great-power confrontation. Despite the unmistakable signs of geopolitical tensions, individuals and organizations from the United States and the Soviet Union, as well as from other countries, were continuing to meet. They shared information and exchanged ideas, thereby confirming the persistence of transnational endeavors in the immediate postwar years.

Besides educational and informational exchanges, perhaps the most impressive instance of organized international effort at this time was in the realm of humanitarian relief, a traditional goal of nongovernmental organizations and international agencies but one that was more urgent than ever because of the scale of destruction and devastation that the Second World War brought about. To care for the wounded, the homeless, the stateless, and additional millions of men and women who had been deprived of an opportunity for normal, decent living, organized international efforts were considered essential. Already in 1943, the Allies had established a United Nations Relief and Rehabilitation Agency (UNRRA) to deal with victims of war, and in 1946, shortly after the founding of the United Nations, this agency was transformed into the International Refugee Organization. At that time the most urgent task appeared to be the settlement of European Jews in Palestine, but the subsequent founding of the state of Israel, and the fighting between Jews and Arabs, gave rise to the complicated question of Arab refugees, those driven out of their homes and living in tents along the west bank of the Jordan River in legal limbo. Without the heroic work of the International Refugee Organization, their situation could have become disastrous. (Jewish settlers were being provided with relief assistance by the World Jewish Congress and other organizations.)[20]

In the meantime, the United Nations International Children's Emergency Fund (UNICEF) was created in December 1946, initially intended for the care of children in war-devastated areas. Graphic reports surfaced, in pictures and movies, of undernourished and starving children in Poland, Czechoslovakia, and elsewhere, and the condition was made even more acute during the severe winter of 1946–1947. The need for food, medicine, and doctors was urgent. (One-half of Polish doctors are said to have died during the war.) But when the United Nations established the new agency, its goals went beyond saving European children. Assistance was to be given to children of all countries, "on the basis of need, without discrimination because of race, creed, nationality, status, or political belief." This included children of former Axis countries and of the colonial areas. Such an ambitious program required large-scale funding, something the United Nations itself was not prepared to provide. Private donations had to be solicited from individuals and organizations, and not surprisingly, the bulk of those donations was raised in the United States. Already in 1946, American donors are said to have given $200 million to UNICEF.[21]

In response to urgent appeals from this and other bodies for funds for humanitarian purposes, new nongovernmental organizations were established in the United States that aimed at international rescue and relief activities. Before and during the war, many such agencies had been connected to Christian churches, but their number had proliferated to such an extent that seventeen Protestant denominations came together in 1946 to create Church World Service, to "do in partnership what none of us could hope to do as well alone." It was, according to a recent history of the organization, "the first inclusive, ecumenical, and coordinating instrument for overseas relief and reconstruction in the history of the Protestant churches in the United States." It took over work that other church organizations had carried out, and already in 1946, it was providing 80 percent of all relief goods shipped from nongovernmental organizations in the United States to Europe and Asia. In 1947 Church World Service began running a program of "friendship trains" that would go through midwestern and southwestern states to collect wheat, beans, and other agricultural products and then transport them to eastern ports, from which they were shipped abroad. The bulk of the relief goods was destined for Europe, but after the Marshall Plan was launched as the major undertaking for reconstruction and development of European countries, church groups in the United States increasingly turned their attention to Asia and the Middle East. For instance, Church World Service sent penicillin and other medical supplies to India, where one out of ten people was said to be dying of violence, sickness, or hunger following the subcontinent's independence in 1947.[22]

Outside the Protestant denominations, the religious charities in the United States most active in postwar international relief were Catholic Relief Services and the American Jewish Joint Distribution Committee. (The Lutheran Church established its own agency, Lutheran World Relief, in October 1945.)[23] From 1946 through 1955, Catholic Relief

Services is said to have shipped the largest volume of goods abroad; Church World Service was third and the Jewish Committee fourth.[24]

The second in rank was the Cooperative for American Remittances to Europe (CARE), launched in the United States in December 1945. It was the largest nonreligious agency sending relief goods overseas. The initiative for its founding came from a group of voluntary organizations in the United States whose representatives had begun considering a nationally coordinated relief program for Europe even before the war ended. The inspiration behind the founding of CARE was similar to that of Church World Service, but because of its nonsectarian nature, it was able to work more closely with the United Nations as well as with the U.S. government. UNRRA transferred millions of the packages it had collected to CARE for distribution in Europe, a process that involved working closely with as many as nine U.S. government agencies that had been involved in collecting and storing packages of foodstuffs and other goods for use by the UN organization. Moreover, the War Assets Corporation, a unit within the Reconstruction Finance Corporation that had legal control over the packages, laid down certain conditions for CARE's work; for instance, the shipments had to enter a recipient country free of duties and other taxes, and families and individuals receiving relief goods could not be denied their normal food rations as a result.[25] These and other bureaucratic hurdles were overcome in time, and after 1947, CARE took over the whole program hitherto administered by UNRRA. The organization's initial focus on Europe was understandable, given that so many Americans had relatives and friends across the Atlantic whom they wanted to help. But just as UNICEF aimed at helping children worldwide, so the "E" in CARE in time came to sand for "Everywhere," so that not just Europeans but also Japanese and Koreans began to benefit from such help.

Although most of the funds and volunteers for international relief work came from the United States in the immediate aftermath of the war, other countries were not far behind. In Europe, especially, organizations that had been created before and during the war continued their work. Among the most famous was the Oxford Committee for Famine Relief, established in 1942 to send food to victims of war-related starvation in Europe. After the war, other countries were to create their own "Oxfam" organizations. The International Red Cross, which had provided assistance to victims of the Spanish civil war, worked energetically after the war to obtain and distribute information regarding missing persons. And Service Civil International resumed its work as soon as France and the Low Countries were liberated in 1944. By 1949 it had established work camps in many parts of Europe, including Czechoslovakia, Germany, Austria, and Italy. While modest, all these activities by international organizations were as much part of postwar international affairs as the emerging rivalry between the United States and the Soviet Union, commonly known as the "origins of the Cold War." Those activities had their origins decades before the Cold War, and just as they had survived many international crises and wars, they were now being carried out with a momentum of their own. Intergovernmental organizations and nongovernmental organizations, whether engaged in cultural exchange or in relief work, were demonstrating that there were other themes in international affairs than the Cold War, that geopolitics defined only one aspect of the postwar world, and that visions of global community had not disappeared.

This does not mean that great-power rivalries and tensions did not intrude on the activities of international organizations. Numerous examples indicate that they did. As early as 1947, for instance, the American Council of Learned Societies had to give up its program for U.S.-Soviet scholarly exchange, and in the following year, Bulgaria and Romania drove out representatives of UNICEF, CARE, and other humanitarian organizations, accusing them of engaging in sabotage and spying.[26] On the U.S. side, some officials and politicians came to see cultural exchange programs as an instrument of waging cold war. From selecting artwork for exhibiting abroad that was considered to be the best representation of democracy to bringing German intellectuals to the United States to inculcate in them pro-American ideas, Washington was actively interested in the work of nongovernmental organizations.[27] Some of them, including such giants as the Rockefeller and Ford Foundations, often collaborated with the government, although their collaboration some-times gave rise to fierce internal debate.[28] There were even nongovern-mental organizations that the state secretly funded; after its establish-ment in 1947, the Central Intelligence Agency covertly subsidized such organizations as the Congress of Cultural Freedom and the Inter-national Confederation of Free Trade Unions. (This latter, consisting of U.S., British, Dutch, and other trade union representatives, had split off from the World Federation of Trade Unions, established in 1945 as the successor to the venerable International Federation of Trade Unions, whose history went back to 1901. While labor leaders from all countries had joined forces to seek to protect workers' rights, the growing tension between the capitalist and socialist countries made it impossible for the organization to retain ideological uniformity.)[29]

Such examples, however, do not show that geopolitical factors alone characterized postwar international relations. The equation could be turned around; rather than Cold War calculations tending to threaten the integrity of activities by intergovernmental organizations and non-governmental organizations, it was frequently the latter that affected, or at least tried to affect, Cold War developments. We can see this in the efforts of some organizations that were determined to keep alive the vision of one world and to resist the growing tendency everywhere to view international affairs in bipolar fashion. For instance, a group of American scientists, many of whom had been involved in the develop-ment of the atomic bomb, began a movement for international control over nuclear and other weapons as soon as the war ended. In November 1945 they organized the Federation of Atomic Scientists to alert the world about the danger of atomic warfare. In an influential book pub-lished in 1946, *One World or None*, these scientists, including Robert Oppenheimer and Albert Einstein, warned that the only way to control atomic weapons and to prevent nuclear war was through international supervision. Even more crucial, from their point of view, was to renew a commitment to internationalism. As Oppenheimer noted, "The vastly increased powers of destruction that atomic weapons give us have brought with them a profound change in the balance between national and international interests. The common interest of all in the prevention of atomic warfare would seem immensely to overshadow any purely national interest, whether of welfare or of security." Einstein agreed, arguing that "real security" in the age of atomic weapons was "tied to the denationalization of military power." Only a "supranational army," not individual national armies, should be entrusted with the task of preserving the peace.[30] Similar ideas had been expressed in the past — and had proved helpless against forces of destruction. But that did not prevent these scientists from trying yet again, believing that the fear of the demise of civilization was now universally shared. And their strategy, to get organized to spread the message, had also been tried before. While these internationalist endeavors were not unique, their significance lay in the fact that the organizations created by these scientists and by others who shared their views were part of an unprecedented scale of organizing that went on in the wake of the Second World War.

The Federation of Atomic Scientists was soon joined by many other organizations, large and small, that were created in the late 1940s to promote the cause of nuclear disarmament or, at the very least, international control over atomic weapons. As Lawrence Wittner, Paul Boyer, Charles DeBenedetti, and others have chronicled, the "ban the bomb" movement was particularly noticeable in the immediate postwar years, which suggests a serious attempt at defining some order in a seemingly chaotic world.[31] Not surprisingly, many individuals and organizations believed that the only solution was through some form of world government, and those who did not consider the United Nations to be the answer pursued other alternatives. The United World Federalists, for instance, was established in the United States in 1947 to serve as the headquarters for world federalists throughout the globe.

But the peace-oriented organizations were not limited to those concerned with the danger of nuclear war. In 1946 the Inter-American

Judicial Committee met to consider "rights and duties of war," the idea being that jurists in the Western Hemisphere ought to take the initiative to reestablish laws of war and peace. Such initiatives led to the 1949 United Nations convention on new laws of war, banning certain categories of weapons and acts toward civilians during a war. In the meantime, the American Friends Service Committee began urging the superpowers to opt for coexistence rather than prepare for war. In 1949 it published a report titled *American-Russian Relations: Some Constructive Considerations* and argued that the United States and the Soviet Union should be less confrontational toward each other and instead seek to promote a relaxation of tensions through cultural exchange and other programs.[32]

Such examples show that the movements to internationalize atomic weapons, to establish a world government, and to promote cultural exchange were all part of the growth of organized international activities that characterized the postwar world. According to one source, the number of intergovernmental organizations increased from 38 in 1940 to 81 in 1950, and that of international nongovernmental organizations from 477 to 795 in the same decade.[33] Various accounts give differing numbers, but they all agree that the decade, or more particularly the five years between 1945 and 1950, saw the reintensification of efforts at international organization. Just as impressive a rate of increase had occurred in the number of such bodies during the 1920s, and yet no one could have foreseen in 1950 that these figures presaged what was to emerge as one of the most impressive stories in the history of the twentieth century: the continued and spectacular growth of international organizations. Even during the late 1940s, however, an astute observer would have noted the unprecedented variety, as well as number, of these organizations.

The three types of activities thus far mentioned — educational and cultural exchange, humanitarian relief, and peace — may be viewed as renewals or continuations of efforts begun earlier, though on a more expanded scale. The years 1945–1950, however, also saw the beginnings of organized activities in many other areas as well. Particularly notable were those that focused on human rights, the environment, and developmental assistance. The protection of human rights before the war had been closely associated with providing relief to victims of wars, natural disasters, or totalitarianism. The League of Nations had spearheaded an international effort to stop the exploitation of female and child laborers. But the experiences of the Second World War, ranging from the strategic bombing of cities to atrocities committed against Jews, Chinese, and other ethnic and national groups, served to develop a more comprehensive notion of human rights. From its inception, the United Nations took it upon itself to serve as the international custodian of human rights, establishing the Commission on Human Rights within the Economic and Social Council. And human rights were now defined much more broadly than before, to include "protection of minorities" as well as "prevention of discrimination on grounds of race, sex, language or religion," terms that were already in use at the San Francisco meeting in the spring of 1945 that prepared for the establishment of the world organization.[34]

Three years later, the General Assembly gave such ideas its ringing endorsement when it adopted the "universal declaration of human rights," which, according to Jack Donnelly, contained as many as twenty-eight rights to which all people everywhere were entitled.[35] (These rights ranged from "the right to own property" to "the right to rest and leisure.") Together with the concept of "crimes against humanity," adopted at the international military tribunals trying Nazi war criminals, the international sponsorship of such a broadened definition of human rights meant that henceforth world affairs would come to entail far more than interstate relations. In reality, member states in the United Nations were still considered sovereign entities, and they would not willingly accept international meddling in their internal affairs, even when apparent violations of human rights took place. Even so, the idea spread with impressive speed, so that virtually all new constitutions of nations or their subdivisions drafted after the war contained references to the principle.[36] And some nongovernmental organizations were from the beginning actively involved in the work of the Human Rights Commission as advisers and consultants. Soon, starting in the 1960s, these organizations would seize the initiative and seek to implement the universal declaration on human rights in many corners of the globe.

The conservation of nature, too, had a prewar history. But it became a sustained international movement only after 1945, although, as will be seen, systematic worldwide activities to protect the environment did not gather momentum till the 1960s. Lynton Keith Caldwell has chronicled how in the immediate postwar years, various attempts were made to revive the international movement to preserve the natural habitat that had remained dormant during the 1930s and the war years. Already in 1946 the International Whaling Commission was established to safeguard "for future generations the great natural resources represented by whale stocks." The reference to "resources" suggests that at that time, there was a serious concern with the depletion of the earth's resources, due in part by the devastation brought about the war and in part by the realization that despite the scores of millions of people killed in the wars of the twentieth century, the world's population had almost doubled in the meantime. What was needed, according to those active in organizing various conferences on conservation at that time, was a truly international effort to use resources wisely. Conservation and utilization were often pursued as twin aims. At the same time, however, others stressed the importance of protecting the natural environment. In 1947 delegates and observers from twenty-four countries and nine international organizations came together in Brunnen, Switzerland, and drafted a proposal for the establishment of a worldwide body "for protection of nature." The result was the founding of the International Union for the Protection of Nature in 1948. ("Protection" in the name of the organization was to change to "Conservation" in 1956.) An international conference that the new organization sponsored jointly with UNESCO in 1949 was, according to Caldwell, a harbinger of the 1968 international biosphere conference.[37] These developments were still very tentative, but one already sees here a far more concerted international movement for nature conservation than that which had existed after the First World War.

Organizations and conferences dealing with developmental assistance in the years immediately after 1945 were even fewer than those concerned with the environment. Even so, the formal name for the World Bank, established in 1945, was the International Bank for Reconstruction and Development. Reconstruction was clearly the priority item for a few years after the war, but from around 1949, economic assistance to poorer countries, many of them recently decolonized, came to claim the Bank's increasing attention. In 1948, the United Nations General Assembly passed a resolution calling for the establishment of a technical assistance program for these as well as other economically poorer nations.[38] In the meantime, President Harry S. Truman initiated the so-called Point Four program for technical assistance to newly independent countries. Even so, at that time developmental assistance was very limited in scope, and few, if any, nongovernmental organizations devoted themselves to this project. Indeed, even the term "development" does not seem to have been widespread. True, the United Nations' Economic and Social Council had a "subcommission on economic development," but at that time economic development seems to have been discussed in connection with the proposed establishment of an international trade organization. At a series of meetings in Cuba in 1947 and 1948 to draft the charter of the new organization, it was proposed that member states were not to impose "unreasonable impediments that would prevent other members from obtaining access to facilities required for their economic development."[39] In other words, developmental assistance to "backward countries" was to be seen as an integral part of the system of world trade that was to be set up. The United States and other "highly industrialized countries" considered such a proposal as too ambitious, and the proposed international trade organization was scuttled for the time being. Consensus could not be reached that developmental assistance was an international obligation.[40] All this was to change with dramatic suddenness after 1950.

For this reason, the following chapters include the discussion of development-oriented organizations as well as those focusing on five other types of issues that have been mentioned in this chapter: cultural exchange, humanitarian relief, peace, human rights, and environmentalism. An examination of these six categories of international organizations, through an admittedly small number of examples, enables us to see what their activities may have added to international affairs, what contributions they may have made, individually and collectively, to developing global consciousness and a global community, and what problems they may have encountered in the process.

CHAPTER 3

Beyond the Cold War

The 1950s are usually seen as a period when the Cold War intensified. According to this view, during the second half of the 1940s, the confrontation between the United States and the Soviet Union had been largely confined to Europe, and the two sides had mostly employed non-military means to combat each other's influence, whereas between 1949 and the early 1950s, the Cold War became both more global and militarized. With China falling to the communists and a war breaking out in the Korean peninsula, Asia now became a major theater of the superpower conflict. Other parts of the world, too, came to be seen as arenas for the struggle for power between the two sides. With Germany and Japan, the common foes of the United States and the Soviet Union in the Second World War, now being rearmed and incorporated into the superpowers' global strategies, the postwar phase of international history was clearly giving way to a new era. Both the United States and the Soviet Union reinforced their respective nuclear arsenals and built up alliance systems so that by 1953, the year when Joseph Stalin died and Harry S. Truman left the White House, a bipolar world had come into existence, with both halves preparing for a third world war. And their successors — Nikita Khrushchev in the Soviet Union and Dwight D. Eisenhower in the United States — did not alter the basic picture. They employed various means for continuing to wage cold war, and their nations increased their nuclear armament to such an extent that by 1960, the American president was frankly admitting that a war with the Soviet adversary would annihilate the whole world.[1]

In such a view, virtually all developments in the world during the 1950s tend to be seen in relation to this major drama. Every episode in international affairs is put in the framework of the Cold War and viewed according to whether it added to, or subtracted from, the power of one side or the other in this struggle. In domestic developments, too, the politics, economy, society, and culture of each country have been pictured as having been shaped by, and in turn having contributed to the further enhancement of, Cold War tensions. The bipolar confrontation on a global scale is seen as having been reflected in domestic affairs, between forces and movements struggling for victory of one global coalition or the other.

Inevitably, such Cold War–centered accounts stress the role of the state: governmental agencies, the military, and segments of the society that they co-opt for waging this war. The state, in this view, vastly extended its scope and its power, and there was less and less room for private initiatives apart from the national strategy of winning the Cold War. In the case of the United States, such a development has been termed a "national security state," a nation where the energies of government and people are pictured as having been directed toward the overriding foreign policy objective.[2] President Eisenhower himself referred to the "military-industrial complex" as something that had developed in the nation as a result of its absorption with waging the Cold War.[3] Other studies likewise suggest that during the 1950s, if not earlier, the Cold War came to define national educational endeavors, scientific development, and popular entertainment as well.[4] The obverse of this picture, of course, is that civil society's autonomy became jeopardized, as the state intruded upon private organizations with an unprecedented degree of power and determination. If such a phenomenon could be said to be taking place in the United States, a nation traditionally noted for the vigor and autonomy of its civil society, then other countries, whether allied to the United States or to the Soviet Union, could be expected to have become even more state-centered and even more preoccupied with the Cold War.[5]

As with the immediate postwar years, such a Cold War–centered view of the 1950s is misleading. It compels us to see all events and episodes at that time in the framework of the geopolitical drama and blinds us to the possibility that many developments in the world might have taken place regardless of the Cold War. If we examine those developments in their own terms, not as reflections of, or episodes in, the U.S.-U.S.S.R. confrontation, we shall be able to arrive at a different view of the period, to recognize that there were many forces in the world of which the geopolitical tensions were only one, albeit an important one. Of all such forces, the momentum toward globalization was, as earlier, the most conspicuous. The relationship between the Cold War and globalization was a complex one, just like the relationship between the World Wars and globalization. But the argument can be made that globalization was a more pervasive force than the geopolitical realities during the 1950s, producing a number of developments outside the drama of the Cold War.

For instance, surely one of the most remarkable phenomena in international affairs during the 1950s was the building of the momentum for European integration, culminating in the signing of the Treaty of Rome in 1957, which established the European Economic Community. The origins of this story had nothing to do with the Cold War. The idea of European community went back to the eighteenth century and was an important part of the internationalist movement after the First World War. It was given renewed impetus after the Second World War because of the urgency to effect reconciliation between Germany and its wartime enemies. Although the United States encouraged the move, and the Soviet Union was hostile to it, some sort of an integrated community, comprising at least several European states, would have emerged regardless of the vicissitudes of the Cold War. In the context of our discussion, it seems possible to say that European integration was a reflection much more of the globalizing trends of world affairs than of the U.S.-USSR rivalry.[6]

Of course, an integrated Western Europe played a crucial role in the U.S. Cold War strategy. In a sense, too, the Cold War itself was a globalizing force. It was global in scope and enveloped the whole world with networks of alliances and military bases. Moreover, both the free world and the socialist bloc espoused universalistic ideologies and visions. Of the two, the ideology of a free world order had much in common with the vision of an interdependent, prosperous, and just international community that generations of internationalists had promoted. By "winning" the Cold War, the United States and its allies undoubtedly facilitated the rapid globalization at the end of the twentieth century. Nonetheless, the Cold War was never a necessary condition for globalization. The geopolitical rivalry between the United States and the Soviet Union divided the globe; it did not unite it. The Cold War cannot be said to have been conducive to an interdependent world community; this was a task left to the European Economic Community and other regional entities, and to international organizations.[7]

The same thing can be said of another significant phenomenon of the 1950s: decolonization. One after another, former colonies, mostly of European states, gained independence and undertook the task of what came to be called "nation building." Even more than European integration, decolonization and nation building developed with their own momentum. These phenomena, too, were aspects of globalization. To divide up the empires that had ruled large parts of the globe and establish a host of independent new states might have appeared to fragment, rather than integrate, the international community, but the spirit behind decolonization everywhere echoed the preamble of the United Nations charter, asserting the principle of "self-determination of peoples." So long as a new state was a product of this principle, believed to be universally valid, decolonization would serve to unite the world. This was what Wendell Willkie had visualized in *One World*; because the newly independent nations would share the same aspirations, together they would contribute to the creation of a global community. In reality, some of the newly independent states became enveloped in the drama of the Cold War, choosing sides in the bipolar confrontation. But just as many were determined to stay out of the conflict.

As early as December 1950, twelve states from Asia and Africa formed an Asian-African bloc within the United Nations to demonstrate their common stand at the world organization. Although the People's Republic of China, which had officially come into being in October 1949, was not represented at the United Nations — indeed, it had been denounced as an aggressor by this body when its troops became involved in the Korean conflict — its leaders, too, in time became interested in joining these other countries to develop an agenda outside the framework of the U.S.-U.S.S.R. struggle for power. In 1955, China, India, Indonesia, Egypt, and other nations sponsored the first conference of Asian and African states in Bandung, Indonesia. Although Cold War tensions and considerations were never totally absent — for one thing, Japan, an ally of the United States, participated — the Bandung conference became an occasion for many of the newly decolonized countries of Asia and Africa to assert their separate interests from those of the superpowers. In their view, they, rather than the superpowers, were forces for a new world order. The Asian and African nations, which soon came to be called the Third World, would remind the two superpowers and their allies that there were global, human interests that were not being met by the accelerating tempo of nuclear armament. Although Third World countries would prove to be just as divided as the others, collectively they were asserting that the Cold War was not the only reality in international relations and that the global community should heed their voices, which, after all, represented the majority of the world's population.[8]

And there *was* a global community in the 1950s made up of international organizations. A Cold War–centered view of the decade tends to give the impression that the overarching hand of the state was stifling nonstate activities and depriving civil society of freedom and initiative. Such, however, was not necessarily the case. The decade saw both inter-governmental organizations and nongovernmental organizations be-coming even more active than earlier. In some areas, their activities were undeniably linked to the Cold War; the United States, the Soviet Union, and their respective allies sought to make use of these organizations as weapons in the worldwide struggle for power. There were occasions when international organizations became arenas for the geopolitical drama, or when the autonomy of nongovernmental organizations was constrained by a state's power-political considerations. But that was not all. Precisely because of the seriousness of the global confrontation, both intergovernmental organizations and nongovernmental organizations frequently stirred themselves into action so as to mitigate its impact. In that sense, these organizations were actors in the Cold War drama, albeit playing antithetical roles to those of the main protagonists. They were seeking to move the world away from a bipolar division toward an interdependent community.

In the same spirit, these agencies became involved in many other tasks, such as assisting newly independent nations and promoting edu-cational and cultural exchanges. These were continuations of earlier efforts, but their significance was, if anything, even greater because of the very seriousness of the Cold War. Altogether, international organi-zations of various types continued the efforts to interconnect nations, rather than dividing them against one another. They were forces for the preservation and strengthening of internationalism. Whether as self-conscious opponents of the Cold War or as promoters of agendas out-side the Cold War framework, most of these agencies kept alive the vision of global community. Thanks to them, the history of the 1950s became far more complex as well as promising, looking to a future where integration and unity, rather than confrontation and division, would emerge as more relevant themes in international affairs.

One could write a history of international relations during the 1950s by giving prominent play to intergovernmental organizations and nongovernmental organizations as they sought to preserve some sense of international order despite the tensions of the Cold War, to generate cooperation rather than conflict between the two superpowers and their respective allies. This can most clearly be seen in the movement for limiting, and ultimately halting, nuclear tests and for turning nuclear energy to peaceful use. A great deal of intergovernmental activity occurred in this realm, especially at the United Nations. During the Korean War, the world organization became an arena for acrimonious debate between the two sides in the conflict. The United States and its allies sought to use the body for punishing North Korea, the People's Republic of China, and, by implication, the Soviet Union for their aggression in Korea, while these latter accused the United States of imperialistic designs and killing innocent people. Even so, the United Nations remained a symbol of world unity. The Soviet Union and its satellites never left the organization despite the Korean crisis, and the Chinese communist leadership was adamant in asserting that they, rather than the Nationalists in Taiwan, represented China. Once the Korean conflict wound down, starting with the armistice of 1953, the United Nations could again return to the business of seeking a more peaceful international order.

A new impetus was provided by the coming to power of Dwight D. Eisenhower as U.S. president, followed immediately by the death of Joseph Stalin. Eisenhower, while committed to a nuclear strategy (so-called massive retaliation) in waging the Cold War, did not hesitate to turn to the United Nations to encourage peaceful uses of atomic energy through international cooperation. As early as December 1953, he went before the General Assembly to propose the establishment of a new international agency for carrying out this task. An earlier Atomic Energy Commission had been established by the United Nations General Assembly in 1946, but it had fallen victim to the growing tension between the two Cold War protagonists, and the Soviet Union had withdrawn from the body in 1952. This time, however, the post-Stalin leadership in Moscow was more receptive, and when in 1955 the United

Nations sponsored a conference of scientists in Geneva, the Soviet Union as well as Czechoslovakia sent delegates.[9] The technology was there, the participants agreed; what was lacking was the will, a determination on the part of governments and citizens alike to shift nuclear power away from military to civilian use, not just in the countries that had already developed nuclear weapons but also in others in need of alternative energy supplies. How those countries could be provided with nuclear power without their turning it to military purposes was the crucial question, and remarkably the United States, the Soviet Union, and virtually all member states in the United Nations agreed that the best way to solve the question was through the establishment of an international agency. Such an agency would make sure that nations did not use nuclear energy for other than peaceful ends. In 1956, representatives from twelve countries, including the two superpowers, met in New York to plan for the founding of such an organization, and in the following year, the United Nations officially created the International Atomic Energy Agency.[10]

Nor was this the only instance of big-power cooperation at the world organization. In 1958 the United States and the Soviet Union both submitted proposals to the world organization for "peaceful uses of outer space." Significantly, such steps were taken in the immediate aftermath of the launching of *Sputnik*, the first space satellite. The launch had obvious military implications, and the United States countered by stepping up its own missile program. At the same time, however, Moscow and Washington were willing to cooperate in research in outer space. The General Assembly naturally welcomed such initiatives, and in 1959 it voted to set up a permanent committee on peaceful uses of outer space.[11]

These beginnings, however modest, in international cooperation show that the themes of confrontation and conflict should not blind us to aspects of international affairs during the 1950s that do not fit neatly into the Cold War framework. Moreover, such instances of cooperation were grounded on the activities of individuals and organizations that never gave up their efforts to mitigate geopolitical tensions and to seek areas in which nations could work together. Lawrence S. Wittner has chronicled in detail the existence of informal networks of scientists in the early 1950s and their efforts at organizing themselves as an effective voice for peace.[12] Pacifist organizations in various countries were actively engaged in campaigns to limit the testing and manufacturing of nuclear weapons. A graphic example of a nongovernmental initiative was the grassroots movement in Japan against such weapons. It was triggered by the *Daigo Fukuryū Maru* (*Lucky Dragon, Number Five*) incident of March 1954, when the United States Navy tested hydrogen bombs near the Bikini atoll in the central Pacific. The Japanese fishing vessel was in the area but, its captain later reported, it did not receive warning to stay away. As a result, the crew were exposed to radioactivity from the "black ashes," and one of them subsequently died. The United States Navy as well as the State Department at first sought to ignore the affair and even suggested that the fuss being made in Japan was an anti-U.S. conspiracy that communists and radicals orchestrated.[13] But the Japanese press was persistent in trying to get at the facts and succeeded in interviewing some victims of the nuclear fallout. While the government in Tokyo sought to cope with the crisis through quiet negotiation with Washington, nongovernmental individuals and organizations began to call for a ban on nuclear weapons. The movement was unprecedented in postwar Japanese society in that the initiative came not from communists and radicals, as had been the case earlier, but from citizens and grassroots organizations not affiliated with any of the existing political parties. A nationwide campaign to collect signatures was launched, and in August 1955 a world conference against atomic and hydrogen bombs was convened in Hiroshima. It was preceded by a declaration by Albert Einstein, Bertrand Russell, Yukawa Hideki (a nuclear physicist and Japan's first Nobel laureate), and five other prominent intellectuals to appeal to the powers to stop the manufacture, testing, and use of nuclear weapons.

The Hiroshima gathering, coming on the heels of the declaration, was notable for its scope and for its consequences. It attracted several hundred participants from the United States, Europe, and Asia, all of whom pledged to continue the movement. Within a month, some of the Japanese leaders of the movement organized a Japan Committee against Atomic and Hydrogen Bombs, a permanent nongovernmental organization. Many counterpart organizations were established elsewhere, ranging from the Pugwash Conferences on Science and World Affairs (a periodic gathering of scientists from both sides of the Iron Curtain to discuss nuclear arms control) to grassroots movements in the United States, Britain, and elsewhere for abolition of nuclear weapons. Establishing a direct connection between these movements and the policies of the powers concerning nuclear armament would be difficult, although a recent study by Matthew Evangelista shows that the "transnationalism" of the Pugwash group ultimately succeeded in persuading the Soviet government to change course, "to end the Cold War."[14] (For its work, spanning four decades, the Pugwash Conferences received the Nobel Peace Prize in 1995.) At the very least, we must juxtapose these nongovernmental initiatives with the efforts of the United Nations as well as of various governments to do something about the continued testing, development, and possible proliferation of such weapons. Together, governments, intergovernmental organizations, and nongovernmental organizations were arousing the consciousness of people throughout the world about the dangers of nuclear war. What is particularly significant for our story is that such awareness went beyond concerns with individual countries' well-being and pointed to a worldwide problem whose solution must also be global in scope.

Nowhere was this phenomenon more graphically illustrated than by the energetic participation of women's organizations in the antinuclear movement. Women spoke not simply as representatives of their respective countries but as mothers and grandmothers worried about the possible contamination of milk and other food items given to their children and grandchildren. As a speaker stated at the 1952 national convention of the Young Women's Christian Association, "The desire for peace has always been strong in the hearts of all women, for war brings a special kind of suffering to the mothers, sisters, wives, and sweethearts of men."[15] This had always been the language of women's peace movements, but the threat of nuclear war made it a far more poignant reminder of women's relationship to world peace than ever before.

Concerned over the effects of radiation caused by nuclear tests, an American "wife and mother," Dagmar Wilson, got together with other women and founded Women Strike for Peace in 1961. "End the Arms Race — Not the Human Race" was its slogan, an excellent illustration of the connection among the nuclear question, women's issues, and global awareness.[16] Most of this organization's original female leaders came from SANE (National Committee for a Sane Nuclear Policy), which was established in 1957 through the initiative of Clarence Pickett, of the American Friends Service Committee, and Norman Cousins, editor of the *Saturday Evening Review*. (The Friends, or Quakers, were among the most active participants in the movement against nuclear testing in the Pacific Ocean. Some of them tried to take a ship, named the *Golden Rule*, to stop hydrogen-bomb tests in the South Pacific. Although they were detained in Hawaii and never reached their destination, this episode is often cited as the precedent for the later and more dramatic activities by the *Rainbow Warrior*, the vessel belonging to Greenpeace, the environmental organization established in 1970.)[17]

SANE, too, embraced the language of global community; one of its first public statements, published in the *New York Times*, boldly asserted, "The sovereignty of the human community comes before all others — before the sovereignty of groups, tribes, or nations. In that community, man has natural rights. He has the right to live and grow, to breathe unpoisoned air, to work on uncontaminated soil." The statement was a courageous reassertion of internationalism, now considered of greater value and urgency than ever before because of the threat of nuclear war and contamination. Its authors established an explicit connection, or rather a hierarchy of loyalty, between the sovereign state and the entire globe by declaring, "There can be no security for America unless we can establish and keep vital connections with the world's people, unless there is some moral grandeur to our purposes, unless what we do is directed to the cause of human life and the free man."[18] Given such language, it is not surprising that many female members of SANE went on to provide leadership for their own organizations to promote the cause. Although their activities would become notable only in the 1960s, their origins clearly lay in the initiatives taken during the preceding decade.

Besides seeking to prevent a nuclear catastrophe and to explore ways for peaceful uses of atomic energy, various individuals and organizations sought other ways of bringing the nations and peoples of the world closer together, in particular promoting contact between the two sides in the Cold War. This latter objective was very difficult to carry out, given the tense international atmosphere throughout the 1950s. Any attempt at establishing contact across the Iron Curtain was suspect. Nevertheless, even the governments in Washington and Moscow showed an interest in some exchange programs. True, these would be officially sanctioned and monitored exchanges; as Walter Hixson has shown, "cultural infiltration" and propaganda were considered vital means of waging the Cold War by the United States, and no doubt the same thing could be said of the Soviet Union.[19] Even here, however, the leaders in both countries recognized the importance of what John Foster Dulles called "U.S.-Russian people-to-people relationships." The policy was formulated by the United States Information Agency in 1955 and was endorsed by both Dulles and President Eisenhower. The USIA had an Office of Private Cooperation, which selected citizens to head some forty-two committees to promote contact across national boundaries. For instance, the music committee chose Van Cliburn to enter the Moscow Music Festival in 1957. His winning first prize was a major contribution to private cultural exchange between the United States and the Soviet Union.[20] Eisenhower was an enthusiastic supporter of such programs, for, as he said, "people are what count," and "every international problem is in reality a human problem." [21] Both the president and Secretary of State Dulles endorsed the idea of reciprocal exhibitions "to be devoted to the demonstration of the development of each of its science, technology, and culture."[22] The result was the holding of a Soviet show in New York and an American exhibition of consumer goods in Moscow, both held in 1959. These instances, as well as the two governments being signatories to several student-exchange agreements during the 1950s, suggest that grassroots contact was never lacking even in the middle of an intensified nuclear rivalry and that private individuals and organizations, with governmental support, continued to play important roles in the story. (The estimate is that between 1958 and 1961, over three hundred projects were undertaken by various U.S. organizations that sent close to four thousand Americans to the Soviet Union; a similar number of Soviet citizens came to the United States in connection with their projects. Also during this period, thirty-five hundred American tourists visited the Soviet Union, and twelve hundred Soviets reciprocated.[23] These tours, of course, were arranged through private and semigovernmental organizations, another instance indicating the role of nongovernmental organizations.)

Special mention should be made of the American Friends Service Committee, whose leader, Clarence Pickett, was a cofounder of SANE. With its headquarters in Philadelphia, the organization was among the most influential during the 1950s (and beyond) to engage in nongovernmental activities to mitigate the seriousness of the Cold War. In a report published in 1949, *American-Russian Relations: Some Constructive Considerations,* the Committee had asserted that the United States and the Soviet Union, instead of confronting one another all over the world, should accept the idea of coexistence.[24] To carry out what they were preaching, a group of Quakers, led by Pickett, traveled to Russia in 1955 and visited several provincial cities as well as Moscow. (They were not, however, the first Quaker group to travel to the Soviet Union. Seven English Friends went to Moscow and Kiev in 1951, and a reciprocal group of Russians visited Britain in 1954.) Pickett's group later published a ninety-four-page booklet about their experience, *Meeting the Russians: American Quakers Visit the Soviet Union.* The authors were not naïve; they clearly understood the nature of the Soviet system of government whose stress on ideological conformity and military preparedness seemed to preclude any possibility of an accommodation with the capitalist countries. Still, the Friends believed that "the very emphasis [the Soviets] put on the cult of science and on the dialectical nature of all phenomena may make it easier for them eventually to recognize the contradictions between their Marxist interpretations of reality and reality itself." Even more fundamentally, "Communists could not avoid being human beings even if they wished to, and as human beings they are far too complex to be adequately explained by their own doctrines." Such views were confirmed when the American visitors traveled across the Soviet Union, visiting Moscow, Leningrad, Alma-Ata, Tashkent, Stalingrad, and other citics. They were met with "innumerable examples of . . . unaffected friendliness and hospitality," and came away convinced that if, "instead of rivalry and suspicion, we are to look forward with hope that our two great powers can learn to work toward the common welfare of the world," efforts should be redoubled by "voluntary forces" and "small groups" within the United States to reach out to Soviet society.[25]

Voluntary forces and small groups — these were precisely the nongovernmental organizations that were seeking to contribute to an alternative definition of international affairs, away from the superpower confrontation. Their activities — antinuclear movements, efforts to develop peaceful uses of atomic energy, and grassroots contact across the Iron Curtain — were responses to the heightened tensions of the Cold War. They were attempts at mitigating the tensions and developing a vision of human, global community.

It was not just in connection with the Cold War, however, that international nongovernmental organizations as well as intergovernmental organizations asserted themselves as important actors throughout the 1950s. They continued to be involved in such traditional transnational activities as humanitarian relief and cultural exchange, and many of them began to focus on relatively newer areas such as development, human rights, and the environment. Most of these activities had little or nothing to do with big-power politics, but they affected the fortunes and well-being of the world's population just as critically as the Cold War.

To start with, humanitarian relief remained as important as earlier. Relief of areas devastated during the Second World War was now of lesser urgency, but newer wars and civil strife, ranging from the Korean War to the famine in China during the period of the "great leap forward" (1958–1962), invited humanitarian activities. Moreover, decolonization of Asia and the Middle East was often accompanied by civil war and disorder, necessitating efforts to alleviate hunger and disease. Many migrated from former colonies to metropolitan countries; for instance, the number of immigrant workers from former British colonies in the Caribbean, South Asia, and Africa numbered over 200,000 in 1951, and nearly 550,000 ten years later.[26] These people needed special care in health, housing, and education. Where governmental programs proved inadequate, intergovernmental and nongovernmental organizations had to step in.

Among the most notable achievements in humanitarian relief was in the medical field. The World Health Organization was the most active, thanks to its status as an agency of the United Nations. Already at the beginning of the 1950s, over seventy nations had joined the organization. Both at its headquarters in Geneva and in various regional offices, it devoted itself to collaborative research for the eradication of epidemic and endemic diseases and to service to many countries, especially those that became newly independent, in carrying out public health programs.[27] The organization standardized the system of issuing certificates of vaccination (against smallpox, cholera, and other diseases) that all travelers would carry with them when going abroad. The health organization also spearheaded a movement to eradicate malaria by distributing DDT to kill mosquitoes.[28] Although this goal was not (and still has not been) achieved, the campaign was important because it expressed the first significant challenge by an international body to what many considered the most grave danger to human health. Such efforts went on irrespective of the nuclear arms buildup and other incidents of the Cold War. True, the United States, as the major donor of funds to the World

Health Organization, tended to see the eradication of malaria as a worthy cause that would demonstrate the West's stronger commitment to Third World welfare in the global competition with the Soviet Union. But the latter was also a member of the organization, as were most other socialist countries, and little is gained from viewing this and other international bodies simply as arenas for the drama of the Cold War. Without denying that Cold War considerations frequently intruded upon humanitarian endeavors, we should recognize that at the very moment when humankind was becoming frightened of the spectacle of a nuclear war, serious and at least partially successful attempts were being made to save lives through international cooperation.

Other agencies supplemented the work of the World Health Organization. In 1954 the Medical Assistance Programs International was founded, bringing together doctors and nurses from Europe and North America for service overseas. In Asia, the Colombo Plan, adopted at a meeting of the foreign ministers of the British Commonwealth in January 1950, became an instrument for interregional cooperation in health care. Although initially only the member states of the Commonwealth participated in the Plan, it soon came to involve other countries, including Japan. The latter had sufficiently recovered from the war that in 1955, it began sending specialists to countries in the Middle East and Africa to help them deal with the scourge of tuberculosis. Service Civil International, whose history, as noted earlier, went back to 1920, began to shift its attention from relief of war-devastated areas of Europe to that in other parts of the world. During the 1950s, the organization sent volunteers to Pakistan, Algeria, Tunisia, Morocco, and other countries suffering from political disorder and economic chaos following their decolonization. Local branches were set up in India, Algeria, Lebanon, and Jordan. Work camps were established in Israel and Japan to bring volunteers of these and other countries together for cooperative activities. There was even a joint work camp with Polish youth organizations in 1955, and another that opened in the Soviet Union in 1958 through cooperation with the Union of Soviet Youth. (Interestingly, in that year the United States government allowed conscientious objectors to work for Service Civil International.)[29]

The list of nongovernmental organizations established during the 1950s primarily for undertaking humanitarian projects is long. To cite a few notable examples, in 1953 the International Voluntary Service was created by Protestant and Catholic groups in Europe and North America to provide emergency relief to victims of civil wars as well as of natural disasters and malnutrition. A few years later, Robert Andrew Hingson, director of anesthesia at the University Hospitals of Cleveland, conducted a medical survey of the world's poorer countries and, on returning home, founded My Brother's Keeper, "a volunteer, non-sectarian group dedicated to the purpose of linking America's vast medical resources to global health care needs." The organization, which soon changed its name to the Brother's Brother Foundation (a Nigerian student told Hingson, "We don't need a keeper; we need a brother."), initially focused on providing immunizations in developing nations, until the World Health Organization took over most of the work. (In the subsequent decades, the Brother's Brother Foundation was to grow into one of the major organizations to send volunteer medical service personnel to needy countries.)[30] Outside the United States, there were equally important developments. In France, the Association Mondiale de Lutte contre la Faim was established in 1956. One of many humanitarian organizations that emerged in France, its founding was inspired by the Catholic Church. Although vexing problems of Vietnam, Algeria, and elsewhere were still plaguing the nation, the Church was ready to take the initiative in organizing relief efforts. While the Association Mondiale was designed as an international body, as an expression of Catholic charity throughout the world, a more nationally focused agency, the Comité Française contre la Faim, was set up in 1960 to help Algerian victims of the colonial war.[31] In the meantime, Voluntary Service Overseas was founded in Britain in 1958, and Campaign against Hunger and Disease in the World in Germany in the same year. These instances show that by the late 1950s, Western European nations, including West Germany, had sufficiently recovered from the devastation of the Second World War that their citizens and private organizations were willing to undertake systematic efforts to alleviate medical and nutritional problems in the rest of the world. Japan, too, began to participate in international relief activities. In 1960 some of its Christian leaders organized the Overseas Christian Medical Cooperation Service, which observers regard as the first postwar Japanese nongovernmental organization in the field of international humanitarian service.

In such a list of humanitarian organizations, one notices the absence of those concerned with the disabled. The 1948 Universal Declaration on Human Rights asserted the principle of nondiscrimination of all categories of people (women, minorities, political dissidents) except for the disabled.[32] This is a puzzling omission, considering that the disabled — physically, mentally, and emotionally — make up a significant portion (some say as much as 3 percent) of the world's population. About the only international organization that addressed the needs of the disabled was Rehabilitation International, established in Geneva in 1929 to help war veterans who had been wounded and otherwise incapacitated reintegrate into society. The same organization worked with veterans of the Second World War, but during the 1950s, it began to concern itself with nonveterans as well, especially those injured in workplaces. Stressing the need to "rehabilitate" such people, Rehabilitation International held conferences in Sweden, the Netherlands, Britain, Denmark, and Germany. That only European countries hosted these gatherings suggests that at that time, there was as yet no worldwide concern with the disabled — something that would have to wait till the following decades.

In the meantime, some organizations were going beyond traditional humanitarian relief and beginning to concern themselves with what came to be known as "developmental assistance," offering economic, technical, and other types of aid to "developing" (often referred to as "underdeveloped") countries. Programs for developmental assistance, as distinct from economic relief and rehabilitation, were slow to develop in the immediate postwar years; such assistance implied a long-term commitment, not a temporary alleviation of suffering from war or civil war, and involved a perception of international relations in which richer, technologically more advanced countries were expected to help less developed countries. This was a major commitment and required a reconceptualization of international affairs. It was by no means certain that such reconceptualization would occur at a time when Cold War tensions increased after 1949, especially with the outbreak of the Korean War in 1950. Precisely for that reason, however, prominent leaders from developing nations, such as Abdel Nasser of Egypt, Jawaharlal Nehru of India, and Achmed Sukarno of Indonesia, insisted time and again that their needs and priorities were different from those of the protagonists in the Cold War, and that the richer countries, instead of trying to divert their resources to improving their respective nuclear arsenals, should share their technology, resources, and wealth with poorer countries eager to transform themselves.

Taking heed of such voices, the United Nations established a Special United Nations Fund for Economic Development in 1951 and a Committee for Industrial Development in 1960. These organizations provided the institutional apparatus for the study of developmental assistance. What they envisaged was no less than the creation of a network of countries and agencies throughout the world that would promote the economic development of nations as an international objective, not as a means for waging Cold War. Much of the funding for the realization of such a vision would come from the United Nations and, therefore, from its member states with their own interests and agendas. Moreover, during the 1950s the main source of funds was the World Bank, which established an International Finance Corporation in 1956 to subsidize private enterprise projects in Third World countries.[33] Because the World Bank was dominated by the United States and its European allies, and because it emphasized private enterprises, one could argue that these activities still were not far removed from the geopolitical realities of the world. Nevertheless, both the United Nations and the World

Bank pursued aid policies that were oriented differently from the waging of the Cold War. For instance, the massive economic and technical assistance these organizations extended to India was based on different criteria from its perceived position in the bipolar world. Indeed, the aid programs were designed to unite the world community, not to keep it divided.[34] Likewise, the Asian and African nations participating in the Bandung conference of 1955 considered various proposals for promoting regional cooperation with regard to economic development and trade expansion.[35] Little of anything specific emerged at this time, and the Bandung group of nations did not succeed in creating a system comparable to the European Economic Community. Nevertheless, economic development was by then a widely used concept. China and Japan both sent delegates to the conference, and they agreed with their counterparts from other countries (including India and Pakistan, with their conflicting geopolitical interests) that there was room for cooperation in this realm, irrespective of the vicissitudes of the Cold War.

That developmental assistance was becoming an international concern of nongovernmental organizations as well may be seen in the founding, in 1957, of the Society for International Development. It started from a meeting of development specialists in Washington to exchange information and experience. That professional personnel specializing in developmental problems already existed is an interesting phenomenon, suggesting that by the middle of the decade, these problems were beginning to be seen as requiring training. (Haverford College, a small liberal arts institution, was then offering a graduate program in technical assistance.) However, as the Society's official history admits, at first "it was uncertain" specifically how "international development" could be promoted.[36] It was only during the 1960s that the organization became larger, more international, and better equipped with intellectual expertise and administrative skills to carry out its objectives. But it was not alone in calling the nation's and the world's attention to Third World problems. The Ford Foundation, by far the largest philanthropic body in the United States at that time (in 1954 it dispensed some $68 million, four times the amount expended by the next largest organization, the Rockefeller Foundation) became very interested in developmental issues. Under the presidency of H. Rowan Gaither (1953–1956), the Ford Foundation established an Overseas Development Office to fund development projects abroad, which were being undertaken not only by U.S. but also by European organizations.[37] The estimate is that by 1960, some 69 percent of private funds for overseas assistance was going to Asian countries, while 11 percent went to Latin America and 6 percent to Africa.[38] It may be surmised that the bulk of these amounts was earmarked for developmental programs.

To say that such activities were totally private initiatives, independent of governmental input or intervention, would be an exaggeration. As Brian Smith has pointed out, governments periodically contributed funds to various organizations engaged in developmental assistance, and in so doing sought to make use of the latter in implementing projects that were in line with state policy. Sometimes officials found it prudent to make use of nongovernmental organizations to work with their counterparts abroad as recipients of economic assistance, rather than dealing directly with host governments. But these were by no means cases of nongovernmental organizations automatically doing their respective governments' bidding. Smith notes that more often than not, the former took the latter's money but followed their own sense of priorities. Indeed, by encouraging the establishment of networks of nongovernmental organizations among aid giving and receiving countries, officials may indeed have been unwittingly promoting the growth of such organizations.[39]

At bottom was a vision, shared by intergovernmental organizations and international nongovernmental organizations alike, that the developing nations of the world should be closely integrated into the international economy. Theories of economic development were in their infancy at that time, and one of the most influential writings on the subject, W. W. Rostow's *Stages of Economic Growth* (1960), was less an argument for internationalism than "a non-Communist manifesto," as the book's subtitle indicated. The MIT economist saw development as the key theme in the global contest between the West and the Soviet Union and asserted that the best strategy to prevent the latter from dominating the non-Western parts of the world was to ensure that their economic development took place through the infusion of capital and technology from the West. This kind of developmentalism was clearly seen as an instrument for waging the Cold War, not as a call for an integrated global society.

Nevertheless, even such ideas could serve internationalist purposes. The underlying assumption was that all countries went through "stages of economic growth," the stage of "modernization" being the crucial one. A country became "modernized" when its economy "took off," departing from centuries of agricultural production for industrialization. Although modernization theory was and has been criticized as Eurocentric, imagining a teleology in which all countries followed the same path of historical evolution as the West, at least it suggested the possibility of conceptually linking different parts of the world, with their different histories, in an overarching framework.[40] (An entry in the *International Encyclopedia of the Social Sciences*, published in 1968, defined *modernization* as "the process of social change whereby less developed societies acquire characteristics common to more developed societies."[41] Such a notion would be subjected to increasing criticism during the 1960s, but the definition may have been an accurate reflection of the thinking in the 1950s that saw possibilities for global transformation through modernization.)

Even the critics of developmentalism and modernization theory at that time sought to formulate an alternative viewpoint that was also global in scope. For instance, the assumption that somehow development would take place in all parts of the world through capital investment and technology transfer was challenged by the Argentine economist and banker, Raul Prebisch, who chaired the United Nations Economic Commission for Latin America at that time. He and his colleagues argued that the relationship between the developed and underdeveloped parts of the world was one of the latter's "dependency" on the former, and that this disparity could be overcome only through the state-led strategy of "import substitution" by which less developed nations would seek to reduce their dependence on the industrial economies.[42] Such a view, postulating a world economic system consisting of the "center" and the "periphery," proved extremely influential, but this, too, was an attempt at developing a global view of economic affairs. Whether inspired by Rostow, Prebisch, or others, the nations of the world did come to consider development a global concern, to such an extent that in 1961, the United Nations decided to call the new decade "a decade of development."

Reflecting the global scope of the problem of development, developmental assistance frequently entailed exchange programs to bring officials, intellectuals, businesspeople, and others from Third World countries to more advanced nations for education and training. Not surprisingly, the Ford Foundation saw one of its principal missions as the promotion both of economic development and of educational exchange. The foundation had, immediately after the war, funded exchange programs with European nations and would continue to do so in the 1950s. At the same time, this and other organizations increasingly shifted their attention to the Third World and funded programs for exchanges of persons between the United States on one hand and Asian, African, and Latin American countries on the other. The purpose was to help produce a sufficient number of Third World experts in economics, engineering, applied mathematics, and related subjects so that they would play a role in the development of their respective countries. But such programs were not confined to the United States. Great Britain, France, Germany, and other European countries, as well as the Soviet Union likewise interested themselves in bringing young leaders from Asia and Africa for training purposes. The Cold War was undeniably one context in which such exchanges took place, but only one. In the history of international organizations, these programs held significance in that rather than perpetuating the division of the world into two geopolitical camps, they served to establish additional networks among different parts of the world.

Exchanges between developed and developing nations were part of a larger phenomenon: the educational and cultural exchanges throughout the world were regaining their prewar level of intensity and were already beginning to surpass it. Perhaps the most famous example, the Fulbright program, expanded spectacularly during the 1950s. At its inception in 1948, there were faculty and student exchanges under the program with only five countries, and only forty-eight Americans and thirty-six overseas participants were its beneficiaries. By 1958, thirty-six countries, 1,734 Americans, and 2,670 foreign nationals were involved.[43] That the increase took place despite vehement attacks by Senator Joseph R. McCarthy, who insinuated that communists and subversives had been selected as participants, suggests widespread acceptance of educational exchanges.[44]

The Fulbright program was only one of many undertakings that sent American scholars and students abroad and invited their counterparts to the United States. During the 1950s, U.S. foundations, colleges and universities, and other organizations brought thousands of additional visitors for study and travel. They seem to have paid particular attention to exchanges with Germany and Japan as a way to bring about postwar reconciliation and cooperation. The estimate is that more Germans were being invited to visit the United States under governmental and nongovernmental auspices than individuals from any other country. Altogether some fifteen thousand Germans (including over two thousand Fulbrighters) crossed the Atlantic during the decade and, as Oliver Schmidt has shown, they were instrumental in establishing networks of communication between Germany and the United States — and, equally important, between Germany and other Western European countries. For such exchanges were part of a larger phenomenon: the intellectual and cultural reintegration of West Germany into the postwar Atlantic community.[45] This was not just cultural window dressing for the military alliance that was being forged, however. Germans and Americans who were involved in exchange programs were convinced that solid intellectual and cultural understanding was the key to a stable relationship. Such

a relationship had to be an equal one; while the bulk of the initial funding came from the United States, German exchange scholars, journalists, and students were encouraged to make their own input. After they
went home, they would do their part in building bridges, with their
compatriots as well as with Americans and other Europeans residing in
the country. In this process, not just Germans but Americans and others
were also being transformed.

Such transformation as a consequence of the self-conscious, sponsored intermingling across national boundaries in peacetime made the
post-1945 years unique. Earlier, in most instances only the rich and the
privileged had an opportunity to associate themselves with people of
other lands, the local rich and the privileged. Now, however, governments and nongovernmental institutions were encouraging private associations on a massive scale. The implications of such a phenomenon for
international relations were far-reaching. It may be more accurate to say
that the meaning of international relations became broader because of
these interchanges. They were creating a sense of transnational experience to a degree unprecedented in history, and this sense was subtly
transforming the world community. David Lodge, the English writer,
has captured the significance of this transformation in his autobiograph-
ical novel *Out of the Shelter* (1970). Lodge was sixteen years old when he
visited Heidelberg in 1951 to see his aunt, who was working for the
United States Army. The trip was, he writes, "one of the formative experiences" of his life. Not just for him alone, but for the British and
Americans he saw, a new world seemed to be opening up. "Back home,"
an American in Heidelberg observes in the novel, many of his compatriots residing in Germany would be "nobodies, sitting in their back-
yards, wondering if they could afford to change their cars this year, planning a vacation in Atlantic City. But here they can live like kings. Europe
is their playground."[46] That captures the emerging transnationalism of
the age, affecting both victors and vanquished in the last war.[47]

Similar developments could be observed in exchange programs
involving Japan, although the scale was less than that for Germany, and

the bulk of educational exchanges was with the United States, with far fewer opportunities to forge links with Asian countries at that time. Some twenty-eight hundred Japanese students and scholars were invited to study in the United States under the Fulbright program between 1951 and 1962, and over five hundred American Fulbrighters went to Japan.[48] But even before 1951, when the San Francisco peace treaty officially terminated the state of war between the two countries, GARIOA (Government and Relief in Occupied Areas) funds had been made available for these purposes. Equally important were a number of private initiatives that enabled Japanese and Americans to resume their peacetime exchanges. St. Paul's School in Concord, New Hampshire, for instance, invited high school students from Japan for two years of education.[49] The idea of bringing teenagers from Japan, to have them serve as symbols of the two countries' reconciliation and renewed friendship, harked back to the prewar years, when a number of private programs had financed study for young Japanese in the United States. One example had been the Edgar A. Bancroft Foundation, established in honor of an American ambassador who served in Japan during the 1920s. The foundation had sent several young men to study in American colleges, and the program was resumed in 1953. Another prewar ambassador, Joseph C. Grew, was instrumental in setting up a foundation that bore his name, for similar purposes.[50] The first four students in the program, having just graduated from high school, left for the United States in 1953. A larger-scale organization devoted to shorter-term exchanges was Youth for Understanding International Exchange, established in 1951 to promote world peace and understanding through young people's "home-stay" experiences. Japan and Germany were active participants in the program from early on.

The American Friends Service Committee, which was actively seeking to build bridges to the Soviet-bloc nations, was also organizing international seminars and workshops in Germany and Japan as well as other countries. At a time when nongovernmental international gatherings were still rare, it energetically sought to bring young people of various countries together to share their ideas and to work together on humanitarian projects. By the mid-1950s Friends' international seminars and workshops were arenas for the gathering of young men and women from all over the world. College students from the United States began to attend them in Japan starting in 1955, living with local families or in university dormitories for a common experience with people from Japan and other countries of Asia, Africa, and Europe. Here again, besides opening new channels of communication between Americans and Japanese, such opportunities were instrumental in effecting the first phase of postwar reconciliation between Japan and the countries it had occupied.

Within Europe, in the meantime, cultural exchange was being viewed as equally important to economic integration. In 1957, the year when France, West Germany, Italy, Belgium, the Netherlands, and Luxembourg established the European Economic Community, these countries also set up a European Atomic Community (Euratom) for cooperative development of nuclear power. Such regional organizations stood outside the framework of the Cold War. These same nations, together with the United States, Britain, and others, were also working to strengthen their collective defenses against the Soviet-bloc countries, which established their own regional security system, the Warsaw Pact, in 1955, the same year that West Germany was admitted to the North Atlantic Treaty Organization. In the history of international nongovernmental organizations, however, what is significant is that economic and cultural cooperation was being promoted just as vigorously as military coordination, and that negotiations that culminated in regional economic and atomic communities had little to do with the vicissitudes in the Cold War drama. In fact, some initiatives in the cultural direction were intended to mitigate the geopolitical tensions of a divided Europe. In 1954 European nations signed a cultural convention, the first of its kind after the war, to promote exchange programs not just among Western Europeans but also between them and the people of Eastern Europe. From the agreement resulted a number of initiatives by teachers and scholars of various countries to come together to discuss the teaching of history and other subjects. The teaching of history was particularly important, as educators understood the significant roles history textbooks had played in strengthening exclusionary nationalism. With the lessons of the two wars fresh on their minds, French and German historians and teachers conferred frequently to find ways of writing joint textbooks. For Germans this involved the rewriting of much recent history to repudiate the Nazi version of their nation's past. They were willing to undertake the task in cooperation not only with their French counterparts but also with Polish teachers and scholars. Textbooks jointly authored by German and Polish historians began to be written in the 1950s, a sure sign that not every aspect of European international affairs had to do with the U.S.-Soviet confrontation.[51]

Outside of the United States and Europe, too, cultural exchange attracted the attention of many countries. This could best be seen in the workings of UNESCO, whose membership increased from fifty-nine nations in 1950 to ninety-nine by 1960. The increase reflected the coming into existence of newly independent states, all of which were eager to play a role in international cultural relations and establish their respective national commissions. Their self-consciousness and assertive self-identity, as well as their eagerness to promote cultural exchange, were evident already at a conference organized by UNESCO in New Delhi in 1954 on the theme of "the concept of man and the philosophy of education in East and West."[52] The dichotomizing of East and West was nothing new; most recently, wartime Japanese propaganda had made much of the alleged contrast between Eastern and Western values. The war had discredited the Japanese construction of the dichotomy, but not the fascination with the question of the relationship between East and West itself. India's Nehru, for instance, was deeply interested in the question, as was virtually every leader of the newly independent Asian states. The reason may well have been that the East was becoming more and more a concrete reality, as a result of the decolonization of European empires. With China under a communist regime and India and Indonesia asserting their "third" way in the Cold War, it was important to try to see if these countries could still communicate with Western nations. But even apart from such Cold War considerations, there was a sense that international understanding hinged increasingly on mutual appreciation among different cultures. The widespread belief was that not just by spreading Western values or transferring Western technology to the East, but also by bringing the two perspectives together, would it become possible for the countries of the world to build a solid basis for a stable international order.

These ideas were reiterated at a meeting of the Indian national commission of UNESCO, held in 1954. Representatives from Afghanistan, Ceylon, Egypt, Indonesia, Iran, Iraq, Japan, Lebanon, Nepal, and Syria were invited to attend, a good indication of the degree to which postcolonial societies were evincing an interest in international cultural relations. (Japan was an exception, but its presence in New Delhi — two years before the nation was admitted into the United Nations — was one of the first instances of the country's participation in an international conference after it regained sovereignty.) At the meeting, the participants once again stressed the importance of fostering communication between Eastern and Western civilizations. An interesting question is whether such an emphasis would have been there if delegates from the People's Republic of China had been invited. China was still represented in UNESCO and most other international organizations by the Nationalist regime in Taiwan, so that mainland Chinese did not participate in the cultural dialogue going on among other Asian countries. (Beijing did participate in the Bandung conference of 1955, where a committee on cultural cooperation considered various ways of promoting Asian-African cultural exchange. Little came of the discussion, however.)[53] To the Chinese communists, "East" may well have meant the Soviet-bloc, not Asian civilization, and "culture" may have had a highly ideological content. Still, during the short period known as the "hundred flowers campaign" of 1956–1957, when Beijing let China's intellectuals voice their views freely, many expressed their curiosity about the extent of the communist country's difference from Western nations, some echoing the sentiment of other Asian countries that China should be a bridge between Eastern and Western civilizations.[54] In any event, Asian countries were clearly doing their share in building their own networks of cultural communication and in that process helping to generate a sense of global community.

That sense was further fostered in two other areas where a great deal of cross-national activity began to develop: human rights and the natural environment. That human rights was already becoming a serious concern of international organizations can be seen in the fact that the United Nations Human Rights Commission held a series of subcommission meetings and working group discussions throughout 1951. The Korean War was still going on, and the United Nations Security Council was an arena of acrimonious debate between the two sides in the Cold War, but that did not prevent Washington and Moscow from sending delegates to these subcommission meetings. And their proceedings provide a valuable glimpse not only into shared as well as contrasting perspectives on human rights, but also into the role of nongovernmental organizations.

As just one example, the Human Rights Commission's "working group on economic, social, and cultural projects" held a series of meetings in Geneva to provide a basis for the drafting of an international covenant of human rights, a document that would give specificity to the 1948 universal declaration on human rights by indicating in what areas those rights should be protected and promoted. Represented at the working group's sessions were eighteen countries, three affiliated agencies of the United Nations (UNESCO, the International Labor Organization, and the World Health Organization), and twenty-three nongovernmental organizations.

Listing these organizations indicates the range of international nongovernmental institutions that were concerned with human rights issues at that time: the World Federation of Free Trade Unions, the International Federation of Free Trade Unions, the International Federation of Christian Trade Unions, the World Federation of United Nations Associations, Caritas Internationalis, the Carnegie Endowment for International Peace, the Catholic International Union for Social Service, the Commission of the Churches on International Affairs, the Consultative Council of Jewish Organizations, Friends' World Committee for Conciliation, the International Bureau of Penal Law, the International Council of Women, the International Federation of University Women, the International Federation of Business and Professional Women, the International League for the Rights of Man, the International Union for Child Welfare, the International Union of Catholic Women's Leagues, the Liaison Committee of Women's International Organizations, Pax Romana, Women's International League for Peace and Freedom, the World Jewish Congress, and the World's Young Women's Christian Association.

A number of these organizations had been around for some time; for instance, the history of the International Council of Women went back to the 1880s.[55] A few were sponsored by governmental agencies, often covertly, to serve their respective national interests. Some associations of free trade unions, for instance, are known to have been funded by the United States Central Intelligence Agency to counter left-leaning tendencies of other countries' labor organizations. Most of the previously listed nongovernmental organizations, including recent creations such as the International League for the Rights of Man and the International Union for Child Welfare, had little to do with the geopolitical dramas of the time. They were deeply interested in the question of human rights, which they, as nongovernmental organizations, believed they were in a unique position to promote. As a delegate of the World Jewish Congress noted at one of these gatherings:

> The United Nations, by its establishment of committees of
> independent experts in various fields and by the grant of consultative
> status to non-governmental bodies, has recognized the legitimacy
> and importance of non-governmental opinion as a factor in the
> shaping of its policies . . . this non-governmental factor should

be encouraged and strengthened as representing elements and
aspirations in international public opinion which must play a
significant role in the development and consolidation of a genuine
world community.[56]

Such a statement, so characteristic of that time, indicated self-consciousness and self-confidence on the part of nongovernmental organizations as important participants in international affairs.

That six out of the twenty-three nongovernmental organizations
whose representatives attended the working group meetings were
women's organizations shows a strong interest and determination that
any consideration of human rights must include the principle of the
equality of the sexes. During the 1950s, the International Labor Organization responded to the voices of these and other women's associations
and adopted two conventions barring gender discrimination in the
workplace: the equal remuneration convention (1951) and the employment (discrimination) convention (1958). More than one hundred
nations were to ratify these two conventions during the subsequent
decades.[57] (Historians have noted that in the United States at least, more
traditional ideas of womanhood pervaded domestic politics and social
relations during the 1950s. As such, to the extent that international
organizations were promoting women's rights, they were paving the way
for what would develop as a worldwide movement for women's liberation during the 1960s.)

Outside the principle of gender equality in the workplace, much
debate and disagreement surrounded the issue of what constituted
human rights. At the 1951 working group sessions, Jaime Torres-Bodet,
who had succeeded Julian Huxley as director-general of UNESCO,
stressed the right to education, while Brook Chisolm, director-general
of the World Health Organization, insisted, not surprisingly, that the
"enjoyment of the highest attainable standard of health is one of the fundamental rights of every human being." The delegates from Chile and
Egypt argued that economic, social, and cultural rights should be

specified in any definition of human rights, while Eleanor Roosevelt, representing the United States, demurred, remarking that these "rights" did not come within her government's understanding of human rights. Her viewpoint, which other representatives of the Western world shared — namely, that human rights were principally matters of individual conscience — contrasted sharply with that of Soviet-bloc and Third World delegates, who tended to stress economic and social rights. On this issue, the United States and its allies were willing to make concessions so as to complete the tasks of the working group. As Mrs. Roosevelt said, the United States would be willing to view economic and social rights as a matter of "aspirations," if not as legally binding obligations. The same willingness to compromise was apparent when the delegates disagreed on the means of enforcing the practice of human rights. The Soviet representative insisted that the matter should be left to each government, whereas Mrs. Roosevelt stated that her government was prepared "to surrender a certain amount of national sovereignty in an effort to join with the other nations of the world" in implementing the human rights agreement, should it be ratified. In the end, the matter of enforcement was left vague to accommodate these differences, but despite such disagreement, the working group was able to conclude its task and unanimously adopted a report enumerating a long list of items on which the delegates had achieved agreement.[58]

These discussions, however limited in scope, were initiating a process for implementing the principle of human rights throughout the globe. Nations of the world, whatever their geopolitical policies, were trying to see if they could jointly produce what Richard Falk would later call "a scenario for the attainment of a transformed world order that embodied the chief precepts of cosmopolitan democracy."[59] And the success, modest as it was, of such international efforts owed itself to a great extent to the energetic activities of nongovernmental organizations. That they were already becoming quite visible and being recognized as important contributors to the scenario may be seen in another meeting of the

Human Rights Commission. Its subcommittee on the prevention of discrimination and protection of minorities held a series of meetings in 1952, and at one such meeting, a delegate proposed that a conference of nongovernmental organizations be convened to coordinate their work in the prevention of discrimination against minorities. As he said of these organizations, "Their zeal, independence, and, in some cases, very considerable resources [make] their assistance indispensable."[60] The proposal was approved unanimously, with only one abstention; the delegates of both the United States and the Soviet Union voted for it, indicating that they shared an awareness of the rising importance of nongovernmental bodies in international affairs. It was no accident that the International Federation of Human Rights, originally founded in Paris in 1922, resumed its work in 1958 and began cooperating closely with the United Nations, the Council of Europe, and other international organizations.

Compared with human rights, there was far less international activity dealing with the natural environment. According to statistics made available by the Union of International Associations, there were thirty-three international nongovernmental organizations concerned with human rights in 1953, whereas only two existed in the area of the environment.[61] This low figure is misleading, since it is possible to argue that many antinuclear organizations were seriously concerned with the problem of atmospheric pollution. Moreover, besides the one major international organization, the International Union for the Protection of Nature (its name was changed to the International Union for Conservation of Nature and Natural Resources in 1956), smaller organizations were beginning to appear, even if they were not registered with the Union of International Associations. For instance, in 1957 the Scientific Committee on Oceanic Research was established to focus on the preservation of marine life. And in the following year, the International Council of Scientific Unions (organized in 1919) created two committees, one on space research and the other on Antarctic research.[62] Still, the impression is inescapable that compared with the other types of international activities that this chapter has sketched, the time for international environmental activism had not yet arrived.

Why was this the case? It may well be that environmental consciousness had not yet emerged on a global scale. "Until this point in history," UNESCO noted in 1968, "the nations of the world have lacked considered, comprehensive policies for managing the environment." Although small steps had been taken, "a threshold" would be reached only in the 1960s, generating a public awareness of the serious need for concerted action.[63] We should, however, not jump to the conclusion that the slow development of international environmentalism was because of the Cold War. After all, the intensification of the Cold War did not prevent the notable expansion of international organizations in so many fields. Even without much to show in this one area, they were contributing to redefining international relations during the 1950s. If by "international relations" one means geopolitical realities such as balance of power, armaments, and alliance systems, obviously the manifold activities by the nonstate actors were of merely marginal relevance. But what were the "realities"? After all, the Cold War, in postulating a third world war, was as much in the realm of imagination as of reality. By the same token, activities by international organizations to prevent the imagined world war from becoming a reality, to feed the hungry, to help new nations to undertake economic development, to promote educational exchanges, and to seek ways of protecting human rights — these activities were no less real than the geopolitics of the bipolar confrontation. If that confrontation was creating an atmosphere of fear and insecurity among nations, international organizations were offering hope, suggesting to humankind that goodwill existed even in such a horrible world. They were demonstrating the possibility that an alternative definition of international affairs might be developed, a definition that stressed global interdependence rather than bipolar conflict and shared interests across national boundaries rather than disparate national interests in a zero-sum game of power politics. The intergovernmental organizations and international nongovernmental organizations did not change the geopolitical drama of the Cold War; rather, they were quietly writing a scenario for another drama. In that sense, international organizations were even more subversive of the Cold War than the spies and double agents who worked within that framework. And so, when the Cold War began to be undermined during the 1960s, these organizations were already there, ready to step in and lead the world in a different direction.

CHAPTER 4

More States,
More Nonstate Actors

Self-consciousness about global community may have been a key aspect of international relations of the 1960s, a decade that is usually seen through such geopolitical dramas as the Cuban missile crisis, the Vietnam War, and the Chinese-Soviet rift. Historians speak of the "eyeball-to-eyeball" confrontation between the United States and the Soviet Union over the latter's introduction of missiles into Cuba, which was swiftly followed by the superpowers' agreement to limit nuclear testing and to prevent the proliferation of nuclear arms. By the end of the decade, Washington and Moscow were pledging not to unleash these weapons against each other, and it seemed as if the worst phase of the Cold War was over. On the other hand, the global struggle for power did not disappear, and the long war in Vietnam in which the United States became involved was rationalized as a necessary part of the struggle. Even here, however, the picture was complicated because the Soviet Union and the People's Republic of China did not always coordinate their policies, and their relationship became strained as Beijing refused to accept Moscow's tentative rapprochement with Washington. The Vietnam War intensified in part because, simultaneously with the thawing of U.S.-U.S.S.R. relations, the United States came to view the containment of China in Southeast Asia as a major objective of its Cold War strategy, and even more so after the successful Chinese testing of nuclear devices in 1964. The Chinese touted the development as a victory of anti-imperialist forces everywhere. When, in the second half of the decade, the Chinese erupted in the Great Proletarian Cultural Revolution, denouncing both U.S. "imperialism" and Soviet "revisionism," it seemed as if Asia would remain a major arena of instability, nuclear armament, and ideological confrontation.

Such dramatic developments might give the impression that the globe remained more seriously divided than ever, rendering the vision of international society extremely difficult to envision, let alone bring to fruition. Nevertheless, in the story of the making of a global community, the 1960s constitute an important chapter. Precisely because the world's geopolitics appeared so volatile and dangerous, forces and movements that had desperately sought an alternative world order during the 1950s redoubled their efforts. Ad hoc nongovernmental organizations mushroomed in North America and Western Europe to protest the continuing war in Southeast Asia, their combined pressure ultimately leading to a change of policy in Washington. New student organizations such as Students for a Democratic Society, established in 1964 in Port Huron, Michigan, were merely among the most visible, and they were joined by countless others that together made up a potent movement for an alternative to the Cold War. Even within the Soviet bloc, there grew a powerful movement, spearheaded by nongovernmental organizations in Poland and Czechoslovakia, for a new domestic order more liberated from communist control. In the meantime, there were successful attempts at regional organization, the most notable examples being the European Community and the Association of Southeast Asian Nations, both established in 1967. These developments, too, are usually understood in the context of the history of the Cold War. However, intergovernmental and nongovernmental initiatives were becoming a pervasive global phenomenon, continuing the trend that had begun in the 1950s and earlier. A history of international relations during the 1960s that ignores this phenomenon, as most studies still do, pays attention only to the surface drama of international politics and is oblivious to some fundamental changes that were taking place just below the surface.

To begin with, the number of intergovernmental organizations increased from 154 to 280 between 1960 and 1970, and that of international nongovernmental organizations from 1,268 to 2,795, according to data collected by the Union of International Associations.[1] More than doubling the number of international nongovernmental organizations is particularly noteworthy. If we count the various branches of intergovernmental organizations and international nongovernmental organizations, there were 3,116 and 24,136 of them, respectively, at the beginning of the decade. By 1966, their numbers had increased to 4,616 and 36,336. What is particularly striking is that during the 1960s, many of these branches were established in the Third World: newly independent states of Asia and Africa, as well as the older countries of Latin America. Thus, more than ever before, various parts of the globe were becoming interconnected.

A graphic example of how private organizations were seeking to establish nonstate networks despite the apparently continuing intensity of Cold War tensions may be seen in the activities of several United States nongovernmental associations in Vietnam. While the war escalated, a host of organizations, many of them religious, created programs to train volunteers for humanitarian work in Southeast Asia. The American Friends Service Committee, for instance, began sending humanitarian missions to South Vietnam in 1965 under its Voluntary International Service Assignment (VISA) program, originally founded in the late 1940s to provide help to postwar Germany. By the 1960s VISA volunteers were working in more than forty countries, including India, Tanzania, and Guatemala. The Quaker organization from the beginning was intent upon working with nongovernmental organizations in Vietnam — indeed to place its personnel within and under Vietnamese agencies. VISA workers even established contact with representatives of the National Liberation Front to apprise the latter of their work. Although such activities inevitably had political connotations, the volunteers stuck to the position that their purpose in Vietnam was "not . . . protest, but service," as one of them stated.[2]

In the meantime, Church World Service took the initiative in 1966 to work with thirty Protestant denominations, including the Mennonite Central Committee, which had been sending service workers to Vietnam since the 1950s. It organized a Vietnam Christian Service, one of the major attempts at helping Vietnamese refugees, now numbering over one million. Volunteers worked in hospitals, refugee camps, and city slums to alleviate suffering. While these were U.S. organizations, the volunteers included Europeans and Asians as well as Americans.[3] The spirit that motivated the volunteers is evident in a little pamphlet written by Atlee and Winifred Beechy, two leaders of Vietnam Christian Service, and published in 1968. Vietnam, they noted, "symbolizes the military mentality and the military dominance in our world. The resulting forces of hate and fear are real in the lives of the people here." It was all the more important, therefore, to "remind the nations that there is another kind of power, another way for men to relate to each other, another kingdom which transcends national and racial lines."[4] Similarly, Mary Sue Rosenberger, who worked in Vietnam for Brethren Volunteer Service, organized by the Church of Brethren, wrote, "I am . . . eager for the challenge of putting Christian-American concerns for the Vietnamese people into action without guns and killing." The "need for care, love, peace, and a responsibility for a brother or sister's need" were human phenomena and knew no national boundaries or ideological differences.[5] The religious and nongovernmental organizations that shared such internationalism and sent volunteers to Vietnam were demonstrating, once again, that conflicts and wars would provide an impetus for transnational movements that would seek to preserve and strengthen global consciousness.

Relief work in Vietnam, however, must also be seen as part of a larger picture: the expanding role of nongovernmental organizations throughout the world. During the 1960s, humanitarian programs were as critically important as ever; many local conflicts arose that had less to do with the Cold War than with the fact that some forty countries became independent during the decade. Many of them, especially in Africa, had been devastated through years of anticolonial struggles, and even after independence they were plagued by internecine warfare, both domestic and external. The problems of these countries were serious enough to command the attention of the United Nations and other intergovernmental organizations, but it was international nongovernmental organizations that played key roles in seeking to provide relief. For instance, Service Civil International was active in Algeria, reconstructing villages destroyed by many years of its war for independence. The British branch of this organization sent long-term volunteers to such countries as Cameroon, Botswana, Swaziland, Lesotho, and Senegal. In Asia, Service Civil International workers were busy in Malaysia, Thailand, and Nepal. The parent organization was eager to send missions to South and North Vietnam, though at that time little was accomplished. But throughout the 1960s, this organization was conspicuous among international nongovernmental organizations because of its activism in newly independent countries.[6]

In the meantime, new nongovernmental organizations were being established to join the existing ones to engage in humanitarian work. Unquestionably, this reflected the widening gap during the 1960s between rich and poor countries; the economies of North America, Western Europe, Japan, and Oceania were growing much faster than the rest of the world, and many people in the former countries were keenly aware of the need to do something about the situation. It was no accident that in the United States, the new administration of John F. Kennedy, asserting its determination to be active in "new frontiers" in foreign affairs, established the Peace Corps, an agency for recruiting and sending volunteers to engage in humanitarian efforts abroad. Thousands of young men and women, inspired by the vision of service to humanity, went to countries in Latin America, Africa, the Middle East, and Asia as teachers, social workers, and agricultural experts to help those countries overcome their misery. Because the Peace Corps was a governmental program, cynics then and since dismissed it as just another tool of foreign policy, a nonmilitary means for winning the Cold War. In the context of our discussion, however, the program's voluntary nature should be noted; its participants were all volunteers, and moreover, private agencies worked closely with it. Even before the Peace Corps was officially launched in early 1961, for instance, the American Council of Voluntary Agencies for Foreign Service (created in 1943) established its own Peace Corps committee to provide input into the organization and functioning of the federal program. The relationship between the two was not always smooth; the Peace Corps announced in November 1961 that while it desired nongovernmental organizations' "continued cooperation and support . . . church-related organizations would not receive contracts to administer programs abroad."[7] An inherent tension existed between international humanitarian work carried out by private volunteers and by governmental agencies. Nevertheless, in the context of our discussion, the Peace Corps represented an internationalist antidote to the struggle for power with the Soviet Union that had divided the world. Historian Elizabeth Cobbs Hoffman is unquestionably right when she writes that the Peace Corps represented a universalistic impulse in a geopolitical age. In U.S. foreign affairs, she notes, the exercise of power often "calls forth a compensatory impulse." Thus the extension of military power during the war in Vietnam coincided with the growth of Peace Corps activities.[8]

Moreover, the officially sponsored project was only one out of numerous programs for international relief, most of which continued to be carried out by nongovernmental organizations, old and new. In the United States, the 1960s saw the establishment of such voluntary agencies as Project Concern International and American Near East Refugee Aid, which supplemented the work of existing organizations such as Church World Service and Lutheran World Relief in promoting humanitarian activities. While some of these groups were not, strictly speaking, international nongovernmental organizations, they established overseas offices to coordinate the activities of volunteers who, of course, served in different parts of the world. A major characteristic of organized relief programs during the 1960s was that many groups began to focus their attention on poorer areas and countries in Asia, Africa, the Middle East, and Latin America. Project Concern International, for instance, was established in the early 1960s in San Diego to help save children's lives in Africa by providing medicine and food, while American Near East Refugee Aid, founded in the wake of the 1967 Arab-Israeli war, aimed at "improving lives, relieving suffering, building communities, investing in peace in the West Bank, Gaza strip, and Lebanon."[9] All such activities were making networks of humanitarian internationalism more global than ever before.

That network was being expanded through the activities of non-governmental organizations outside the United States. In Canada, Compassion of Canada, Leprosy Relief/Canada, International Medical Assistance (Canada), and the Christian World Relief Committee (Canada) all came into being during the 1960s. In Europe, the Oxford Committee for Famine Relief (founded during the war) came to be widely known as Oxfam at this time and established branches elsewhere (such as Oxfam Belgique, founded in 1964). In France the Catholic Church took the initiative in setting up various humanitarian organizations. The social activism of Pope John XXIII (1958–1963), who had a strong interest in combating poverty and hunger in the world, was undoubtedly a major force behind the trend. But the lay community was no less involved, and in 1961 Comité des Jeunes contre la Faim was created, followed two years later by the founding of Terres des Hommes France and Frères des Hommes. (In 1968 these two were combined into Les Hommes pour les Hommes.) Also in 1968, local associations providing help to lepers became federated.[10] In Australia, in the meantime, a humanitarian organization named Austcare was founded in 1967 to provide private funds for the care of the hungry abroad. The names of these organizations suggest that, as in the United States or Canada, there was sensitivity to the persistence of hunger in poorer areas of the globe and that the vision of common humanity inspired an earnest effort at alleviating the suffering of fellow humans.

Far more than during the 1950s, however, international humanitarian relief now tended to merge into, or be overshadowed by, developmental assistance. It was typical that in France, Comité Catholique contre la Faim, founded in 1961, was renamed Comité Catholique contre la Faim et pour le Développement four years later. And, also in France, several older and newer organizations concerned with popular education came together to pool their resources for work in the Third World.[11] It was becoming evident to religious and lay people alike that only sustained programs of developmental assistance would provide permanent solutions to the problems of poverty and hunger in Third World countries.

It was in 1961 that a group of newly independent nations met in Cairo and defined themselves for the first time as "developing countries."[12] And in the same year, the United Nations determined that the 1960s were to be called "a decade of development," postulating that the gross national products of the developing countries would grow at the annual rate of 5 percent throughout the decade. The initiative taken by the world organization suggested that development was a global phenomenon and that more advanced countries had an obligation to help those that were struggling to transform themselves. These ideas had emerged during the 1950s, and the United Nations as well as the World Bank had begun to turn their attention to the problems of nation building. What distinguished the 1960s was that development entered the vocabulary of international affairs as a key concept, often even overshadowing geopolitical concerns. This in turn reflected the fact that while more countries, especially in Africa, gained independence, the disparity between the richer and the poorer nations did not cease and, if anything, widened during the decade. How to assist the nation-building efforts of the former colonies, when the metropolitan governments no longer undertook to care for them, was now a major international issue.

Not just the newly independent countries, however, but many others in the Middle East, Asia, and Latin America came to focus on developmental assistance as a principal framework in which they related themselves to the more advanced nations of the world. They also related themselves to the Cold War; countries such as India, Egypt, and Ghana often played the United States and the Soviet Union against each other to obtain maximum amounts of aid. To view developmental assistance merely as an episode in the Cold War, however, would be to ignore the role played by international organizations, especially the United Nations, in coping with developmental issues. The Economic and Social Council, in particular, became an arena where Third World countries, which now made up more than half the membership, expressed their collective interests and concerns. Throughout the decade the Council grew enormously in scope, attaching to itself a large number of committees and commissions. Regional economic commissions — for Europe, for Latin America, for Asia and the Pacific, for Western Asia, and for Africa — had been established before 1960, but in the new decade others, oriented toward development, were added — for instance, the Committee on International Development (1960), the Industrial Development Organization (1965), and the Capital Development Fund (1966). In 1964 the United Nations held its first conference on trade and development (UNCTAD), a sure sign that the world body was going to involve itself directly in the question of development. Seventy-five countries from Asia, Africa, and Latin America attended, and they organized themselves as a group (later known as Group 77 when two additional nations joined them) to speak with one voice on international trade and investment issues. The UN's Food and Agricultural Organization (FAO), in the meantime, expanded its operations during the 1960s so that its membership increased from 88 in 1960 to 119 ten years later, its budget from $9.5 million to $40.0 million, and its staff from 1,454 to 3,410.[13]

The United Nations and its agencies were not the only international organizations concerned with developmental assistance. The Organization for Economic Cooperation and Development, established in 1961 by the richer countries of Europe, North America, and Oceania (joined by Japan in 1963), sought to coordinate their various foreign aid programs, while the World Bank, which had earlier focused its attention on assisting the countries of Europe to recover from the devastation brought about by the war, began to interest itself in developmental questions. In 1962 it set up the International Development Association as an affiliate body that would offer funds to developing countries at low interest rates. It extended loans amounting to $300 million in 1964, while the World Bank itself lent some $600 million, mostly to developing nations. By 1970, World Bank lending total amounted to $2 billion.[14]

The 1960s were also notable because various governments undertook to incorporate developmental assistance as an integral part of their foreign policies. This alone indicates that the Cold War was not the only concern of these nations; at the very least, the growth in official developmental assistance programs (ODAs) during the decade suggests that the foreign policies of some of the major powers, especially in the more advanced West, were becoming diversified to include far more than purely military, geopolitical strategies. The best example of this new trend was President Kennedy's initiation of the Alliance for Progress and the establishment of the Agency for International Development. Kennedy was willing to sponsor developmental assistance for its own sake, although he and his aides firmly believed that it would win the United States friends in the Third World.

The theories of modernization and of economic development, popularized by W. W. Rostow and others in the 1950s, had provided an intellectual underpinning for technical and economic assistance. These theories remained influential, but they were now less directly linked to a Cold War strategy. Geopolitical considerations were not totally absent from foreign aid programs, but it may be argued that developmental assistance began to generate its own momentum and came to affect formulations of foreign policy. The belief was that wealthy countries had an obligation as well as the capacity to implement ambitious developmental projects abroad. When, in 1969, the World Bank adopted a report recommending that advanced countries earmark 0.5 percent of their respective gross national products for official developmental assistance, the idea did not sound too idealistic. Indeed, throughout the so-called decade of development, developing nations grew by an average of 5.7 percent per year, thanks in no small degree to the massive infusion of such aid. The realization was that a stable world order could be attained only if the glaring disparity in standards of living throughout the world could be eliminated.

Thus the Alliance for Progress and other official aid programs undertaken by the United States, amounting to $10 billion during the 1960s, were in a sense part of a global effort to change the nature of international affairs, away from traditional concerns with balance of power and national interests toward the promotion of a more interdependent, integrated world order. The decade also saw similar programs implemented by other wealthier countries. Canada, for instance, established an International Development Agency in 1968, while the government of West Germany began offering grants to private organizations engaged in developmental assistance projects. Australia did not have a separate governmental agency dealing with foreign aid, but it consistently spent over 2 percent of national budgets (more than 0.5 percent of national income) on developmental assistance, focusing on the countries of Southeast Asia.[15] Perhaps it was symbolic that Robert McNamara, in many ways the architect of U.S. strategy in Vietnam, abruptly shifted course in 1968 by resigning from the government and assuming the presidency of the World Bank. It was as if one era, characterized by the ready use of force to establish order, was giving way to another, in which more peaceful means would be employed to restructure international affairs.

Nongovernmental organizations played a minor, but nevertheless significant, role in the story. This was so in part because public funds in the donor nations that were spent on developmental assistance never matched the lofty visions or grandiose rhetoric. Even President Kennedy, who showed a stronger interest in developmental assistance

than any president who preceded him, found it necessary to trim economic aid budgets in the face of a skeptical Congress whose members
were not convinced of the need to spend so much on foreign assistance
when domestic projects were claiming increased governmental attention
and outlays. Not just the war in Vietnam, or a determination to maintain
nuclear superiority over the Soviet Union, but also more fundamentally
fiscal and balance-of-payments deficits that became noticeable in the late
1960s prevented the United States from implementing a more massive
aid policy. Other countries, even those enjoying unprecedented trade
surpluses, also had their priorities, so that it was very difficult for them
to meet the goal, set by a United Nations resolution in 1970, of devoting 0.7 percent of their gross national products on official developmental assistance.

Under the circumstances, the private sector steadily increased in
importance as a source of money and expertise for developmental assistance, especially since many more countries now needed such aid. Some
of the nongovernmental organizations in the donor nations that focused
on development had long been engaged in missionary, educational,
medical, and philanthropic activities. But many new ones were created
during the 1960s. In the United States, for instance, the Pan American
Development Foundation was established in 1962 to do through private
initiatives what the government was attempting to carry out through the
Alliance for Progress. The National Association of Partners of the
Alliance, created two years later, served similar purposes. Also in 1964,
an African-American Labor Center was established to train African
labor leaders in the United States.

Other countries were no less active in establishing new nongovernmental organizations to focus on developmental assistance. In West
Germany, the Protestant Association for Cooperation and Development
was organized in 1962; two years later saw the founding of the International Association for Cooperation and Rural Development in
Belgium, as well as the Interchurch Coordinating Committee for Development Projects in the Netherlands. They were followed by the estab-

lishment in 1965 of the Australian Council for Overseas Aid and Switzerland's Pan-African Institute for Development. Japan, which lagged behind other developed countries in organizing nongovernmental organizations, began to stir itself during the same decade. Reparations and other settlements with the Asian countries that Japan had occupied during the war were being completed, and Japanese businesspeople as well as tourists began turning their attention to the promise and problems of those countries. The long war in Vietnam may also have provided the Japanese, now enjoying rapid economic expansion, with an opportunity to try to do something for their Asian neighbors. In 1961 a philanthropic organization called OISCA International was established to train development personnel in Japan and other Asian countries. About the same time, small-scale centers were created outside Tokyo to focus on the education and exchange of agricultural experts in Japan and the rest of Asia. The stress on Asia and on agriculture suggests that at that time, improvement in the productivity of rice and other grains was considered a priority for the economic development of the region.[16]

The mushrooming of these development-oriented nongovernmental organizations was a distinctive feature of international relations during the 1960s. They were creating a community of individuals and groups committed to development, and they were coming into frequent contact with one another. In their view, development was becoming a "global project," to be carried out through transnational efforts.[17] In some such way, the decade saw the coming together of the themes of globalization, development, and international organization. One may see such a connection, for instance, in the activities of the Society for International Development, which had been founded in Washington in the late 1950s as a forum for the exchange of information among development professionals. The organization expanded its scope considerably during the 1960s; it held regional conferences in Calcutta, Brussels, Athens, Milan, and New Delhi in which development specialists from various organizations participated. By the end of the decade, more than half of the

Society's members, now numbering over five thousand, came from outside the United States, and its journal, *International Development Review*, served to professionalize and internationalize thinking about development.[18]

The same process may be seen in the fact that developmental nongovernmental organizations established a large number of branch offices in aid-receiving countries. Because many countries in Africa achieved independence during the 1960s, the number of these branches in Africa, not surprisingly, increased rapidly; there were about two thousand of them in 1960, and by 1966 the number had increased to over forty-two hundred.[19] Most such branches included representatives sent from aid-giving organizations, but they were staffed primarily by local individuals. Of course, the degree to which locals participated in such projects varied from country to country. In countries with a weak civil society or with a low literacy rate, organizing autonomous nongovernmental bodies or recruiting staff to work for international nongovernmental organizations was extremely difficult. (In Ghana, when President Kwame Nkrumah declared in 1961 that there was to be free and compulsory education for all, finding trained teachers, especially in rural villages, was very difficult, and anyone who could read had to be recruited.)[20] Still, the mere fact that these branch offices were established throughout Africa (as well as in Latin America, the Middle East, and Asia) is significant as an indication of the political and social change in such countries that accompanied economic development. Moreover, whereas official developmental assistance channeled aid from a donor government to a recipient government, private organizations could, where conditions permitted, make use of their funds in ways they considered most suitable to local circumstances.

Nongovernmental organizations, however, did not operate in a vacuum. In both donor and recipient countries, they somehow had to cope with the presence of the state. Depending on the nature of the political system in a country, autonomy and freedom of action on the part of private organizations could be restricted. Even in the United States, private organizations often found it frustrating to work with agencies such as the Peace Corps and the Agency for International Development. These agencies were sources of funding to which voluntary groups applied for grants, in addition to soliciting private donations, to carry out their aid activities. But numerous bureaucratic rules and restrictions governed the contractual relationship between voluntary associations and the government.[21] The latter, on its part, was interested in monitoring the activities of nongovernmental organizations and in ensuring their accountability. Moreover, as Brian Smith has shown, officials in Washington often sought to co-opt these organizations to promote an officially defined foreign policy agenda. For instance, the State Department and the Agency for International Development often sought to persuade development-oriented associations to specialize in certain areas of developmental assistance that were not part of official aid programs. Professional expertise and voluntary workers, however, were more abundant in the private sector than within the government, so that more often than not, the initiative came from nongovernmental organizations to prod officials to design or refine governmental programs.

Smith cites a very good example of the interaction between public and private bodies: a 1968 project organized by Massachusetts Institute of Technology to bring together officials from the Agency for International Development and representatives of nongovernmental organizations for a six-week session. One conclusion the participants reached was that private organizations were going to play an increasingly important role in developmental assistance programs. Private agencies and volunteers were "in daily and significant touch with precisely those elements of host-country populations with which U.S. [AID] mission personnel least come into contact: the urban poor, the peasants, the forgotten of the earth."[22] It was exactly these categories of people that nongovernmental organizations targeted, so that some kind of symbiosis existed between governmental and nongovernmental activities, the former focusing on state-to-state aid and the latter on marginalized segments of recipient populations.

Such thinking suggests that there was an increasing awareness of the close connection between postcolonial development and human rights. After all, "the urban poor, the peasants, the forgotten of the earth" represented the bulk of people in newly independent as well as still-colonized parts of the world. And their problems could be comprehended as much in the framework of human rights as of postcolonialism. Thus one interesting development during the 1960s was the growing influence of the vocabulary of human rights in the discussion of international relations. Decolonization, nation building, postcolonial poverty — all these could be put in the framework of the search for, or the abuse of, human rights. Because human rights embraced many other issues as well — such as the rights of women and children — it seemed that the concept could be applied to all aspects of international, indeed human, affairs. This was an important stage in discourses about world events, for human rights, not just national interests, was coming to be seen as a critical issue. Indeed, the broader concept of international affairs as human affairs could revolutionize the way governments and nongovernmental organizations alike considered their own activities. The more traditional definition of international relations as interstate relations was making room for, though by no means giving way to, an alternative proposition — that the world consisted of far more than sovereign states. A global community defined by human rights was being proposed — "imagined," to use a term that would become widely used in a subsequent decade.

Of course, such a community was not seen as altogether replacing the older, geopolitically conceived world order. But the 1960s, for many reasons, witnessed the first powerful wave that pushed nations and peoples in this direction. Indeed, it may even be argued that the Cold War that had seemed to define the "real" state of international affairs now began to appear to belong more and more in the realm of "imagination" (inasmuch as the third world war never came), whereas postcolonialism, human rights, and a host of other nongeopolitical issues were coming to the surface, as the more "real" phenomena. And international organizations were ready to recognize the changing circumstances and give such phenomena their focused attention.

At a session of the United Nations General Assembly in 1960, a resolution on human rights was adopted, declaring, in part, that "the subjection of peoples to alien subjugation, domination and exploitation constitutes a denial of fundamental human rights . . . and is an impediment to the promotion of world peace and cooperation."[23] The coupling of colonialism and the denial of human rights, which had been implicit in the discussions at Human Rights Commission meetings, was now becoming explicit. It seemed axiomatic that any abuse of human rights, including colonialism, was a concern for the world organization — and by implication for the entire world community. The 1960 United Nations declaration was followed by another, in 1963, on "the elimination of all forms of racial discrimination" and, in 1967, on "the elimination of discrimination against women." Such initiatives revealed that something like a universal awareness of human rights abuses was dawning on people everywhere, who recognized that those rights transcended national distinctions and that discrimination in any form was an offense against a decent international order to whose realization they aspired.

One concrete manifestation of this global concern with human rights abuses was the founding of Amnesty International in 1961. It was initially established in London to protest the jailing of some Portuguese student dissidents, but it quickly became committed to a campaign against political imprisonment and also for fair trials of prisoners everywhere. The organization's main activity at that time was letter writing; members sent letters to officials of countries where "prisoners of conscience" were believed to exist. From the beginning, Amnesty International defined itself as a movement on behalf of the human rights of prisoners that "transcend national, cultural, religious, and ideological boundaries," according to its official statement.[24] This focus on the rights of prisoners was particularly well chosen in a decade that saw massive incarcerations, from those in China during the Cultural Revolution to Chile under a military dictatorship, not to mention the continuing existence of gulags (slave camps) in the Soviet Union. Although Amnesty International was unable to significantly alter conditions in these camps, its headquarters in London, as well as rapidly increasing branches in other countries, served as transnational voices of conscience. Some of these branches were small-scale operations, staffed mostly with volunteers and funded by individual donors. Even so, they organized symposiums, exhibits, and tours to obtain and disseminate information, and by 1970 a worldwide network had been established to represent a global civil society with a public opinion that transcended those of individual countries.

We may better understand such a phenomenon if we put it in the context of the cultural turmoil that affected the West and many other parts of the world during the 1960s. The sixties are usually associated with a cultural revolution that manifested itself in a number of ways in different countries: the "counterculture" movement of the new left in the United States, "the generation of 1968" in France and Germany, "the Prague spring" of 1968 in Czechoslovakia, student radicalism in Japan, and even the Cultural Revolution in China, which not only turned the country's youth against traditional culture but also gave rise to a Maoist cult in Western Europe and North America. Everywhere student radicals and their sympathizers appeared to be questioning accepted wisdom and to be determined to develop a new cultural consciousness.

In parts of the world, especially in Western Europe and the United States, this phenomenon was a response to the long war in Vietnam and, more fundamentally, to the Cold War. In that sense, these movements can be seen as a reaction against the continued preoccupation of the powers with nuclear armaments and balance of power. But viewing them simply as a by-product of the Cold War would be wrong, for that would assume that without the geopolitical drama, there would have been no global cultural revolution of the 1960s. On the contrary, in the context of our story, it may be said that the consciousness of a global community had been generated by the manifold activities of intergovernmental organizations and nongovernmental organizations since the end of the Second World War, and that this consciousness had reached a stage where it was asserting itself against the geopolitical mind-sets that continued to shape the policies of the major powers. Put this way, the anti-Vietnam and anti–Cold War movements were products of the new global consciousness, rather than the other way around. Also true is that these movements further strengthened this consciousness, to such an extent that it would remain in force long after the Vietnam War, and indeed the Cold War, would come to an end.

Roland Robertson, a sociologist and one of the leading students of globalization, notes that the process of globalization entered a new phase in the late 1960s because of such phenomena as the "heightening of global consciousness" and the "[conceptions] of individuals [that were being] rendered more complex by gender, ethnic and racial considerations."[25] While rather vague, such a perspective points to the significance of certain global trends that became apparent during the 1960s and continued into the subsequent decades. The juxtaposition of "global consciousness" and "gender, ethnic and racial considerations" is interesting; it suggests that these may have been two sides of the same coin. Global cultural transformation was being promoted through an aroused consciousness about gender, racial, and ethnic diversity. Globality and particularity reinforced each other so that the reformist and protest movements that enveloped many parts of the world, promoting women's liberation, civil rights, and other causes against the existing norms, were generating a sense of transnational interconnectedness. Even the emergence, in the late 1960s, of a new conservatism in the United States — a development that some historians view as having been as significant as the cultural revolution of the decade — may be put in the same context and seen as a reaction against the global trends. Many of those whom Lisa McGirr calls "suburban warriors" identified with the Cold War and a strong military establishment, and at the same time, they were adamantly opposed to an activist state eager to promote racial justice and other causes.[26] The conservatives established their own private associations to help elect politicians who shared their ideas. These associations pitted themselves against those, national and international, that stressed cross-national solidarity. Understanding this phenomenon in the framework of an ongoing dialogue on cultural and social globalization seems possible.

In any event, the antiwar protests of the 1960s can be interpreted as having been part of the global forces that were producing a large number of transnational movements dedicated to humanitarian relief, developmental assistance, and the protection of human rights. For the most striking thing about the antiwar movement was its global character. Although the United States was the only major power involved in the Vietnam War, global forces served to expand antiwar protests in the nation into a worldwide cultural movement. The protesters in the United States were joined by those elsewhere, and they combined to develop a transnational network of protest, which from the beginning never limited its target to the war but quickly became a cultural movement, thus becoming part of the existing international forces promoting global agendas. True, some of the forces became noticeably radical, even self-consciously revolutionary, during the 1960s. Extremist student organizations in North America, Western Europe, Japan, and elsewhere sought to rise against the establishment to reconstruct social order at home and abroad. For them the Maoist revolution in China seemed an apt model, as students denounced their teachers, children their parents, and "people" their erstwhile political and intellectual leaders in the name of revolt against the status quo. But most individuals and groups engaged in the new cultural activities are better characterized as internationalists rather than as extremists: internationalists in that they viewed their thought and behavior not simply in the framework of national affairs but within an international network of reformers they envisaged themselves to be constructing. As typically expressed in the Port Huron statement by Students for a Democratic Society, "Science and scholarship should be seen less as an apparatus of conflicting power blocs, but [sic] as a bridge toward supra-national community." The

United States, the student group asserted, must "progress now toward internationalizing rather than localizing, its educational system — children and adults studying everywhere in the world . . . would go far to create mutual understanding."[27] Such language of internationalism was transforming the ways in which people looked at world affairs.

That international organizations were willing to embrace such language and actively pursue agendas that might contradict the domestic priorities of many countries may be seen in the activities of the environmental, antinuclear, and women's movements that continued throughout the 1960s. All these movements were in a sense related; concern with pollution, for instance, was at the heart of the movement against the atmospheric testing of nuclear weapons, which in turn was strongly promoted by women worried about its health hazards to their children. The link between the movements for peace and for the environment was graphically demonstrated when a new organization, Greenpeace, was established in Vancouver in 1970. Its founders, Canadians as well as American expatriates living in Canada, were concerned with the environmental effects of past and planned nuclear tests off the coast of Alaska, and they adopted the strategy of drawing public attention to the problem by sailing to the test site in their vessels. (A nuclear test four thousand feet beneath the island of Amchitka in the Aleutian Island chain had taken place in 1969, and Greenpeace undertook its first voyage to protest against future tests in 1971.)[28]

Within a few years, Greenpeace grew to become one of the most active environmental and antinuclear testing organizations in the world. But they were not alone. They were joined in their movement against nuclear tests by many others, including Pope John XXIII, whose encyclical of 1963, "Pacem in terris," called for a halt to such tests. Scientists from the Soviet Union, the United States, and other countries that had established the Pugwash movement (see chapter 3) stepped up their efforts for banning nuclear tests. Although their efforts were not entirely successful, Matthew Evangelista's careful study shows that the partial test-ban treaty of 1963 owed itself to a great extent to the groundwork that these scientists laid.[29] In the meantime, American women who had organized Women Strike for Peace traveled to the Soviet Union in 1961 to promote the cause, and in 1964 they met their European counterpart in Prague to protest against the nuclear armament of NATO's fleet. At the same time, even while the major nuclear powers were suspending atmospheric tests, a parallel movement for peaceful uses of nuclear energy gained momentum. The International Atomic Energy Agency became particularly active, with a membership of 74 countries in 1960 increasing to 103 by 1970. The Agency established a system of inspection of nuclear installations to ensure that power plants using atomic energy confined its use to nonmilitary purposes, and the system was strengthened by the provisions in the nuclear nonproliferation treaty of 1968, mandating that all signatory nations that did not possess nuclear arms accept the Agency-promoted safeguards. Although countries that were not covered by these provisions still remained, a powerful step was being taken collectively to minimize the hazards of nuclear pollution.[30]

Other environmental initiatives formed as well. The previous chapter noted that during the 1950s, there were as yet few international movements and organizations dedicating themselves to the protection of the physical environment. The situation changed dramatically in the new decade. That the world was ready for a new initiative in environmentalism was clearly demonstrated when Rachel Carson's *Silent Spring*, first published in the United States in 1962, became an instant best-seller and was read by millions in many countries. Her warning that the "ecosystem" that had established an equilibrium between humankind and nature over hundreds of thousands of years, enabling humans to cohabit the earth with other living organisms, was being threatened with destruction because of chemical fertilizers and anti-insect sprays (such as DDT), provided the first clarion call to focus people's attention on the dilemma of modernization — that the increasing productivity of food through the "green revolution" (the use of new fertilizers) and the eradication of diseases through the use of DDT and other chemicals were ironically making the earth less inhabitable for all beings. The suggestion has been made that more than any other document, this book popularized the word "environment."[31] The timing was perfect, and soon, not just fertilizers and sprays but also urban and industrial waste began to attract the attention of concerned citizens; urban congestion and industrialization, they pointed out, were contaminating the world's lakes, rivers, and oceans, making the air dirtier and the water poisonous.

Such awareness resulted in the founding of various movements and organizations dedicated to coping with the perceived environmental crisis. According to Margaret Keck and Cathryn Sikkink, in 1953 there had been two international nongovernmental organizations with a focus on environmental issues, whereas the number had increased to five by 1963 and would reach ten by 1973.[32] These numbers were still small, but the steady growth of the international environmental movement is undeniable. The best evidence for this growth may be seen in a 1968 United Nations resolution on the human environment, calling on the nations of the world to convene a worldwide conference on the natural environment. The resolution eventually led to the landmark Stockholm conference of 1972. In conjunction with such initiatives, in 1967 the World Meteorological Organization, a venerable international nongovernmental organization, sponsored a "global atmospheric research program" to conduct surveys of the earth's atmosphere to ascertain the degree to which it might have become polluted. In the meantime, in 1961 the World Wildlife Fund was established to provide funding for preservation initiatives, such as those carried out by the International Union for Conservation of Nature and Natural Resources. The Fund was especially concerned with preserving wildlife in Africa, in particular elephants, and began to lobby governments and intergovernmental organizations to persuade them to prohibit trade in ivory. (Julian Huxley, former head of UNESCO, played a key role in this regard, warning that unless effective measure were taken to protect Africa's wildlife, it could disappear in twenty years.) One specific outcome of such activities was the signing in 1968 of the African Convention on the Conservation of

Nature and Natural Resources in Algiers by thirty-eight member states of the Organization of African Unity.[33] The convention provided the international legal framework for the protection of the natural habitat in the African continent through the subsequent decades.

These environmentalist initiatives, whether undertaken by intergovernmental or by nongovernmental organizations, were open to all countries, and quite often the organizations could provide arenas for cooperation between the United States and its allies, on one hand, and the Soviet Union and its allies, on the other. On the environmental question, to be sure, such cooperation would not materialize till the early 1970s. The two military blocs in Europe (NATO and the Warsaw Pact) developed their respective research programs for coping with environmental issues independently of each other.[34] Moreover, as Robert G. Darst has suggested, while the Soviet Union boasted stringent regulations concerning the disposal of industrial and agricultural wastes, they were never implemented until much later. Nevertheless, by the end of the 1960s, the Soviet leadership was beginning to consider environmental cooperation with the Western powers as part of the process of easing Cold War tensions.[35]

Indeed, it is possible to argue that while at one level the Cold War continued to provide the framework for great-power relations, that framework was being eroded by numerous instances of bridge building across the geopolitical divide. Achievements in cultural exchange, broadly defined, were particularly notable. In the field of technological cooperation, for instance, the two powers worked together through the United Nations to launch a project in 1964 for worldwide satellite communication by setting up an international agency — Intelsat — to administer the program. The Tokyo Olympics held in October of that year made use of the satellite transmission system and broadcast the games as they were being played simultaneously to other parts of the world — the first ever for an Olympics event. In 1968 the United Nations sponsored another conference, in Vienna, to discuss peaceful uses of space, and again the United States and the Soviet Union were among the participating nations, which numbered over seventy. The resulting agreement made it possible for scientists and engineers from different countries to work together to explore outer space. Soviet scientists (as well as other scholars) began visiting the United States, Western Europe, and Japan, and their scholars in turn were hosted by Soviet academies and research institutes.

The decade also witnessed serious attempts at educational and artistic exchanges between the United States and the Soviet Union — something that had been carried on sporadically after 1945 but had been frequently interrupted by Cold War tensions. In the Soviet Union, a new state committee for cultural relations with foreign countries was established to coordinate the activities of ministries, academies, institutes, and nongovernmental organizations involved in educational and cultural exchanges. Some of those activities, such as the training of foreign students (about twenty-five thousand of them were studying at Soviet universities in 1963), were obviously calculated to enhance the U.S.S.R.'s prestige and influence relative to those of the United States, but others were less directly tied to Cold War strategy. Philip H. Coombs, who headed the State Department's office of cultural affairs, reported in 1964 that "only some" of Soviet objectives in promoting cultural and educational exchanges were "associated with the cold war." Especially with regard to Western countries, there was "heavier emphasis now on genuine intellectual, technical, and artistic exchange without immediate ideological connotations."[36] During the 1960s, the Bolshoi Ballet, the Leningrad Symphony Orchestra, and other artistic organizations toured Western Europe and North America, and the nongovernmental organizations in the host countries provided their hospitality and logistical support. And these countries in turn sent some of their best musicians, artists, and dancers for a tour of the Soviet Union and its allies.

It may well be, as Coombs suggests, that the "cultural rapprochement" between the two camps in the Cold War had something to do with the deterioration in Chinese-Soviet relations that became noticeable already in the early 1960s.[37] While the split between the principal

socialist allies had obvious implications for the global geopolitical picture, in the context of our discussion what is most interesting about the
situation is the possibility that the Chinese-Soviet estrangement may
have served to strengthen, rather than weaken, the sense of global consciousness that was a hallmark of the 1960s. That one socialist country
was now accusing another of "revisionism" and "social imperialism" was
a fascinating phenomenon for observers in the rest of the world and in a
way forced them to clarify their own positions on international and
national affairs. Many undoubtedly seized the opportunity to promote
further exchanges between the West and the Soviet-bloc nations.
Others, however, were fascinated by China's adamant resistance to the
U.S.-U.S.S.R. rapprochement and its increasingly vehement opposition
to what was considered the decadent bourgeois culture of the West that
appeared to be permeating the Soviet Union and its allies. Student radicals, black militants, anti–Vietnam War protesters, and many others in
the United States and elsewhere established a vicarious sense of solidarity with the Red Guards in China during the Cultural Revolution. They
seemed to share a sense of disdain for capitalism and middle-class values
and envisaged their movement as a worldwide undertaking to remake
society, to turn the world back to an idyllic existence where life was sim-
pler and purer. The "counterculture" movement would soon run out of
steam, in China as well as elsewhere, but it was clearly part of the phenomenon of the rising global consciousness. As pointed out earlier, the
"revolution" of the 1960s must be understood in that context; it served
to establish psychological and mental connections between different
parts of the world, even as the Cold War and the Chinese-Soviet split
were keeping the globe divided and subdivided.

Underneath the drama of radical movements in many parts of the
world, more traditional types of cultural exchange were also being promoted with even greater vigor than before. UNESCO, for instance,
completed its ten-year project "on mutual appreciation of Eastern and
Western cultural values" in 1966. The project had been launched in
1957 under the initiative of India. It was one of the major enterprises

undertaken by the organization, and during the 1960s various symposiums continued to be held, and research conferences convened, to promote cultural "interpenetration," to borrow a word from the final report by UNESCO. Thus, to cite a few examples, in 1963 a colloquium was organized in Athens on the theme of "reciprocal influences of Eastern and Western architecture," in 1964 a conference was held in Baghdad on "Arab music in relation to other Oriental music and to Western music," and throughout the decade, the Research Council for Cultural Studies in New Delhi undertook studies on such subjects as "changing attitudes towards work as a social and cultural value," "the tradition of non-violence in East and West," and "science and technology in relation to cultural values and institutions of South and South-East Asia."

In summing up all such activities, UNESCO acknowledged "the invaluable role of international non-governmental organizations in the implementation of the project." These organizations often cosponsored gatherings with UNESCO, and their leaders frequently served on the latter's committees. Lest these gatherings and activities should give the impression of elitism, efforts were made to disseminate translated literary works, visual arts, and musical recordings among the general public. These were truly worldwide efforts, reaching out to people in Eastern as well as Western Europe, Latin America as well as Africa. Whether all these efforts really brought about a situation in which, as the UNESCO report concluded, "no well-informed or cultivated person would dream in 1967 of describing the Orient as a block massively opposed to a monolithic Occident," would be debatable.[38] In the context of our discussion, the important thing is that international organizations continued to play a key role during the 1960s in building bridges across cultural as well as geopolitical boundaries.

At a somewhat different level, the liberalization of policies governing trade, investment, and tourism was making it possible for a growing number of privately financed students and travelers to go abroad, individually and in groups. The number of international tourists grew spectacularly, from approximately 25.3 million in 1950, to 69.3 million in

1960, and to 159.7 million in 1970.[39] However one interprets such figures, relating the phenomenon to the development of cultural globalization in general and of nongovernmental organizations in particular is not difficult. Through international travel, individuals and groups were establishing cross-national links to a degree unprecedented in history. True, some of the more notable links were among scholars and intellectuals, as in the earlier periods. The 1960s seem to have been particularly notable in the internationalization of economics as a field of study; private foundations, universities, and intergovernmental organizations such as the International Monetary Fund and the World Bank encouraged students and scholars from both developed and developing countries to come together for research, so that they were able to develop an international vocabulary for coping with issues ranging from income distribution to industrialization. Most of this vocabulary was non-Marxist, and seeing the process of global intellectual interchanges among economists as an aspect of the Cold War is tempting; but in the context of our study, it is far more important to recognize the role of international organizations in standardizing an academic discipline. While at one level a global cultural revolution was undermining the intellectual presuppositions underlying the great-power rivalry, at another level a globalization of scholarship was also taking place.[40]

Outside North America and Western Europe, Japan became a country that avidly partook of such transnational experiences. It hosted annual meetings of the Econometric Society, an organization that had been established in the United States in the late 1930s but had grown in international membership from the late 1950s onward due to the "econometric revolution." Not surprisingly, Marxist economics began to be overshadowed by neoliberal and Keynesian economics in Japan in the late 1960s, as an increasing number of economists trained in the United States came to occupy key teaching positions.[41] Similarly, political scientists and historians with advanced degrees from American and European universities were beginning to occupy strategic positions in Japanese educational institutions. Many of them were influenced by modernization and other theories and found them applicable to their own country's experience. They played a role in organizing international scholarly conferences. One notable example was a meeting of historians from the United States, Britain, and Japan held in 1969 to discuss the origins of the Pacific War. Some still consider the conference, organized and funded by private associations, to have been the most successful and intellectually exciting of its kind. The participants shared their findings and exchanged their ideas freely, not as representatives of a nation but as fellow scholars seeking the truth.[42]

Such transnational scholarly collaboration may be seen to have been part of the larger phenomenon of cultural globalization in which international organizations played major roles. To cite two further examples from Japan, both the Tokyo Olympics (1964) and the Ōsaka Expo (1970) attested to the expansion of networks of nongovernmental contact to non-Western parts of the world. With the participation of 5,586 athletes from ninety-four countries, the Tokyo Olympics were the largest ever and symbolized the extent to which countries of the world could come together for a celebration of their peacetime pursuits. (Tokyo also hosted what would later come to be called the Paralympics, an international sporting competition for the disabled. The first such event had been organized in conjunction with the Rome Olympics of 1960. Both in Rome and Tokyo, about 400 wheelchaired athletes from over twenty countries took part in the competition, an important aspect of the globalization of sport, blurring not just geographical but physical boundaries.)[43] Four years later, the Olympics moved to Mexico City, the first time that a South American country had ever hosted the games. The year 1968 was a tumultuous one in American, European, and also Mexican politics and foreign policy, with reverberations in the rest of the world, but the athletes competed under the same rules that had governed the world's sports for decades.

Even sport internationalism, however, could not prevent the Tokyo and Mexico City Olympics from being politicized; athletes from North Korea came to Tokyo but were not allowed to compete, and in Mexico

City two African-American runners protested against racial discrimination at home by raising their fists in a Black Power salute during a medal ceremony. In the context of our discussion, however, the globalization of sporting events rather than their politics should be stressed. If nothing else, Tokyo and Mexico City attested to the increasing role of international organizations in bringing nations and peoples of the world into closer contact; besides the International Olympic Committee, numerous local voluntary organizations hosted the visiting athletes and established lasting ties with one another.

At the Ōsaka World's Fair, Tange Kenzō, the architect and principal producer of the event, proclaimed that the Expo aimed at "gathering different people who would communicate their energies to each other and exchange their knowledge and creativity."[44] Such a vision of cross-national interchange had existed for many decades, but it was coming closer and closer to fulfillment, thanks to this and many other activities, which in turn owed their scale and scope to the existence of intergovernmental organizations and international nongovernmental organizations in all parts of the globe, whose number kept increasing even as newly independent states were being created.

CHAPTER 5

The Growth
of Civil Society

Historians agree that international relations entered a new phase during the 1970s. Whereas the period between 1945 and 1970 may possibly be comprehended within the framework of the Cold War — although this book argues that there are other ways of conceptualizing the quarter century — during the 1970s so many drastic changes occurred that the decade may be said to have marked the beginning of a new period of world affairs. Among such transforming events were the rapprochement between the United States and the People's Republic of China, the deterioration in Soviet-Chinese relations, and the détente between Washington and Moscow. The Cold War, in the sense of the bipolar division of the globe, lost whatever meaning it had ever had. As if to symbolize the passing of an era, the U.S. war in Vietnam, fought in the name of containing Soviet and Chinese communism, was brought to an end, to be followed promptly by a Chinese invasion of the newly united Vietnam — something that would have been incomprehensible in a world conceived in the vocabulary of the Cold War.

But that was not all. In the international economic sphere, the 1970s saw such cataclysmic changes that historian Eric Hobsbawm characterizes the history of the world during the twenty years after 1973 as "the crisis decades," in contrast to the "Golden Age," the term he chooses to refer to the period between 1945 and the early 1970s.[1] While it would be difficult to agree with Hobsbawm that world history after the early 1970s became a "landslide," there is no denying that in the economic realm at least, the world order that had prevailed during the 1950s and the 1960s broke down in the 1970s. First the United States government decided in 1971 to decouple the dollar from gold, so that the value of the dollar began falling against the currencies of most European countries as well as of Japan. Profound instability appeared in the international currency market as a result, a departure from the so-called Bretton Woods system that had been based on stable rates of exchange between the dollar and other currencies. In 1973 and again in 1979, the Organization of Petroleum Exporting Countries (OPEC) adopted the policy of reducing their petroleum output, tripling and then quadrupling the wholesale price of crude oil. The result was a worldwide shortage of oil and a soaring inflation as consumer prices rose everywhere. The world economy that had steadily expanded after the Second World War now began to stagnate, and even the United States, Western European countries, and Japan recorded zero or minus growth rates. All these developments indeed impressed contemporary observers that the golden age of economic recovery, growth, and prosperity had come to an end. Just as a fundamental transformation was taking place in the geopolitical sphere, in the economic realm, too, one era was passing and another, presumably less certain and far more disorderly, era was dawning.

That world history, or more specifically the history of international relations, was entering a new epoch in the 1970s is beyond dispute. The nature of the transformation, however, is open to varying interpretations. In the framework of this book, the most striking feature of the changes, both geopolitical and economic, is that they were in effect integrating different parts of the world to a far more extensive and intimate degree than during the preceding period. The rapprochement between the United States and China, and between the United States and the Soviet Union, were bringing the two socialist giants into the international community where before they had largely remained apart from it.

(True, the Soviet Union and the People's Republic of China were seriously estranged, thus dividing the socialist world, a phenomenon that would not fit into the theme of global reintegration, but the Beijing-Moscow rift would prove to be temporary, and besides, they were now more involved in international economic affairs than ever before.) In a similar way, the petroleum-producing countries were asserting their prerogatives as members of the international economic order. Of course, their orientation would be distinct from that of the capitalist industrial nations, but that was precisely the novelty; the world economic order now accommodated a growing number of countries that had hitherto tended to be minor players but that now demanded more say. Likewise, the global currency regime that had been built upon the overwhelming power of the dollar was giving way to a multicurrency system in which rates of exchange would fluctuate constantly.

All this made for unpredictability and even instability, but it did not necessarily spell the coming of an age of crisis. Actually, the volume of international trade continued to grow throughout the 1970s, and the world's major economic powers made much effort to cooperate in solving currency, energy, and other problems — in sharp contrast to the 1930s, when no such cooperation was possible. Nor should it be forgotten that the Third World, which had emerged as a group of underdeveloped (and, in most cases, recently independent) countries, found it difficult to maintain its uniform identity; while, from time to time, its members put up a common front toward the advanced, industrial nations, some of them began taking steps to industrialize themselves to join the ranks of the latter countries. Either way, the Third World was now more than ever part of global developments.

Seen in such a perspective, the 1970s may be considered to have marked a definite phase of globalization, a process that was to continue into the subsequent decades. Forces of globalization that had been manifest during the earlier decades became even more effective in connecting different parts of the world. In that process, a genuine world community was emerging — a world community, however, that was not necessarily identical with the visions that dreamers and idealists long entertained. This is a fascinating story that has not yet ended. For that reason, assessing the historical significance of various facets of international affairs since the 1970s is extremely difficult. In this and the next chapters, I attempt to understand contemporary history through an examination of activities by some intergovernmental organizations and international nongovernmental organizations, old and new. Such examination shows that these organizations have played a decisive role — in some instances even more so than the sovereign states — in the global transformation since the 1970s.

To begin with, the number of both intergovernmental organizations and international nongovernmental organizations, already impressive in the 1960s, grew phenomenally during the 1970s. According to the Union of International Associations, the former increased from 280 in 1972 to 1,530 by 1984, and the latter from 2,795 to 12,686 during the same period. Both types of international organizations had been steadily growing in number, but never with such speed. And if local branches were taken into consideration, the figures were even more spectacular; in 1984 there were altogether 7,073 intergovernmental organizations and 79,786 international nongovernmental organizations, including both their headquarters and various local offices.[2]

Why such a burst of international organizations? One way of understanding this phenomenon would be to put it into the larger framework of the growth of nonstate, nonterritorial actors in the world. For instance, the 1970s began to develop what Hobsbawm calls a "transnational economy" in the world, symbolized by the mushrooming of multinational business enterprises.[3] (There were about nine hundred of them in the early 1980s.) Such enterprises had existed earlier, but their number began to grow quickly only during the 1970s. More and more businesses were turning extraterritorial, operating far away from their original locations and establishing factories and offices with workforces consisting of individuals from several countries. Some scholars have argued that the presence of multinational corporations contributed to a smooth functioning of the international economic system; before the Great War, while globalization was progressing apace, the possibility always existed that the whole mechanism of worldwide transactions could become unhinged, because the majority of manufacturers and trading companies retained their national identities, engaging themselves in fierce competition and in the process generating nationalistic animosities. The growth of multinational enterprises, on the other hand, served to develop transnational interests and solidarities conducive to international order.[4] This is an intriguing argument and fits nicely into the overall picture of the growth of nonstate actors throughout the world. Multinational businesses and international organizations represented forces that were in effect seeking to create an international society that was distinct from the international system, defined as a sum of interactions among sovereign states. The former was challenging the latter's traditional hegemony as the definer of world order.

A similar process, the rise of civil society and the diminishing role of the state, was under way throughout the world as well. Loss of faith in government was a phenomenon witnessed in many countries, most dramatically with the Watergate scandal in the United States, which climaxed with the president's resignation in 1974. But this was not an isolated incident. In many parts of the globe, civil society was asserting itself, willing to challenge the authority of the state and to undertake tasks the latter was either unwilling or unable to perform. In the democratic states of Europe as well as in the United States and Japan, political commentators began discussing the question of governability — the ability of the state to cope with the increasing demands of society.[5] There was less and less optimism that the governments had the will or the capabilities to do so; hence their increasing willingness to turn to civil organizations to share the task. All in all, then, state-society relations were changing rapidly, both within individual countries and in world affairs as a whole. Perhaps it was no accident that religious bodies, especially the Catholic Church, were beginning to regain their influence

in domestic political and social affairs, as if to reclaim the influence they
had lost to the secular authorities.

Even some countries that had not hitherto tolerated anything close to
a civil society began to witness the emergence of nongovernmental associations, thanks in no small degree to the encouragement and support
that the Church provided. Charter 77, an informal group of intellectuals
in Czechoslovakia founded in 1977 to call for respect for human rights,
was one example, and Poland's labor organization, Solidarity, offered
another. Established in 1979, the latter started out as a trade union of
Gdansk dockworkers led by Lech Walesa. But, as an association outside
the government or the Communist Party, it soon attracted a membership
totaling some nine million and became a model for similar organizations
in other socialist states. In the Soviet Union and elsewhere, students,
intellectuals, and dissidents grew steadily bolder and began to organize
themselves. Their associations, many of them clandestine, may not have
been exact replicas of nongovernmental organizations in democratic
countries, but they were clearly becoming self-conscious members of a
civil society that was emerging in Eastern Europe. Indeed, the concept of
civil society came to be developed during the 1970s as representing
forces that were not controlled by the state.[6] Those involved in the construction of nonstate organizations in Eastern Europe were conscious of
the international implications of what they were doing. They were in
increasing contact with developments in the West, and European and
American capital was beginning to be invested in the Soviet Union and
elsewhere to produce larger quantities of consumer goods. There is little doubt that for intellectuals, journalists, labor leaders, and others in
these countries, freedom of association came to be seen as a key aspect of
contemporary Western society and that they believed this was where
they would have to start to become part of global developments.

Civil society also grew outside Europe, although the impetus for the
growth of nongovernmental organizations seems to have been more
social and economic than political. In Latin America, Asia, and Africa, a

large number of voluntary agencies sprang up to cope with problems of poverty, hunger, and health to complement work by the public authorities. Often governments were too weak, corrupt, or inefficient to administer social services, and they willingly turned these tasks over to nonstate bodies. Why their number should have begun to increase during the 1970s is unclear, but it is remarkable that so many community organizations that are active today seem to have originated at that time. Perhaps the world economic disarray of the early 1970s hit particularly hard those Third World countries that were not endowed with rich natural resources. It may also have had something to do with the spectacular rise in cross-national migration. Driven by civil strife, ethnic conflict, and poverty, millions crossed borders, often illegally. Fortunate ones found refuge in richer countries of Europe, North America, Oceania, or the Middle East, but a greater number ended up in refugee camps. In Africa, for instance, the number of refugees grew from three hundred thousand in 1960, to one million in 1970, and to over three million ten years later.[7]

Even among those who stayed home, sprawling slums were a common sight in larger cities. Voluntary work was often the only effective means of dealing with such a critical situation. Small-scale community organizations were founded, and successful ones inevitably grew larger as they expanded the scope of their activities.[8] Even such organizations, however, held political connotations inasmuch as they were involving people — the poor, women, and other marginalized groups — in community affairs. They were engaged in grassroots, bottom-up efforts in contrast to the top-down pattern of governmental programs for relief and economic development. Thus, in many instances community organizations served to empower people who had hitherto been deprived of a voice in their own governance. From there, it was but a step to an active campaign for their rights. Such a development seems to have exemplified many nongovernmental organizations in the Third World during the 1970s. Thus in the non-Western parts of the world, too, self-conscious civil society was emerging.[9]

Nor was the growth of civil society in many parts of the world limited to domestic organizations. Branches of international nongovernmental organizations were established everywhere, their total number increasing from 36,336 in 1966 to 52,074 in 1977, and to 79,786 by 1983. In 1977 the Soviet Union belonged to 43 international nongovernmental organizations, and China to 71.[10] These were much smaller figures than the number of international nongovernmental organizations in the United States (1,106) or in Japan (878), but they were nevertheless indicative of a trend. The figures for Africa, the Western Hemisphere, and Asia (including the Pacific) for that year were 6,830, 11,076, and 9,725, respectively. It was almost as if the whole globe was becoming dotted with domestic and international nongovernmental organizations. Added to them were local offices of intergovernmental organizations, totaling 6,432 in 1977. These numbers show that global consciousness was becoming even more fully institutionalized than earlier. The new international order that was being promoted at the geopolitical level through the rapprochement between the United States and the Soviet Union, and between the former and China, had its counterpart in the emerging global community consisting of thousands of intergovernmental organizations and international nongovernmental organizations, as well as of domestic civil societies.

It is no accident that astute observers of the international scene began to notice this phenomenon. Some of the seminal works on international organizations were published during the 1970s. In 1975 Johan Galtung, a leading scholar of nonstate actors, argued in a pioneering essay, "Nonterritorial Actors and the Problem of Peace," that a "sixth continent" of the world, "the invisible continent of nonterritorial actors," was emerging.[11] Two years later, Evan Luard, a British student of international politics, published *International Agencies*, a guide to the existing intergovernmental organizations that is still useful.[12] The important work by these and other scholars was summed up and put into a comprehensive framework by Harold K. Jacobson, whose *Networks of Interdependence* (1979) may be considered the basic text for the study not simply of international organizations but also of international relations in general during the 1970s. As he wrote in the preface, "Humankind is crafting new political institutions that have already contributed significantly to greater global security, to better material welfare through a larger gross world product, and to higher standards of social welfare."[13] All these authors were noticing a global development that would soon enter the consciousness of millions of people everywhere: the proliferation of international organizations, some of which expanded on the work begun earlier, while others were innovative in that they were not elite bodies but were products of, and responses to, the political, social, economic, and cultural concerns of ordinary individuals

To examine these organizations systematically is beyond the scope of this book. But it seems useful to describe briefly some of their activities in the fields of human rights, humanitarian relief, developmental assistance, environmental protection, and cultural exchange. We have seen in the earlier chapters that these five, plus peace and disarmament, had been among the most important objectives of international organizations. While peace advocacy was by no means inactive, the easing of Cold War tensions may have had the effect of eclipsing it as a central issue for international organizational attention. According to Margaret Keck and Kathryn Sikkink, twenty international nongovernmental organizations were concerned with peace issues in 1963, but the number declined to fourteen ten years later.[14] Further fluctuations would occur in the years to come, and while generalizing may be impossible, one could argue that the five fields just mentioned were now considered more urgent. If such a generalization is tenable, it underscores the fact that beginning in the 1970s, so many issues outside of world peace and arms control came to command the attention of people everywhere, who were increasingly seeing that the solution to these problems lay in international organizations, not sovereign states.

To start with human rights, one remarkable development during the 1970s was the increasing attention that began to be paid to women's rights. The years 1975 to 1985, according to the historian Harriet

Alonso, were "ten years of unprecedented global organizing" among women's groups.[15] These years were designated by the United Nations as the "International Decade of Women," with 1975 as "International Women's Year," an indication that at both nongovernmental and inter-governmental levels, women's movements were becoming an important part of any discussion of world affairs. While such a widened perception of international relations had become notable during the cultural revolutions of the 1960s, the new decade added significant elements to the phenomenon. For one thing, even outside Western Europe and North America, where women's organizations had had long histories, similar movements developed to such an extent that in 1975, an international congress of women was convened in Mexico City. Not surprisingly, the participants resolved to create networks of women's organizations throughout the world. They recognized that women's conditions and lifestyles varied from country to country and from one culture to another, but the common sentiment was that by coming together, women's groups from different parts of the globe could develop a common consciousness — a consciousness of shared concerns and commitments. This was reflected in the publication, starting in 1975, of *Women's International Networks News*, a quarterly journal of information, and in the first "international tribunal on crimes against women," held in Brussels in 1976. This was not a formal trial in the ordinary sense of the term, but an occasion where two thousand participants from forty countries aired their grievances concerning violence against women, including rape and prostitution.[16] Such developments may suggest that while women's international movements had initially focused on peace issues, especially against nuclear armament, the easing of Cold War tensions during the 1970s enabled them to deal with other matters as well, and in so doing, women's organizations became more than ever an integral part of the emerging phenomenon of globalization. For instance, the establishment in 1974 of a new organization in the United States, Women for Racial and Economic Equality, suggests that marginalized and disadvantaged segments of the population could join forces with women everywhere to search for a new order at home and in the world.

Human rights, in that broad sense, were becoming a major theme of international affairs. Three disparate episodes would demonstrate this graphically. One was the 1975 Helsinki accord on human rights, adopted at a meeting of the Conference on Security and Cooperation in Europe (CSCE), a body that had just been organized by members of the North Atlantic Treaty Organization and the Warsaw Pact. The creation of the CSCE was itself a major landmark in postwar international history. Significantly, the declaration defined human rights broadly and referred to "the right of the individual to know and act upon his rights." That such a principle was never wholly accepted, let alone practiced, in socialist regimes was less important than that the nations belonging to opposite sides in the Cold War now put their signatures to the same document, indicating that they were willing to embrace common values regarding the human condition. In 1978 Helsinki Watch was established to monitor the signatory nations' compliance with the 1975 agreement. In that process its staff met, often clandestinely, with dissident individuals and groups, thus encouraging the growth of civil society in the Soviet Union and East European countries.[17]

Another interesting example concerned the rights of those who were physically, mentally, or otherwise disabled and had traditionally been subject to harsh discrimination in many societies. The United Nations' universal declaration on human rights had not asserted the rights of the disabled. At last the world organization made amends when it issued a declaration on the human rights of the mentally disabled in 1971 and another, encompassing all types of disability, in 1975. These declarations called on all countries to improve the conditions of such people. Hitherto, religious organizations, especially various Catholic orders, had been conspicuous because of their attention to the disabled, considering them to be God's special children, but now in many parts of the world, disabled persons and their relatives and friends began to establish organizations to lobby their respective states for more support, financial and moral. In the United States, for instance, people with disabilities asserted their rights as consumers: they should, they insisted, have the right to choose their own rehabilitation programs, hospital and institutional care, and welfare facilities.[18]

Similar movements developed elsewhere, and in time awareness grew that the disabled should organize themselves internationally. The first international nongovernmental organization of the disabled, Disabled Persons International, was not founded until 1981, but in the meantime worldwide awareness of their existence and problems was aroused through international sporting events. Although the first Paralympic games had been held during the Rome Olympics of 1960, and the second in Tokyo in 1964, it was during the 1970s that such activities became more truly international. In 1969 the Stoke Mandeville Sports Stadium for the Paralysed and Other Disabled was opened in Aylesbury, Britain, and in the following year an international competition was held there, attracting four hundred physically disabled athletes from twenty-eight countries.[19] Soon such events came to include the blind and those with cerebral palsy, and in the meantime the mentally disabled began to have their own "special Olympics." The 1980 Olympics for the Disabled, held in Arnhem, the Netherlands, drew twenty-five hundred competitors from forty-two countries. Such an event could not have taken place without the painstaking preparation by a large number of volunteer organizations, and it reflected the fact that human rights during this period were broadening to encompass the well-being of people with disabilities.

A third illustration of the growing influence the human rights question was having on the world was the award, in 1977, of the Nobel Peace Prize to Amnesty International. Since its founding in 1961, the organization had rapidly established branches in various parts of the world and widened the range of its activities. It was particularly active in sending observers to prisons to ensure proper treatment of inmates. When, in 1975, the International Council of Nurses declared that "the nurses in the care of detainees and prisoners" must report all instances of "physical or mental ill-treatment," Amnesty International made sure that such a rule was enforced. It also took seriously a declaration by the World Medical Association at its convention in Tokyo in 1975 that obligated doctors "not to condone, countenance, or participate in torture."[20] That most countries of the world were willing to let Amnesty personnel visit their prisons indicates the tremendous authority this international organization was already beginning to assume in international affairs.

Given the rising global concern with human rights, it is not surprising that the United States government under the presidency of Jimmy Carter (1977–1981) responded to the situation by establishing a bureau of human rights and humanitarian affairs within the State Department. The bureau was headed by the assistant secretary of state for human rights and worked energetically to promote democratization. Although Carter's human rights diplomacy was criticized for its lack of consistency — for instance, he insisted on democratization of South Korea, but not as firmly in China or in Pakistan — we should realize that he had to juggle various demands (geopolitical, economic, humanitarian) and often had to deal with unpredicted occurrences pragmatically. International organizations, not separate states, provided consistency. Where governments could pay only limited attention, nongovernmental organizations made sure that pressure would be kept up on behalf of incarcerated political dissidents and other victims of discrimination and injustice. A great deal of cooperation in this regard also existed between intergovernmental and nongovernmental organizations. The United Nations Center for Human Rights, for instance, was in constant communication with international nongovernmental organizations and was receiving information from them on abuses of human rights in many parts of the globe. Private foundations in Europe and North America, notably the Ford Foundation, for the first time came to interest themselves in funding international human rights work.[21]

All such activities in the human rights field did not mean, however, that international organizations were neglecting other areas of their traditional and recent concern. In the broad area of humanitarian relief, for instance, the United Nations International Children's Emergency Fund (UNICEF) continued to be active in providing health services to children and their mothers. Some seventy million people were reportedly being served by clinics equipped by UNICEF in the mid-1970s.[22] Among international nongovernmental organizations were some notable newcomers, such as Africare and Food for the Hungry International, both established in 1971. The former complemented work by older institutions such as Project Concern International and worked closely with the World Health Organization and other intergovernmental organizations to provide medical service and health care facilities in remote areas of the African continent. Africare's initiative for its founding came from African leaders (such as Diori Hamani, president of Niger) who appealed to African Americans for help. C. Payne Lucas, director of the Peace Corps Office of Returned Volunteers in Washington, took up the challenge and started the project, initially headquartered at his home with a small budget of less than forty thousand dollars. At first envisaged as a relief organization to help victims of drought in West Africa, it soon came to embrace a more ambitious, long-term goal, to offer developmental assistance.[23]

Food for the Hungry, in the meantime, was founded in southern California (and later moved to Arizona) as "an international organization of Christian motivation, committed to working with poor people to overcome hunger and poverty through integrated self-development and relief programs." Soliciting donations from other countries as well as the United States, the organization helped refugees in Bangladesh (which separated itself from Pakistan in 1971), earthquake victims in Nicaragua, and the hungry in West Africa. It also created a Hunger Corps to send volunteers to administer food distribution programs in cooperation with local organizations.[24] In 1976 a new organization was set up in London, the Appropriate Health Resources and Technology Action Group, to serve as a repository of information concerning public health research and administration. Around this time, the notion of primary health care became incorporated into the vocabulary of international organizations.

At an international conference convened by the World Health Organization and UNICEF in Alma-Ata in 1978, attended by representatives of 143 countries as well as sixty-seven international organizations, a declaration was issued, asserting the rights and duties of people everywhere to participate in primary health care "in the spirit of self-reliance and self-determination." "Health for All by the Year 2000" was adopted as the goal toward which nations and international organizations were to strive.[25]

No international nongovernmental organization founded during the 1970s in the field of humanitarian relief has been as well known or influential as Doctors without Borders (Médecins sans Frontières). Its creation in 1971 owed itself to the initiatives of a handful of volunteers and donors (mostly in France) who were committed to the idea that humanitarian activities recognized no national boundaries and that physicians and nurses should go wherever they were needed to help victims of famine, disease, or natural disasters. (The phrase "without frontiers" was so attractive to other organizations that in France alone, more than thirty of them adopted it as a part of their names.) As a founder of the organization wrote, in this way it was frankly "subversive"; it would not always wait for, or go through, government authorization before acting, and it would not hesitate to publicize its activities or the plight of the people it assisted.[26] During the 1970s, doctors and aid workers dispatched by the organization became involved in relief work in Nicaragua after an earthquake, in Vietnam after the long war, in Thailand to provide assistance to refugees from Vietnam and Cambodia, and in several African states to care for refugees fleeing civil strife.

In such activities, Doctors without Borders often frankly confronted the issue of human rights and was willing to disseminate information on violations of those rights. The line between humanitarian relief and human rights activism was thin. The Alma-Ata declaration spoke of the principle of making primary health care accessible to "individuals and families in the community through their full participation." People's involvement in their own health care, and more broadly in their own development, was being asserted as a right, but this could come into conflict with local political ambitions and traditional prejudices. From the beginning, volunteers working for Doctors without Borders and other organizations encountered situations in which the implementation of humanitarian activities experienced difficulties in the absence of a system of governance through which individuals could assert their rights. In such instances, they would have to organize themselves as autonomous entities — something state authorities would not easily tolerate. But it was becoming clearer that the more humanitarian agencies involved themselves in the local scene, the greater the challenge to the existing framework of state sovereignty. Thus here, too, the growth of civil society was emerging as an inevitable by-product of international humanitarian work.

The same was true of developmental assistance. The 1970s witnessed a continued growth in the number of international organizations in this field. This clearly reflected that the rising cost of energy and the fierce trade competition that resulted from it were making the economic conditions of developing countries worse than ever, relative to those of more advanced countries. The former came to be known collectively as the "South," and the latter as the "North," and it seemed as if the North-South rift was becoming even more serious than the geopolitical conflict between East and West. As many Third World countries found it difficult to obtain revenue by marketing their primary exports, whose prices tended to be depressed throughout the decade, they began pressing for what they called a "new international economic order" in which their special circumstances would be given consideration and their products given preferential treatment. Because the governments of the richer countries would make only partial concessions in this regard — for instance, exempting such products from international agreements on mutual lowering of tariffs — private groups would naturally become more deeply involved than ever in providing developmental assistance.

Many of them were organized in France where, as earlier, the Catholic Church expanded the scope of existing organizations and created new ones to extend assistance programs to former French colonies in Africa and in Latin America.[27] One of them, the Comité Catholique contre la Faim et pour le Développement, devised a slogan, "Rien ne changera dans le tiers monde si rien ne change chez nous" (nothing will change in the Third World if nothing changes at home).[28] Such a view expressed the recognition that developmental assistance made sense only in the context of a world that was becoming closely interconnected and in which values such as freedom, justice, and human rights applied everywhere, at home as well as abroad. For this reason, developmental assistance programs and projects came to have an important human rights component, another remarkable phenomenon of the 1970s. We can see this, for instance, in the founding of the Centre for Development and Population Activities in 1975 in Washington (with field offices and "partner organizations and networks" in many countries), aimed at "empowering women at all levels of society to be full partners in development." As the insertion of the word "population" in its title suggests, this organization stressed women's reproductive health and family planning as essential aspects of economic development. These were politically sensitive issues, and, as noted later, the growth of multiculturalism, a parallel development in the same decade, would make them extremely controversial. Of interest to our discussion is that social and cultural questions were becoming inseparable from developmental assistance.

To consider a few other examples, in 1971 a Consultative Group on International Agricultural Research was launched at the behest of the World Bank and of several governments and nongovernmental organizations. Initially designed to help agricultural research, especially in rice production, the Group soon became involved in broader issues such as farming systems, conservation of genetic resources, and other phenomena that had "ecological, economic and social factors."[29] Also about that time, the World Council of Churches established a "program to combat racism" to help individuals and groups in Portuguese Africa as well as Rhodesia and South Africa that were struggling against colonialism and racism. Oxfam America, founded in 1970, often criticized the United

States government for its aid policy that seemed to help existing regimes entrench themselves in power instead of promoting the well-being of ordinary citizens. Reflecting a similar concern, the Society for International Development adopted "jobs and justice" as its objectives for the 1970s, justice being defined as a concept including "cultural diversity and safeguarding the environment."[30]

Cultural diversity and the safeguarding of the environment — these two themes were beginning to claim the serious attention of governments and nonstate actors alike during the 1970s, another distinctive characteristic of the decade's international relations. Not just in connection with humanitarian relief or developmental assistance, but with regard to many other issues, the two subjects were entering into the vocabulary of national and international discourses. Understanding why is not difficult. To discuss environmental protection first, by the early 1970s this issue was apparently becoming urgent, given the polluted skies and waters in so many parts of the world, products of rapid industrial development and population growth during the preceding decade. "Defoliation" and "desertification" were now familiar terms; renowned forests such as the Black Forest in Central Europe began to lose their trees as a result of atmospheric pollution, and deserts spread in Africa because of overgrazing and other causes (including climatic change, although there was no consensus on this point), causing havoc with animal habitats and food shortages for humans. In many cities of the world, as more and more people gained sufficient incomes to own a car, not just gasoline consumption but also air pollution from automobile exhaust grew. Diseases, physical impairment, even deaths were reported in different parts of the world as a result of poisoning by mercury and other industrial chemicals. When nations steadily switched to nuclear power, a move that seemed essential to reduce their dependence on petroleum, they encountered the problem of protecting themselves against radiation.

The connection between environmentalism — the concern with hazards to the biosphere caused by economic activities — and developmentalism was clear. As more and more countries undertook industrialization, they encountered the same environmental issues that plagued the more advanced nations. Would development and environmental protection be compatible? That was becoming a major issue of international affairs. Most Third World countries insisted on the imperatives of economic growth, to remove themselves from the indignity of perpetual poverty. And yet the vocabulary of environmentalism was such that unlimited growth appeared less and less a desirable end — so it seemed to some observers among the already industrialized countries. Such vocabulary came into conflict with the increasingly popular view that it was precisely because the more advanced countries had enriched themselves by relentlessly exploiting the resources of the poorer lands that the earth faced an ecological crisis. Furthermore, some factories from industrialized nations were relocating themselves, partly to take advantage of cheaper labor in Third World countries but also to escape environmental regulations at home. That such factories might be "exporting dirty air" to less advanced countries was a charge that began to be made in the 1970s. But that did not mean that these lands should remain in a perpetual state of underdevelopment. Here was the dilemma: How could nations promote both development and environmentalism? Soon the world would become familiar with the concept of sustainable growth, a pattern of economic development in all nations that did not overburden the earth's resources or injure its biosphere.

It was in the 1970s that the potentially explosive issue of environmental protection was first addressed internationally, at conferences and through new organizations. Despite the deeply divisive nature of the issue, there was agreement that this was a worldwide problem and therefore had to be dealt with in a global framework. A landmark event in internationalizing environmentalism was the United Nations Conference on the Human Environment, convened in Stockholm in 1972. (That the organizers chose to use the term "the human environment" to refer to a conference on the biosphere was indicative of the way in which humans and nature were beginning to be seen as sharing an inseparable destiny.) A product of the UN resolution of 1968 calling for such a gathering, the conference attracted representatives from 114 countries.[31] The gathering was often contentious, as could have been predicted, but remarkably the delegates adopted a resolution calling on the United Nations to establish a special body to deal with environmental issues through international cooperation. The recommendation resulted in the inauguration, in 1973, of the United Nations Environmental Program. This body became a major forum for defining international environmental policy in connection with developmental assistance. Third World countries insisted, and developed countries usually agreed, that the enforcement of environmentally sound programs should not be at the expense of the former's sound economic development or trade, and that the costs of instituting such programs should be largely borne by the richer nations.[32] The objectives of environmentalism and developmentalism could come into conflict, but the new international organization served as a forum where such differences could be aired and, to the extent possible, ironed out. This was a perfect example of the impact of new issues upon international governance.

The Stockholm conference produced almost immediate results in Europe, where the European Community was being established through the addition of Britain, Ireland, and Denmark to the original European Economic Community. From its beginning, the European Community took environmental issues seriously. Through the European Council, the Community's ultimate governing body, the member governments adopted environmental action plans and, at the same time, began coordinating their plans so as to develop common regulations for environmental protection.[33] In the meantime, the European nations as well as others organized a large number of conventions throughout the 1970s dealing with such specific issues as "the prohibition of the emplacement of nuclear weapons and other weapons of mass destruction on the sea-bed and the ocean floor and in the sub soil thereof" (1971), "the prevention of marine pollution by dumping from ships and aircraft" (1972), "international trade in endangered species of wild fauna and flora" (1973), "the protection of animals kept for farming purposes"

(1976), and "the conservation of migratory species of wild animals" (1979). These agreements testified to the willingness of sovereign states, particularly of Europe, to give up part of their national prerogatives to cooperate in pursuit of common objectives.

While national governments became increasingly interested in environmental issues, nongovernmental organizations that had already been active in the field redoubled their efforts, and many new organizations were established during the 1970s. Some of them were represented at the Stockholm conference, while others held their own meetings apart from the United Nations–sponsored gathering. Their agendas were not always compatible, but their presence demonstrated that they could not be ignored in any discussion of environmental problems. The Stockholm conference provided an occasion for internationalizing the activities of many national nongovernmental bodies concerned with the environment. As of 1973, according to a survey, ten international nongovernmental organizations existed in this field, one of the most influential of which was Friends of the Earth, established in the United States in 1969. Its founder, David Brower, had been active in the Sierra Club but felt that this and other conservationist groups were not resisting strongly enough pressures from business and governmental offices for "wise uses" of natural resources. Rather than reform such associations from within, Brower and others decided to create their own organization, which from the beginning would be global in scope.[34] During the 1970s, Friends of the Earth branches were formed in many other countries to disseminate information and campaign actively for the preservation of the natural environment. After the Stockholm conference, additional organizations were created, so that within ten years the number of environmental international nongovernmental organizations reached twenty-six.[35] In 1974 the Center for International Environmental Information was established in New York, and six years later its name was changed to the World Environment Center, a clear indication of the globalizing trend of such activities. These organizations grew so numerous that in 1975, a conference was held in Austria to review the relationship among them, as well as between them and the United Nations, in administering environmental and related social programs.

One of the most energetic and successful organizations founded during this period was the Antarctic and Southern Ocean Coalition, formed in 1977 to try to preserve the Antarctic region from oil drilling and excessive fishing. Its representatives began to lobby nations participating in the Antarctic treaty system, a collection of treaties that governed this area. The Coalition eventually won the right to send observers to these meetings, and in the meantime, they engaged in a worldwide campaign to preserve the Antarctic.[36] Although many political and legal issues complicated their activities, especially regarding the enforcement of any international agreement, the organization was tireless in publicizing the critical situation in the region and promoted, among other objectives, the negotiation of a convention on the conservation of Antarctic marine living resources. Their efforts were to be rewarded in the early 1980s when such a convention was adopted and became part of the treaty system.

The protection of endangered species was an integral part of environmentalism. The safeguarding of wildlife from human encroachment had a long history, but during the 1970s international nongovernmental organizations became even more conspicuous than before in speaking out against the killing of elephants, whales, and a variety of animals, birds, fish, and plants. When various individuals and organizations spoke of the "quality of life," an increasingly popular phrase, they meant not simply that of humans but also of all living beings that shared the "planet earth," another increasingly used term. Reflecting such a trend, the World Wildlife Fund, the International Union for the Conservation of Nature and Natural Resources, and other organizations that had been founded earlier were now more successful than before in persuading national governments and intergovernmental organizations to take wildlife protection seriously. For instance, in 1972, the World Wildlife Fund, in cooperation with Friends of the Earth, spearheaded a campaign to save whales through newspaper advertisements and street marches in

London. (That the Duke of Edinburgh was by then president of the WWF gave the movement much greater visibility.) In response, the British government imposed a ban on the import of products made from baleen whales. This was far from being a complete victory for whale conservationists, and some of them were to move on to become Greenpeace activists. The growing influence of all these nongovernmental organizations is remarkable all the same.[37]

An interesting development of the 1970s was that the preservation of the natural environment was often coupled with that of historical and cultural landmarks. In 1972, at a UNESCO meeting in Paris, a "convention concerning the protection of the world cultural and natural heritage" was signed by seventy-five countries. (The United States was the first nation to ratify the convention.)[38] The coupling of cultural and natural resources showed that culture and nature were beginning to be seen not as opposites, as had long tended to be the case in many parts of the globe, but as closely integrated so that talking of preserving one at the expense of the other would be impossible. An emerging perspective of this period saw culture and nature as interdependent. Moreover, rapid economic growth in many parts of the world had caused serious damage not only to nature and wildlife but also to ancient monuments and works of art. Just as endangered species needed protection, rare historical artifacts had to be treated with care lest they should disintegrate. According to the 1972 convention, individual countries were to prepare a list of historical landmarks within their borders, from which a number would be registered with an international committee on historical preservation. The latter would compile a master list of the world's most precious historical heritages, and those that required immediate care would be provided with funds for restoration and protection. The assumption was that these cultural monuments, just like the natural habitat, belonged to the whole of humanity, and that it was the responsibility of all people to ensure both natural and cultural preservation.[39]

The growing popularity of the notion of multiculturalism, another interesting development of the 1970s, may be said to have been an aspect of the concern with the preservation of historical heritages. Multiculturalism connoted the idea that culture must be seen as pluralistic, consisting of divergent ways of dealing with the human condition. Just as the preservation of pristine oceanic conditions and endangered wildlife was a moral imperative for the whole world, respect for different ways of life and thought came to be seen as an important agenda for international affairs. Pleas for cross-cultural understanding had long existed and produced many important movements and organizations dedicating themselves to a myriad exchange programs. And during the 1960s, a sense of transnational cultural consciousness had emerged. But during the 1970s, multiculturalism gained even greater influence because of its conjunction with other developments such as the rise of global environmentalism and the worldwide mushrooming of nongovernmental organizations. Here were forces pushing for globalization — the term began to be used toward the end of the decade — but the growth of global consciousness was also giving rise to awareness of diversity. Globalization and multiculturalism as twin themes — this was an idea that would eventually come to seem commonsensical. In the 1970s the picture was not yet so clearly recognized, but even so, individuals and organizations promoting educational and cultural exchanges were becoming keenly aware of the connection.

The continued growth of exchange programs during the 1970s and subsequently tends to be overlooked by students of international organization because of their fascination with the more dramatic activities by advocacy groups, such as those concerned with human rights and environmentalism. Purely in terms of number, however, exchange organizations continued to overshadow these other associations. International organizations promoting educational and cultural exchanges grew just as rapidly as the latter, and together they contributed to strengthening transnational networks.

For one thing, the 1970s saw significant developments in exchange programs between the two sides in the (already waning) Cold War, as well as between the West and the People's Republic of China. In 1971

UNESCO began the World Scientific and Technical Information Service to provide bibliographic information on published articles, numbering over one million a year, in seventy thousand specialized journals, which provided an opportunity for scientists from the Soviet Union, China, and other socialist countries to join the international community of scientists. The 1975 Helsinki accord contained the so-called Basket III, which dealt with cultural relations and endorsed exchange programs between NATO and Warsaw Pact countries. About this time, cultural exchange between socialist and capitalist nations picked up momentum. For instance, American and Soviet scientists began collaborating in energy and space research, as exemplified by the *Apollo-Soyuz* joint space mission undertaken in 1975. Two years later, two Soviet historians coauthored a book, an account of the history of U.S.-Russian relations, that was published by the University of Chicago Press; while the book struck many American reviewers as biased, its very publication indicated that the transnational interchange of ideas across ideological divides was becoming accepted.[40]

Likewise, the rapprochement between the United States and the People's Republic of China after 1971 reopened channels of communication between the two that had all but disappeared during the preceding two decades. The Committee on Scholarly Exchange with the People's Republic of China, which had been set up in 1966 under the auspices of the National Science Foundation in anticipation of the resumption of scholarly contact, now established a Beijing office to oversee the renewed exchanges. In cooperation with the Council for International Exchange of Scholars, the Washington organization that administered the Fulbright program, the Committee served as a liaison between Chinese and American students, academics, and professionals as they visited each other's country. On the Chinese side, the Chinese Academy of Social Science, a Beijing organization, played the key role in hosting visiting Americans and coordinating plans for scholarly cooperation. At this time such cooperation was still very limited, but at least the beginnings of the U.S.-Chinese cultural exchange, coming on the heels of the worldwide cultural revolution of the 1960s, served to make international intellectual cooperation and communication more nearly global than had been the case earlier. Moreover, in the United States and elsewhere, new nongovernmental organizations sprang up with a focus on the promotion of exchanges with the People's Republic. Foundations, universities, and professional societies began establishing offices and training staff to serve this purpose. While no exact counterpart to such organizations existed in China, these private initiatives from abroad sowed the seed for what would soon blossom into a large-scale exchange between the Chinese and the rest of the world.

That the growth in the number, scope, and diversity of international exchange programs was giving rise to serious questions may be seen in the fact that during the 1970s, the governments of the United States, Britain, France, and Germany commissioned studies to reexamine their respective cultural policies.[41] In the United States, an "independent panel on international information, education and cultural relations," funded from private sources, recommended that the dissemination of information about the nation should be combined with exchange programs under a single administration. For this purpose, the United States Information Agency was renamed the United States International Communication Agency, starting in 1978. Although the former name was restored after only four years, the stress on communication and exchange, not just on information, was to remain. This change reflected the recognition that the spread of information as an aspect of Cold War diplomacy was now of secondary importance compared with the sharing of ideas and experiences with all countries. In the meantime, an officially sponsored review undertaken in Britain recommended, in its report of 1977, that the British Council be either abolished or scaled down. Such a radical idea was more in response to severe economic problems at home than the product of a new view of international cultural relations, and the government did not accept the recommendation. But the review did reflect the growing sentiment that cultural affairs could mostly be left in private hands rather than officially promoted. In any event, the official response to the report pointed to the importance of "educational and cultural work" in "stimulating the use of the English language" abroad.

This, apparently rather mundane, point was becoming a matter of serious concern to French officials concerned with cultural affairs. A report written in 1979 by a committee headed by Jacques Rigaud acknowledged that English had overtaken French as the language of international communication. The report suggested that France's cultural heritage and ideas could be promoted by languages other than just French. The world was changing, the report pointed out, because of "the involvement of people in international affairs," and it was therefore imperative to consider French cultural centers abroad as places of exchange with the local populace. This did not mean that the teaching of French in other countries should be neglected, but that the training of teachers of French abroad should be emphasized, linked to the concept of *francophonie*.[42] A German report, published by the Foreign Ministry in 1978, admitted that German was not an international language, but it was even more emphatic than the documents of the other countries in stressing the significance of "international cooperation in the cultural sector" so as to "create ties between peoples of different nationalities." Echoing the French report, the German statement asserted, "All nations are today, more than ever before, dependent on one another for their existence. . . . The value of what we give is only worth as much as our willingness to take. Thus, an open attitude towards others is a principle of our cultural policy abroad."[43]

It was against such a background that organizations, national and international, faced the issue of cultural diversity. Those espousing multiculturalism insisted on the autonomy of each culture, defined by religion, ethnicity, race, gender, sexual orientation, and other factors. The world, in such a view, consisted of a variety of specifically definable cultures, each with its own values and agendas. No one culture was inherently superior to others. To the extent that one culture, for instance Western civilization (characterized by exponents of multiculturalism as having traditionally been dominated by white males), tended to claim superiority (or "hegemony," another word gaining currency), it must be rejected. To push such an argument to its extreme, multiculturalism would deny the existence of universal truths or values; all cultures were equally valid. The validity or authenticity of a culture must be recognized before constructing any device for cross-cultural communication and cooperation.

Such an assertion presented a serious challenge not only to cultural exchange but also to human rights, environmentalism, and a host of other causes that were being promoted by intergovernmental organizations and nongovernmental organizations. If there were no universal human rights or a shared commitment to the protection of the natural habitat, how could a global community of men and women with common interests and agendas develop? Was it ever possible to conceptualize such a community to begin with? Was not the idea itself a hegemonic one, coming from a dominant civilization to impose its definition of the world on others? If the globe was becoming subdivided into self-defining cultures with their own local loyalties, should communication and dialogue among these cultures be even attempted? Was a multicultural world compatible with a viable international civil society?

These were serious questions, and they added complexity to international affairs in general and to the workings of international organizations in particular during the 1970s. The very idea of cultural exchange came to be assaulted as a product of Western civilization, even a maneuver by the powerful European and North American countries to hang on to their position of worldwide influence. Although during the 1950s UNESCO had stressed humanity's diverse cultural heritage and sponsored conferences on Eastern and Western values, the assumption was that dialogue was possible and desirable among such diverse heritage and civilizations. All countries and cultures, cultural internationalists had believed (and continued to believe), shared a commitment to mutual communication and understanding. During the 1970s, however, some of the more outspoken leaders of Third World countries began to insist that they did not necessarily share Western ideas about such matters, and that any attempt at cross-cultural cooperation must reflect their perspectives also. Some intellectuals — among the most influential was the Algerian writer Franz Fanon, whose book *The Wretched of the Earth* (1965) was among the first systematic presentations of the argument — asserted that their first task was to liberate themselves from the cultural vocabulary that had provided them with words and concepts to comprehend the world, indeed to describe themselves. The time had come, they argued, for them to develop their own vocabulary if they were to be fully independent of the colonial past. Similar ideas were expressed in a scholarly fashion by Edward Said, the American scholar of Palestinian background, whose *Orientalism* (1978) became something of a bible of multiculturalism. In such a perspective, freeing Third World people from their dependence on the West for knowledge and information would be vitally important.

These views were aired at UNESCO and other international settings, making cross-cultural exchange a far more complex undertaking than earlier. Some observers considered the situation so serious as to nullify all attempts at international cultural cooperation. Add to this the rise, in the late 1970s, of postmodernist theory, which argued against the ideas of progress, modernization, and evolutionary historical processes but stressed the essential meaninglessness of concepts, terms, and words, except in the context of the individual uttering (or hearing) them. Postmodernism could present a serious intellectual challenge confronting all attempts at global community by intergovernmental and nongovernmental organizations.

The crisis would continue into the subsequent decades, but remarkably it did not prevent the further promotion of international exchange programs. The governments of the United States, Britain, France, and Germany continued to recognize the importance of cultural and educational exchange, although they were also aware of the need to refine and reformulate their exchange programs to cope with the challenges of the age. The 1970s saw many new initiatives undertaken by these and other countries, both officially and privately, to promote communication and understanding among nations. In 1971, for instance, the European Federation for Intercultural Learning was established as the umbrella organization of American Field Service offices throughout Europe. These offices had been engaged in providing "home-stay" experiences for young people as a way to foster transnational learning and under-standing.[44] In the United States, many programs designed for encour-aging cross-cultural understanding were created, such as the Educa-tional Resource Development Trust, the Educational Foundation for Foreign Study, and Friendship Force. All were established during the 1970s to bring Americans into closer contact with people elsewhere, especially from non-Western parts of the world. In 1977 the Fulbright Association was founded in Washington to facilitate interaction among former Fulbright scholars. And in 1979 the International Student Exchange Program was organized to provide funding and logistical sup-port for interchange among American and overseas students and young faculty members.[45]

Even among European nations that had been traditionally active in cultural exchange programs, there were so many of them that in 1976, a conference of cabinet ministers in charge of cultural affairs was held in Oslo to coordinate European cultural exchange. In the meantime, the French-American Foundation was established to initiate a program of exchange professors between French and American universities, while the German Historical Institute opened its offices in Washington, London, Tokyo, and elsewhere to undertake cultural exchanges. And in 1972 the Japan Foundation was created by the Ministry of Foreign Affairs to encourage the development of Japanese studies abroad as well as the exchange of scholars, artists, journalists, and many others between Japan and other countries. Around this time, research organizations, or think tanks, began to be set up in Japan, after the pattern of those in the West. The National Institute for Research Advancement was one of the first such organizations, and from the beginning it engaged in projects that were predominantly international in character.

All such efforts suggest that the challenge of multiculturalism was being met in a constructive fashion by promoters of international exchange programs. Rather than give up such programs as hopeless, anachronistic, or misguided in a rapidly changing world of self-conscious diversity, they persisted in the faith that it was possible to incorporate cultural diversity in an interdependent world community and that for this purpose, cross-national, cross-cultural exchange was still the best way. Together with individuals and organizations involved in human rights, environmental, and other international movements, promoters of cultural and educational exchange paved the way for a stronger emergence of global consciousness toward the end of the twentieth century.

In 1970 an Italian spokesman noted that his country's policy on cultural exchange had "evolved from a Euro-centric and elitist view" toward "an attitude of mass-enlightenment and scientifically oriented technical cooperation." Italy, he said, favored a "constructive approach towards understanding between different civilisations" as well as combating "illiteracy in the developing world."[46] The statement neatly summed up the broadening of the scope of cultural exchange in the 1970s. Promoting understanding among divergent civilizations and trying to eradicate illiteracy were now among enterprises that were at the core of cross-cultural relations. These efforts were filled with conceptual difficulties and political obstacles, and yet there were intergovernmental organizations and international nongovernmental organizations ready to meet the challenge. In so doing, these organizations were continuing their attempt at reformulating international affairs.

CHAPTER 6

Toward Global
Community

International organizations, both governmental and nongovernmental, continued to grow in number and scope during the 1980s and the 1990s. Little was qualitatively different about their activities from what they had been in the preceding decade, but their cumulative and combined importance in the world increased because of the dramatic turn of events at the level of interstate affairs. In most accounts of the last two decades of the twentieth century, the erosion and eventual end of the Cold War are presented as the key themes of international relations, which are then considered to have ushered in a new age known as the post–Cold War period. But, as I have argued throughout this book, these terms look at only one level of international affairs and do not help us understand many other developments that were equally significant to, if not more significant than, such dramatic episodes as the crumbling of the Berlin Wall or the collapse of the Soviet Union. In addition to seeing these episodes in the framework of the history of the Cold War, we must make an effort to see them as aspects of some other, nongeopolitical developments as well. All these developments may be said to have combined together to generate a greater global consciousness, the idea that there were transnational themes that affected people everywhere and produced universal standards for judging the behavior of nations. The emergence of such consciousness was an unexpected but in many ways a fitting climax of a century that had been characterized, at the interstate level, by conflict and violence.

The focus on international organizations may help us understand certain continuous themes in international relations during the 1980s and the 1990s. There is still a tendency to view the last years of the 1970s and the first half of the 1980s as a period in which Cold War tensions revived.[1] The difficulty of explaining why the détente of the early 1970s led to the "new Cold War" at the end of the decade, only to usher in a sudden end of the Cold War a few years later, remains so long as one focuses on geopolitical developments. In the history of international organizations, there was in fact no reversal of the trend; they continued to be active throughout the two decades, and it makes little sense to single out the period of the "new Cold War" (around 1978 to 1985) for special attention — except to show that the efforts by these organizations had a great deal to do with the easing of tensions after 1986.

And yet, most writers then and since have paid little attention to such developments. Many have continued to dwell on geopolitical themes. Appearing just before the final curtain was to drop on the Cold War drama, Paul Kennedy's *The Rise and Fall of the Great Powers* (1987) showed an unchanging fascination with power struggles among nations. The great powers were still the central players that defined the international system. The underlying assumption was that the story of interpower rivalries that had begun in Europe in the seventeenth century or even earlier had not ended; players might change from time to time, but not the fact that they determined the shape of the world. Shortly after the publication of the book, the Cold War was officially proclaimed over by President George H. Bush, but Henry Kissinger, writing in *Diplomacy* (1994), continued to argue that power relations among the major states would continue to be the key to world affairs. These were traditional views, presented in conventional vocabulary and frameworks, but the books' popularity suggested how difficult it was to recognize that an alter-

native definition of international relations had been gaining strength and
that a new vocabulary might be needed to note that development.

The gap between the realities of international developments and the
vocabulary to comprehend them was, however, being quietly filled by a
number of imaginative scholars who began publishing important analyses of world affairs in the 1980s. Continuing the work of some pioneering authors who, as we have seen, had written major studies of international organizations during the 1970s and even earlier, several political
scientists published important and prescient works. Johan Galtung's *The
True Worlds*, making its appearance in 1980, indicated the direction that
other studies would take in the coming decades by stressing the roles of
"non-territorial actors" in meeting the needs of individual human
beings.[2] This seminal work was followed by an increasing number of
monographs on international organizations and transnational issues.[3] By
the 1990s there were so many of them that specialized monographs as
well as general accounts of these subjects were filling library shelves. The
bulk of this literature, however, was written by nonhistorians. In the
meantime, the term "global" was becoming a preferred adjective, often
superseding "international" and "transnational." Indeed, "globalization"
emerged as perhaps the key terminology of the end of the century,
embracing international organizations and transnational concerns along
with economic and technological interconnections being strengthened
throughout the world. Not only political scientists but also anthropologists, sociologists, and philosophers — but few historians — wrote one
essay after another discussing the nature and significance of the
phenomenon.[4]

Amid all this scholarly activity, Kenneth Boulding, an economist,
could still write in 1989 that "the rise of international non-governmental organizations [is] perhaps one of the most spectacular developments
of the twentieth century, although it has happened so quickly that it is
seldom noticed."[5] He was at least correct as far as writings by historians
were concerned. As the introduction noted, they, along with more tra-

ditionally oriented social scientists, continued to discuss international relations without taking these organizations — and, for that matter, intergovernmental organizations — into serious consideration. One reason may have been that, as Boulding's statement suggests, there was the impression that the emergence of international nongovernmental organizations had been a recent phenomenon so that they were not yet objects of historical inquiry. Many writers saw them simply as an aspect of post–Cold War history.

An examination of international organizations during the 1980s and the 1990s shows, however, that they were carrying on work that had begun earlier and that the apparently sudden burst of energy by such organizations, especially of the nongovernmental variety, became more conspicuous toward the end of the century, only because the attention-grabbing interstate dramas that had tended to obscure them were losing their centrality in international affairs. International organizations could often find themselves in the spotlight, however, because they became more extensively involved than earlier in local political and social scenes, even giving rise to the view that they were replacing governmental authorities in providing law and order. Moreover, in some instances nongovernmental organizations came into conflict with intergovernmental organizations such as the United Nations in carrying out their missions. While some began to criticize the expanding spheres and deepening levels of activities by these organizations, such criticism was evidence that international organizations had indeed come of age, that no discussion of world affairs could now do without paying them serious attention.

In the pages that follow, only a brief outline of the activities by international organizations in the recent decades can be given. As in the other chapters, these activities are grouped in six subject areas. The concluding chapter mentions the serious scholarly reassessment of these organizations, especially the nongovernmental variety, that began to make its appearance toward the end of the twentieth century.

No history of the ending of the Cold War would be adequate without due attention to the protests of numerous organizations against what appeared to be a resumed nuclear arms race during the early 1980s. One of the most dramatic protests was staged by Greenpeace in 1985 against French nuclear testing in the South Pacific. The organization had drawn world attention by fitting out vessels against such tests as well as against the killing of whales and other endangered species. By the mid-1980s, Greenpeace had a fleet of four ships, the largest of which was the *Rainbow Warrior*. The ships arrived at Auckland harbor, New Zealand, in July 1985 on their way to Mururoa, in the French Polynesian chain, to initiate a new round of protest demonstrations. But while at anchor, the flagship was blown up by agents of the French intelligence service, sinking the boat and killing one member of the crew.[6] The incident made sensational news, and it severely strained relations between France and New Zealand. It also made Greenpeace more visible than ever.

Greenpeace was by no means alone in engaging in an active antinuclear campaign. The first half of the 1980s seemed to witness a resumed arms race among the nuclear powers, and it revitalized worldwide peace movements after they had been relatively quiescent during the détente era of the 1970s. Catholic bishops in North America and elsewhere strongly opposed the placement by the United States and the Soviet Union of intermediate-range tactical nuclear weapons in Europe, and some women activists organized the Women's Encampment for a Future of Peace and Justice, establishing camps outside military bases.[7] This was a new organization, but it was joined by many others that had long been in existence, such as the Pugwash group, in which Soviet and American scientists cooperated to propose alternatives to nuclear armament, so that peace activism was in a sense reaching a new climax, playing a role, however indirect, in the ending of the Cold War.[8]

But this milestone in international relations did not diminish the importance of international organizations in the cause of peace, for outside of the superpower Cold War, numerous other conflicts were crying out for peaceful settlement. At a gathering of representatives of nongovernmental organizations in Nairobi, Kenya, held in 1985 in conjunction with a United Nations conference on women, it was reported, "Here Soviet and American women pledged to work together. . . . Here also Palestinian and Israeli women came together in search of ways to end the conflict [in Palestine]."[9] In reality, of course, the Arab-Israeli conflict proved even more intractable than the U.S.-Soviet confrontation, but to the extent that tensions were to begin to ease in the Middle East, much credit was due to women's organizations, educational institutions, and other international agencies that worked tirelessly to find a peaceful solution.[10]

Even when peace was reestablished, whether in U.S.-Soviet relations or in local conflicts, that did not mean the end of problems, for there were many legacies of such strife, ranging from the land mines that still dotted war-torn nations to the millions of refugees driven out of their homelands in search of food and jobs. International organizations sprang to action to cope with such crises. Among the most impressive was the campaign to ban antihuman land mines. Various national nongovernmental organizations had been created in protest against the continued existence and use of such devices, and six of them — including Handicap International and Human Rights Watch — came together in 1992 to set up an international coordinating body, the International Campaign to Ban Landmines.[11] It worked energetically for the cause and was instrumental in persuading a large number of governments to come together to negotiate a treaty banning antihuman land mines. The Canadian government was receptive to the movement and hosted a conference in 1997 out of which a new treaty emerged. The International Campaign mobilized world opinion in support of the treaty; to say that the pressure succeeded in moving most countries of the world to sign the agreement would be no exaggeration. Some countries refused, including the United States, China, and India. When this organization received the Nobel Peace Prize for 1997, the Russian government declared its intention of adhering to the treaty. Even without these absentee nations, the treaty was a landmark in demonstrating what an international nongovernmental organization could accomplish in partnership with governments in bringing about a change in the ways in which nations conducted themselves.

Closely linked to the campaigns against nuclear weapons, land mines, and other devices for indiscriminate killing was the continued vigor of humanitarian activities carried on by international organizations working in cooperation. Among the new organizations undertaking such coordination was the Center for International Health and Cooperation, founded in New York in 1992, with a European office in Geneva, to "promote healing and peace in countries shattered by war, regional conflicts and ethnic violence." As a volunteer association, the Center cooperated with other nongovernmental organizations as well as with the United Nations High Commissioner for Refugees and the World Health Organization to bring health and healing to the warring parties in Somalia and the former Yugoslavia as the best way for "initiating dialogue, understanding and cooperation" among them.[12]

One of the most serious consequences of war and civil strife was the increasing number of refugees. Their number nearly doubled between 1980 and 1990, from eight to fifteen million worldwide, and by 1995 it had reached twenty-seven million.[13] These included both interstate migrants and internally displaced persons. The bulk of them were victims not so much of major international conflicts as of local violence. The crisis that these displaced persons created was so grave as to tax the energies of the United Nations High Commissioner for Refugees, the highest international agency. The assistance of private humanitarian organizations was imperative, and they expanded their scope considerably. Amnesty International, for instance, had by the 1990s established over four thousand branches throughout the world, and one million members from nearly every country worked in various capacities or made donations. It concerned itself with human rights violations inflicted upon the refugees because, as its 1997 report noted, "many states talk about the rights of refugees, while in practice devoting their energies to keeping refugees away from their borders."[14] Almost by default, but also thanks to their dedicated staff and the funds collected from their supporters, Amnesty International and many sister organizations were emerging as de facto authorities in the governance of some areas of the world.

During the 1980s significant international relief work was carried out in Southeast Asia, where the long war in Vietnam and the civil war in Cambodia resulted in huge numbers of refugees. Only a tiny minority could be resettled in Australia, Canada, the United States, and Europe; the majority were in dilapidated camps in Thailand and elsewhere. Those who returned to their own lands found no home. Into such a situation, voluntary associations of Europe, North America, Oceania, Israel, and Japan appeared and set up medical facilities, founded schools for children, and undertook many activities the local governments were incapable of performing. Activities by Japanese organizations are particularly notable, since the nation had not hitherto been engaged in much volunteer work abroad. But such groups now mushroomed, sending doctors, teachers, students, and others to Thailand, Laos, and elsewhere to cooperate with other international organizations to provide relief. According to the records of one Japanese group, a Buddhist organization, the lack of prior experience was a serious handicap, as was the unwillingness of the Japanese government to give it support. However, the organization made steady headway, particularly through its emphasis on education, bringing textbooks, printing presses, and mobile libraries to local children. Such modest beginnings served to establish close connections between the people of Japan, Southeast Asia, and the West in ways no official relations could have hoped to accomplish.[15]

These organizations often encountered serious problems because of their deeper involvement in the internal affairs of many countries. As their representatives engaged themselves in relief activities in areas where civil strife, banditry, and terrorism were rampant, they were not exempted from resistance and even physical attack from local authorities. In Sudan, for instance, where people throughout the country were suffering from food shortages because of a long civil war, various nongovernmental organizations devised a scheme (called Operation Rainbow) in 1986 to ensure that relief goods actually reached their intended recipients. The government in Khartoum refused to accept the scheme, instead using its own army to distribute food. Doctors without Borders, one of the organizations behind the operation, accused the government of intentionally impeding shipments to people in areas under the control of the opposition forces. Two years later, when a cease-fire was declared, the United Nations and international nongovernmental organizations succeeded in establishing a neutral zone in Sudan from which food would be sent to all parts of the country. Even so, relief goods were often used by the two factions as means for controlling the population, and when in 1992 several UNICEF workers appeared to stand in their way, they were peremptorily murdered by soldiers belonging to the Sudanese People's Liberation Army.[16]

In such instances, aid organizations found it necessary to appeal not just to the United Nations but also to various governments for support. Indeed, reports by Doctors without Borders are filled with expressions of dismay at the United Nation's impotence in the face of adamant local resistance. In the Sudan case, for instance, the nongovernmental organizations involved called upon various nations to push, either through or outside the United Nations, for an effective implementation of the Sudanese food distribution program. The United States was receptive, its Congress adopting a resolution condemning Sudanese violations of human rights. The United States Department of Defense also established a special office to plan for possible assistance to international organizations engaged in humanitarian relief activities. This was symbolic of the age. When chances for major wars of global scale appeared to diminish, and when civil strife, local border disputes, and terrorist attacks came to characterize so much of international affairs — although "international" would hardly be an appropriate term in this context — the role of the state and its armed forces was also changing. At least for the majority of nations as well as the United Nations, peacekeeping and humanitarian efforts were becoming important functions of military power. Until now, humanitarianism and military force had tended to be seen as polar opposites, the former being more "human" and therefore transnational, and the latter considered first and foremost to be the instrument of the state for geopolitical purposes. But now power was increasingly being called on to help in international humanitarian causes.

The complications to which such a conjunction of force and humanitarianism could give rise were made evident in Somalia, where a long reign by a dictatorial regime collapsed and led to a brutal civil war in the early 1990s, in the process starving over a million people and driving them out of the country to become refugees in neighboring states. Here was a clearly recognized case in need of international humanitarian intervention, but how could relief personnel engage in such activities in a situation of complete chaos? Aid workers sent by UNICEF, the International Red Cross, and other organizations had to turn to armed militia for protection as they distributed food, but a United Nations–sponsored cease-fire led to their disarmament, while armed bands and factions continued to plunder aid goods. The United Nations dispatched a peacekeeping force in 1992, but it was helpless against the continuing plundering and terrorism exercised by the contending factions. Finally, in December 1992, the world organization authorized the employment of regular forces by several countries, including the United States. An international force consisting of more than thirty thousand troops was sent to restore order in Somalia so as to enable the implementation of humanitarian projects. Shooting incidents involving United Nations and indigenous forces occurred; according to Doctors without Borders, several hundred Somalian citizens were killed by the international expeditionary force, leading in some instances to protests by nongovernmental organizations of alleged violations of human rights.[17] In the meantime, the United States withdrew its forces in view of a rising domestic criticism; neither the public nor Congress was persuaded that humanitarian purposes justified such a massive use of force.

The Somalian intervention, perhaps more than anything else, demonstrated the dilemma of international efforts involved in establishing local order as a precondition for administering relief. For nongovernmental organizations, the problem was particularly acute because by definition they did not have their own armed force and had to rely on local, national, or international military power to protect their activities. Often they criticized the behavior of United Nations forces or of various nations' troops, but at the same time they had to recognize their own helplessness without some military protection. Could international nongovernmental organizations continue to function without compromising their status as voluntary, nonmilitary agencies for humanitarianism? There was no fast and easy answer.

Under the circumstances, it is all the more striking that, far from being discouraged by their experiences in Sudan, Somalia, and elsewhere, nongovernmental organizations continued to grow in number and scope throughout the 1980s and the 1990s. For the basic reasons for their existence — the need for private funds for carrying out important programs, the unwillingness of sovereign states to undertake certain projects, the growth of global issues for which only transnational solutions were possible — never disappeared but, if anything, became even more urgent toward the end of the century. For one thing, private funds for international nongovernmental organizations were more imperative than ever, because during the 1980s and the 1990s many governments in Europe and North America began to redefine their roles and, in the process, change direction from a welfare state to "small government," reducing governmental expenditures and thereby their fiscal deficits. This shift away from extensive state involvement in social welfare implied that the social and human needs of society, at home and abroad, would now, more than ever, have to be met through private initiatives.

The phenomenon could be detected in other countries as well. In Japan, a country that had traditionally relied on public authorities to look after the needs of the poor and the disadvantaged, business corporations began showing an interest in philanthropy, establishing a "1 percent club," a symbolic gesture that called upon larger firms to set aside 1 percent of their revenues for nonbusiness related activities, including charity. Although the number and scale of nongovernmental organizations engaged in humanitarian work in Japan were still much smaller than those in North America or Europe, already by 1990 some 290 philanthropic organizations had been established. While individual donations were meager compared with those elsewhere — at that time the estimate was that an average American contributed over one hundred dollars a year to charity, whereas an average figure for Japan was only six dollars — the awareness was growing that private individuals would have to play a larger role in social services than in the past. The Kōbe earthquake of 1995 confirmed this trend as volunteers from all over the country — and from abroad — offered their assistance.[18]

During the 1980s and the 1990s, international humanitarian activities became particularly notable in two relatively new areas: the care of AIDS patients and the promotion of the rights of disabled persons. AIDS began to spread with alarming rapidity during the 1980s, especially in Africa where, at the end of the 1990s, 3 percent of young adults were said to be dying of HIV. The catastrophic spread of the disease raised serious moral, as well as medical and scientific, issues for the world community, since AIDS treatment was very costly, and few outside the advanced industrialized nations could afford the expensive drugs. Rich countries and corporations would have to be asked to help, and, not surprisingly, international corporations provided the framework for soliciting and administering funds. In 1996 the United Nations established a program (UNAIDS) "to take on AIDS as a core issue," as its executive director said. In 2000 the United Nations sponsored a world AIDS conference in Durban, South Africa, where the delegates called for "globalization of HIV treatment." The problem was considered so serious that the 2001 "G-8" conference at Genoa paid close attention to it, the first time that the leaders of the world's richest countries, who had been meeting annually to consider global economic issues, collectively confronted the crisis.[19]

Equally remarkable was the expanding recognition of the rights of the disabled. That the state had a special responsibility to care for the disabled was graphically demonstrated when the United States Congress passed the Americans with Disabilities Act in 1990, making it illegal to discriminate against disabled persons in jobs, workplaces, transportation, and public accommodations. Public buildings, for instance, had to be made accessible to wheelchair users. In other countries, too, accessibility became a policy objective, although it was never fully implemented. Not just wheelchair users but also people with many other disabilities were steadily gaining recognition as individuals with all the same rights and privileges as other citizens. This increasing awareness of the disabled may have reflected the fact that in many countries, especially in Europe and Japan, life expectancy was increasing, and as a result the care of the aging population was becoming a serious public issue. The rights of older people were given new emphasis in the United States and other industrial societies. (The American Association of Retired Persons, one of the largest nonprofit organizations in the nation, had a budget of nearly $500 million in the mid-1990s.) In many ways aging people developed physical and mental problems comparable to those of younger disabled persons, and together they were beginning to make up an increasingly large portion of the world's population. Just as able-bodied elderly people often develop various disabilities that entitle them to special medical care, the disabled, too, must be seen as an integral part of the community, rather than being marginalized. Not surprisingly, reflecting these and other trends, the United Nations declared 1980 the "year of the handicapped," and its Economic and Social Council as well as the International Labor Organization provided special funds to promote public awareness of the landmark.

From the beginning, however, private organizations were particularly active in promoting the cause of the disabled and planning various activities on their behalf. In 1981 four hundred persons with disabilities from more than sixty countries came together in Winnipeg, Canada, to found the first international nongovernmental organization for the disabled, Disabled Persons International. Its initial funds came not only from the Canadian government but also from such nongovernmental organizations as the Coalition of Provincial Organizations of the Handicapped, the Mennonite Central Committee, and the Catholic Committee for Development and Peace.[20] Within four years, Disabled Persons International had come to include members from over a hundred countries, representing millions of people throughout the world who were considered disabled. In close coordination with national committees, the international organization devoted itself to educational campaigns to arouse public awareness about the rights and needs of people with disabilities, and to community programs where such people would receive special education, rehabilitation, and, where feasible, job training.

With one out of every thousand individuals in the world being considered disabled — and this was clearly an underestimation — it is not surprising that such people should seek their empowerment just like other groups that had been marginalized. One of the most dramatic ways in which they tried to arouse public consciousness was through sporting events. Although such events had first been organized in conjunction with the Olympic games during the 1960s, it was not until the 1980s that successful efforts were made to incorporate Paralympic games as an integral part of the quadrennial sporting event. In 1984 the International Coordinating Committee of World Sports Organizations for the Disabled was set up, to bring together many organizations that had served the needs of different types of disabilities: the blind, the deaf, those with cerebral palsy, and many others. The Coordinating Committee was able to persuade the national committees hosting the summer and winter Olympics to include parallel events for the disabled. Thus in 1984, while the Olympic games were taking place in Los Angeles, "international games for the disabled" were opened by President Ronald Reagan and attracted the participation of eighteen hundred athletes from fifty countries. Another event, games for wheelchair users, was to have been held in Champaign, Illinois, but the event had to be moved to Britain for lack of adequate equipment. It was at the British games that the term "Paralympics" was used for the first time.[21] But Paralympic games became an integral part of the Olympics only at the 1988 games in Seoul, Korea. By the time of the Barcelona Olympics in 1992, the presence of disabled athletes in the same city, engaged in their own games, had become a familiar sight.

Disabled persons obviously need more assistance, logistically and financially, to participate in international sporting events. At both Seoul and Barcelona, hundreds of volunteers gave their time to serve these athletes, and private donations supplemented subsidies from the hosting Olympic committees for funding. Although Paralympics were no more free of political issues than the regular Olympics — for instance, at Seoul the Iranian goal-ball team refused to play the Israeli team and was told to return home immediately — the history of these games is a powerful reminder that transnational identities can lead to impressive results when provided with institutional frameworks.[22]

Apart from sporting events, the role of international organizations in caring for the disabled was especially notable in poorer countries with limited resources devoted to social programs. Such countries have far fewer doctors per capita, and inadequate medical facilities tend to result in a higher rate of birth defects. In Bangladesh, for instance, in the early 1990s three-quarters of national budgets still depended on aid from other countries, and most of the funding for hospitals and rehabilitation centers came from nongovernmental organizations, domestic and foreign. In 1993 an Asia-Pacific conference of Disabled Persons International was held in Dacca, and an ambitious program was adopted for protecting the rights of the disabled. Even so, many categories of disabilities, including mental retardation, were not yet adequately served. Still, the clear recognition was that the problems of disabled persons worldwide could be dealt with only through international efforts.[23]

Such efforts were now more desperately needed than ever, because during the 1980s and the 1990s, the gap between rich and poor countries widened. True, this was not a new trend, but it was now being exacerbated by the increasing globalization of the world economy. A qualitative difference became apparent between the economies that were integrated into the international networks of production, distribution, and consumption and those that were not. The former economies were electronically connected through computer networks and were able to instantly access information via the Internet, while the latter did not partake in such technological advances. Moreover, while large parts of the world were becoming a huge arena for a global flow of capital, some remained unaffected. Private capital moved from one country to another with increasing speed, and in the late 1990s the total outstanding issues of international loans and bonds amounted to almost $7 trillion.[24]

And yet this huge investment was unevenly distributed. Countries in Latin America, for instance, were regular recipients of foreign private loans and investments, and those in the formerly Soviet bloc (so-called transition countries, shifting from a socialist to a free enterprise system) likewise were becoming integrated into the global financial system. However, as the authors of *Global Transformations* (1999) noted, "The poorest countries have remained on the margins of private international finance and reliant on official aid flows."[25] In 1990 and 1995, for instance, total capital flows to developing countries amounted to $57.1 billion and $211.2 billion, respectively. Africa's share, however, was only $2.5 billion and $11.8 billion in these years. Even countries that received large amounts of foreign investments and loans, however, often fell into a financial crisis, during which they were incapable of making debt payments to foreign lenders. Mexico, Brazil, Argentina, and other countries in Latin America were hit particularly severely by the debt crisis precisely because they had been connected to the world financial network. The upshot of all these developments was that the 1980s were a decade of poor economic growth in most Third World countries; those that did better, such as the newly industrial economies of East Asia (South Korea, Taiwan, Hong Kong, and Singapore), were no longer considered members of the Third World.

Under the circumstances, it was obvious that for the poorest countries in Africa as well as the debt-ridden countries in parts of Asia and Latin America, assistance from abroad was the only means left to enable them to cope with their social and economic crises. Unfortunately for them, this was the very moment when the donor nations were reducing their official assistance, for a number of reasons: their own domestic economic problems, political pressures for "smaller government," and resistance to using public funds for foreign aid in the absence of a geopolitical justification in view of the waning and ending of the Cold War. It was evident that if the poorer countries were to solve their problems, not to mention undertake economic development, they would need aid from international organizations more than ever before. And these organizations were clearly aware of the critical roles they would have to play in those countries' affairs. For instance, UNICEF and the World Health Organization began pooling their resources for polio elimination throughout the world. UNICEF had, since the 1960s, focused its energies on infrastructure development and primary health care programs, rather than on disease eradication, but during the 1980s it recognized that given the civil strife, debt crisis, and other afflictions in the poorer countries, their health conditions, especially of children, were deteriorating. UNICEF thus increased its budget for obtaining and distributing polio vaccine to Asia, Africa, and Latin America, and the World Health Organization administered the immunization program, which proved to be immensely successful.[26] In the meantime, the World Bank and the International Monetary Fund became particularly active during the last two decades of the century, providing not only funds but also guidance for domestic economic policies and trade strategies. Such guidance often came into conflict with local regimes pursuing their own agendas, but the overall picture is clear: poverty and indebtedness in any part of the world were seen as matters for global concern, to be dealt with in an international framework.

The same thing could be said of international nongovernmental organizations concerned with developmental assistance. They were becoming so central to developmental projects in many parts of the world that in 1998 a group of French scholars published a massive volume giving a detailed analysis of this phenomenon. One theme that emerged out of the book's essays was that development-oriented international nongovernmental organizations had grown so much and had become involved in the affairs of other countries so deeply that it no longer made sense to refer to them as though they shared many common characteristics.[27] In the United States, 160 private agencies involved in international relief, development, and refugee efforts formed InterAction, with its headquarters in Washington, to coordinate publicity and fund-raising activities of these organizations through the Internet. Only 16 out of the 160 members (as of the year 2000) had the word "development" in their names, but most of the others were as concerned with development as they were with relief issues. To effect cooperation between these and overseas nongovernmental organizations, the Institute for Development Research actively promoted "global civil society alliances through participation in civil society networks."[28]

Such an objective assumed, of course, that civil society was becoming robust in all parts of the world, especially among developing states. Whether this was in fact the case was not always clear, but there was little doubt that economic development was more than ever connected to the problem of local governance. Case studies of newly independent countries in Central Asia found, for instance, that the trend toward democratization was never unidirectional. Kazakstan, for instance, which gained independence from the Soviet Union in 1991, had a democratic constitution, but freedom of the press began to be suppressed in the mid-1990s, and the country's nongovernmental organizations appealed to the international community for support. A few, including Amnesty International, responded, but none of the democratic states challenged the government of Kazakstan.[29] Such a situation made it difficult for the international community to involve itself in the country's economic affairs. Likewise, aid activities by European and Canadian organizations in Central America during the 1980s provided an example of the difficulties involved when nongovernmental organizations and governmental agencies worked at cross purposes. The region was rocked by internal strife and civil war in Nicaragua, El Salvador, Guatemala, and elsewhere, and the United States government sought to restore order by supporting forces opposed to the Sandinista government in Nicaragua, heir to the movement for social change initially led by Agustino Sandino during the 1920s. Nongovernmental organizations from Europe and North America came into contact with grassroots organizations and helped establish local nongovernmental organizations, seeing them as forces for reform and democratization. Some nongovernmental organizations from the United States, on the other hand, assisted Washington's strategy of counterinsurgency and aided anti-Sandinista groups. The Sandinista regime, however, lost power in the early 1990s following national elections, and many foreign aid organizations had to reassess their objectives and priorities. As a study of their activities in Central America noted, "Long-term planning and strategy were absent from the Central America desks of most European NGOs at this time."[30] An episode such as this demonstrated the enormity of the tasks the nongovernmental organizations were now carrying out, as well as the frequent lack of cooperation between these organizations and the governmental apparatus, both of the aid-giving and aid-receiving nations.

The potentially conflictual relationship between civil society and the state, as well as efforts to bring the two together, could also be seen in the movement to protect the environment. During the 1970s international environmentalism had grown in response to the ecological crises produced by rapid industrialization. But those countries that had not partaken of such growth — some had failed to maintain a reasonable rate of growth even to feed their increasing population — continued to press for economic development as their cardinal objective. The tension between environmentalism and development was symbolized during the 1980s and the 1990s by the worldwide dispute over the building of huge dams. As Sanjeev Khagram has shown, the construction of dams was of symbolic importance in less developed countries, where hydropower was the main source of electricity as well as irrigation and drinking water.[31] However, dams not only could be injurious to the ecological system but also could violate human rights, as their construction often involved forced removal of inhabitants from the construction sites. For these reasons, both in advanced countries and in developing states there grew movements against the building of dams, and Khagram credits "domestic and transnational civil society organizations" for having slowed the pace of their construction. They were particularly successful in putting pressure on the World Bank to reduce its financing of big dam projects. Here again, however, the success of the anti-dam campaign depended on the viability of domestic civil society, as can be seen most clearly in the Three Gorges dam project on the Yangtze River in China. Despite voices of protest from abroad and some scattered opposition at home, the authorities in Beijing pushed ahead with the scheme, involving the destruction of dwellings for hundreds of thousands of people on both sides of the river and the removal and relocation of the residents. The Chinese government insisted that the dam was absolutely essential for preventing floods and generating power for millions of people in central China.

That was the dilemma. Virtually all countries were committed to growth, while the world needed to protect the environment. What was needed was a formula for accommodating the demands for both development and environmentalism. It was typical of the age that the concept of "sustainable growth" seemed to satisfy both these demands. According to Lynton Keith Caldwell, the words "sustainable growth" first appeared in a 1980 publication of the International Union for the Conservation of Nature and Natural Resources, *World Conservation Strategy: Living Resource Conservation for Sustainable Development*. As he notes, the term was defined as "the meeting of today's true needs and opportunities without jeopardizing the integrity of the planetary life-support base — the environment — and diminishing its ability to provide for needs, opportunities, and quality of life in the future."[32] Such an agenda would perhaps necessitate a slower rate of growth for more advanced countries but would also ensure that less developed nations not be left far behind. As a report by the Consultative Group on International Agricultural Research noted, during the 1980s its research agenda focused on "increasing sustainable food production in the developing countries in such a way that the nutritional level and general economic well-being of the poor are improved." For the 1990s the organization defined its mission as "sustainable improvements in the productivity of agriculture, forestry and fisheries in developing countries in ways that enhance nutrition and well-being, especially of low-income people."[33]

Given such an orientation in devising developmental agendas, it is not surprising that much more was accomplished in the environmental area during the 1980s and the 1990s than ever before. The number of international nongovernmental organizations concerned with the environment showed impressive gains during these decades. According to Keck and Sikkink, there were ten of them in 1973, but ten years later the number had increased to twenty-six, and within still another ten years, to ninety.[34] This was a faster rate of growth than any other category of nongovernmental organizations and indicated the influence, assertiveness, and self-confidence of environmental movements. Thanks in no small part to their activism, in 1987 the European Community's "single European act" called for unified environmental standards to be applied to all member states. The year 1989 was declared the "European year of the environment," and four years later, when the European Community became the European Union, the European Environmental Agency was established as the environmental arm of the Union. The European Commission, the legislative body, designated one of its directors general for overseeing environmental issues ranging from security of nuclear installations to soil conservation.[35]

By its very growth and activism, however, the environmental movement came face-to-face with problems that had not been experienced when it was in its infancy. To compare the second (1992) United Nations conference on environment and development (the so-called earth summit), held in Rio de Janeiro, with the landmark Stockholm conference of 1972 is to become aware of the distance the nations and international organizations had traveled in gaining a sophisticated understanding of many complicated problems as well as their determination to try to solve them. The 1992 conference was notable in the history of international nongovernmental organizations because their representatives were included in at least fourteen official delegations, marking a point where the lines separating governmental and nongovernmental personnel became more blurred than ever. Moreover, a large number of environmentally oriented nongovernmental organizations — as many as 1,420 of them, according to a study — gained access to the preparatory meetings that preceded the Rio conference.[36] The 120 individuals that made up the working party of these meetings included representatives from Greenpeace, the International Union for the Conservation of Nature and Natural Resources, and several other organizations. The Worldwide Fund for Nature, the World Resources Institute, and others drafted a comprehensive treaty on preserving biodiversity. While most nongovernmental organizations did not gain access to the formal conference itself, they — over 2,000 of them from 150 countries — held their own meeting in Rio, called Global Forum. The World Commission on Environment and Development, originally founded in Sweden, served as liaison between these two gatherings. Predictably, the meeting of nongovernmental organizations was more forthright in pointing to the dangers of too rapid a pace of economic growth, but the delegates were as critical of the advanced nations' practices as of the other countries'. For instance, they castigated the developed nations for indiscriminately building factories in less advanced countries to make use of their cheaper labor, resulting in forests being denuded and oceans polluted from industrial waste. The nongovernmental organizations adopted an "earth charter," calling upon industrial nations to invest in the preservation of rain forests, the protection of endangered species, and research in oceanography and climatology to guard against the warming trend of the earth.[37]

The final report, called the "Rio declaration on environment and development," did not go that far in giving priority to a transnational partnership on behalf of environmentalism, but it nevertheless was an important landmark in pointing to the responsibility of all nations and peoples to safeguard their natural habitat even as they undertook economic development. Proclaiming the need for "establishing a new and equitable global partnership through the creation of new levels of cooperation among States, key sectors of societies and people," the document reiterated that "Human beings are at the center of concerns for sustainable development. They are entitled to a healthy and productive life in harmony with nature." More specifically, the declaration took note of the different needs and responsibilities of developed and developing nations. The former, the Rio statement said, must "acknowledge the responsibility that they bear in the international pursuit of sustainable development in view of the pressures their societies place on the global environment and of the technological and financial resources they command." Echoing the voices of women and indigenous groups of people heard at the Global Forum, the final document asserted their "vital role" in environmental management. Even more striking was the assertion that "peace, development and environmental protection are interdependent and indivisible." Warfare was declared to be inherently destructive of sustainable development so that in the event of an armed conflict, the states involved were exhorted to "respect international law providing protection for the environment."[38]

From this time onward, it became a familiar scene for an international conference on environmental issues to include representatives of nongovernmental organizations as advisers to, even as members of, governmental delegations. When the United States and Canada negotiated for a North American Free Trade Area, environmental groups worked through congressional and public opinion to ensure that the two nations would couple the free-trade accord with a water-quality agreement to ensure the good condition of rivers and lakes in both countries. The result was the establishment of a North American Commission on Environmental Cooperation.[39] The June 1997 United Nations special assembly on the environment, held in New York as a sequel to the Rio de Janeiro gathering, was notable because representatives of many more nongovernmental organizations were included among national delegations than at Rio. Instead of meeting concurrently with the official conference, now states and nonstate actors were cooperating together to cope with urgent issues of the day. It was just a step from here to the point where nongovernmental organizations would come to play a crucial, even a dominant, role at international meetings. At a 1994 conference on prevention of desertification, nongovernmental organizations not only sent observers and cooperated with official representatives of the respective participatory governments, but they even provided part of the funds for the gathering. The 1995 Berlin conference on climate change attracted one thousand representatives of nongovernmental organizations, some of whom joined seventy thousand Berliners in a bicycling demonstration to warn the world about the hazards of climate change as a result of urbanization and industrialization.[40]

The Kyoto conference on the earth's warming trend, which met in December 1997, was a consequence of these efforts by international organizations to cope with the problem of climate change. All together, 161 countries, 40 international organizations, and 236 nongovernmental organizations were represented. They worked closely together to have the governments adopt specific targets for reducing the level of carbon dioxide emission in each country. The final agreement was a compromise. Thus the members of the European Union pledged to reduce their level of carbon dioxide emission by 10 percent by the year 2010, Japan by 6 percent, and the United States by 7 percent. Even such a modest program would not have been possible if representatives of nongovernmental organizations had not lobbied energetically on behalf of their objectives. Because this was the first large-scale conference on the environment held in Japan, the nation's 200 nongovernmental organizations involved themselves in the event, distributing their newsletter, providing information to the media, and exchanging ideas with their overseas counterparts.[41]

That such an important gathering took place in Japan was symbolic of Asia's steady involvement in the international environmental movement. Much of the movement's initiative, organization, funding, and activity had previously been confined to Western Europe and North America. But the deleterious impact of industrialization on the environment was being taken more and more seriously by the Asian countries with their fast-growing economies. In 1983 a nongovernmental organization, Development Alternatives, was established in New Delhi to engage in research and informational activities on climate change and related issues. In the following year, Climate Action Network–South Asia was created in Dhaka, Bangladesh. A Japanese branch of Greenpeace was organized in 1989, and in 1990 a media symposium on "communications for environment" was held in Bangkok. Four years later a nongovernmental Asia-Pacific conference on the environment was convened in Kyoto, resulting in the creation of the Asian Environmental Council in 1995. Also that year, a new nongovernmental organization, the Action Federation for Environment, was established in Korea.[42] These were but a small sample of Asian organizations that mushroomed in the last decades of the century, indicating not simply that environmental issues were attracting the increasing attention of Asian countries but also that nongovernmental organizations were proliferating in the region. Asia was becoming an important part of the global networks of civil societies.

Related to environmentalism, the movements to protect wildlife continued their momentum throughout the 1980s and the 1990s. The World Wildlife Fund, Greenpeace, Friends of the Animals, Defenders of Wildlife, the Humane Society, and other international nongovernmental organizations formed a coalition to protect elephants in Africa. They worked with local nongovernmental organizations to prevent the indiscriminate killing of elephants, and after a 1989 international agreement to prohibit ivory trade was signed, they made sure that the ban would be enforced. The role of international nongovernmental organizations in the protection of elephants was recognized by Zimbabwe's minister of natural resources and tourism when he complained that those organizations "took it upon themselves to initiate a major study of the ivory trade" and "persuaded international NGOs that they should call for a world ban on the ivory trade."[43] Such a statement shows how subversive of state authority some nongovernmental organizations could become, a matter of considerable concern to governments that saw their power being usurped by private associations that spoke in the name of "the international community." There were numerous instances of open collision between an environmentally oriented nongovernmental organization and a state, as seen most dramatically in the 1985 *Rainbow Warrior* affair, triggered by Greenpeace's concern that French nuclear tests would destroy marine life in the Pacific. Instances like this, however, were rare, and in most cases, at least regarding the preservation of biodiversity, the usual pattern was collaboration between governmental and nongovernmental organizations. Thus their representatives continued to hold meetings to renew the ban on ivory trade. The 1992 convention on biological diversity, which called on each nation to devise a strategy for the preservation of genetic resources, was a product of many years' research and preparation undertaken by the International Union for the Conservation of Nature and Natural Resources.[44]

It was not just national governments, however, that had to reckon with the growing activism of nongovernmental organizations in the environmental arena. Business enterprises, in particular multinational corporations, saw their interests and prerogatives being challenged by these organizations as well. The expansion of multinational businesses and of nongovernmental organizations were twin phenomena of globalization, and these were both nonstate actors, pursuing their agendas independently of governmental authority. And yet their agendas and ideologies often proved to be in conflict. Economic globalization was being promoted energetically by private enterprises, and they resisted undue restriction of their activities, whether coming from governmental agencies or from nonprofit organizations. Nowhere was this clash more evident than in the environmental area. While international nongovernmental organizations pushed for an international convention on biodiversity and biosafety, businesses feared that such an agreement would impede their research into pharmaceutical projects and limit their intellectual property rights; internationalizing biomedical information could damage the interests of holders of such rights. Added to this was a division between business corporations of developed nations, frequently backed by their governments, that insisted on private rights to patented materials, and the developing states, with the support of many international nongovernmental organizations, that argued that genetic resources should be shared by all nations.[45]

The conflict between environmental nongovernmental organizations and business enterprises became dramatically clear when, at a 1999 meeting of the World Trade Organization in Seattle, many private organizations staged huge demonstrations to protest against what they took to be big businesses' insatiable appetite for profits even at the expense of the natural environment. The Seattle episode revealed that political, economic, social, and cultural aspects of globalization had not all cohered. Indeed, some nongovernmental organizations even protested against the very phenomenon of globalization. The relationship between international nongovernmental organizations, on one hand, and globalization, on the other, would remain a contentious issue, as discussed further in the concluding chapter. In an age when so many issues tended to be globalized, whether or not one approved of the development, there was as yet no mechanism to reconcile different aspects of globalization. By the same token, precisely because of these difficulties, nongovernmental organizations were being called on to become even more self-conscious than earlier and to clarify their position on global issues. In that sense, too, they were becoming more global than ever, however much some of them may have begun to question the wisdom of globalization.

The complex interconnectedness among different strands of globalization was evident at a number of international women's conferences. The Third World Conference on Women, convened in Nairobi in 1985, brought together over two thousand delegates from 157 countries. There was also a parallel forum, attended by fourteen thousand women representing nongovernmental organizations from some 150 countries. Significantly, at Nairobi an action paper was adopted unanimously, whereas at the two earlier conferences (in Mexico City in 1975 and Copenhagen in 1980), no consensus had emerged about specific measures to enhance the status of women.[46] The thrust of that document was to ensure that an international discussion of any topic should include a women's dimension. One immediate consequence of this assertiveness was an active effort on the part of women's organizations throughout the world to meet and arrive at some shared viewpoints in preparation for the Cairo conference on population and development, convened by the United Nations in 1994.

The coupling of the themes of population and development, apparent already at some conferences during the 1970s, was now widely accepted as axiomatic. The problem of population growth, it was believed, had to be tackled in the context of economic development. The argument was that as nations grew economically and their per capita incomes increased, people would give birth to fewer offspring as their outlook on life changed; birth control would become more readily available, the overall level of education would be enhanced, and children would primarily become objects of education and care rather than sources of labor. Although different religions and belief systems had divergent views on birth control, the status of children, and, above all, the position of women as wives and mothers, women's groups were instrumental in ensuring the success of the conference. The drafting and adoption of the "Cairo program of action," targeting as a goal a slower rate of population growth throughout the world, were made possible, according to a report on the conference written by the International Women's Health Coalition (established in 1980), by the fact that "women [were] engaged at every stage of conference preparations and at every level to gain access to negotiations." Because, the report concluded, "women have been most affected by population policies and programs, they emerged as an unassailable moral force."[47] Also significant at this conference was that many representatives of nongovernmental organizations were included in official delegations. For instance, Japan, which had hitherto not established a close working relationship between government and nongovernmental organizations, sent a delegation to Cairo consisting of representatives of both. A new pattern of close cooperation on women's issues among states, intergovernmental organizations, and international nongovernmental organizations was developing.

The pattern was confirmed at the 1995 Beijing conference on women, officially called the Fourth World Conference on Women: Equality, Development, and Peace. That China hosted such a gathering, not just of representatives of various governments but also of nonstate actors, was significant, indicating that even for a country that severely restricted the formation of private organizations, the state had come to recognize the worldwide trend toward civil society. The Beijing gathering was preceded by a 1990 forum on Asian women held in Kitakyūshū, Japan, and by the establishment of an Asia-Pacific human rights information center in Ōsaka in 1994. Japan's Kanagawa prefecture hosted an East Asian women's forum just prior to the Beijing conference, which was followed by an Asia-Pacific conference on women and development in Djakarta. Asian women were clearly beginning to assert their rights, and to do so they were following their Western counterparts in organizing themselves. Many of these organizations sent their representatives to Beijing. Some served as advisers to official delegations, but the vast majority joined those from other parts of the world and met separately at a nongovernmental forum held outside the city. Numbering twenty thousand, they experienced some physical discomfort and, worse, personal indignities as they were often treated by local officials as unwelcome visitors, but even so, women's groups from Asia, the West, Latin America, and elsewhere strengthened their networks and reconfirmed their commitment to global dialogue in coping with population, health, and many other questions that concerned them.

As Leon Gordenker and Thomas G. Weiss wrote in 1996, during the 1980s and the 1990s, "human rights advocates, gender activists, developmentalists, groups of indigenous peoples and representatives of other defined interests have become active in political work once reserved for representatives of states."[48] Women's organizations were asserting themselves to such an extent that state authorities would ignore them at their own risk. Even more than humanitarian relief or environmental protection, however, women's issues were wide-ranging and complex. Going far beyond their traditional concern with peace or voting rights, women's groups were increasingly paying attention to various types of domestic violence (including infanticide, abortion, and child molestation), migration (frequently, women outnumbered men among immigrants in advanced countries), family care, discrimination in the workplace, and many problems toward which attitudes would vary from country to country. Not just contemporary issues but also past injustices could become a matter of concern, as happened when the Asia Solidarity Network on the Forced Military Comfort Women Problem was established in 1992 to deal with the problem of forced prostitution practiced by the Japanese army during the war.[49] Because of the political nature of their work, these organizations gave rise to much controversy, another indication of the tendency on the part of nongovernmental organizations to intrude upon spheres traditionally preserved for official governmental action.

To note such a trend, however, is not to argue that nongovernmental organizations as nonstate actors were in fact becoming political players. Much of their activity was indeed becoming indistinguishable from politics. But that was not the total picture, for the politically active advocacy groups and their conferences were only a fraction of the transnational movements that were establishing connections throughout the world. Global interconnectedness was moving at a fast pace, and part of this phenomenon involved politics, in the process perhaps transforming the nature of politics itself. In the context of our discussion, however, it is equally important to note the growth and vigor of nongovernmental organizations engaged in educational and grassroots exchange programs. These were among the more traditional efforts by individuals and organizations to build bridges across nations; they were the ones that had kept alive the vision of global community throughout the turbulent century. And their activities remained just as important as ever in the 1980s and the 1990s.

Intellectual cooperation and grassroots understanding — the twin themes of cross-national exchanges going back to the 1920s — took on new significance in an age of rapid advances in communication and information technology. Satellite television, the Internet, mobile telephones, and facsimile transmission were revolutionizing the way individuals and organizations dealt with one another by linking all parts of the globe into systems of instant contact. Millions were sharing the same information and exchanging opinions electronically, something unprecedented in that this flow of information and opinion was virtually autonomous, not controllable by any state. This provided the setting for expanded communication at both the intellectual and the popular levels.

The revolution in information technology did have some negative consequences. The instantaneous spread of pornography through the Internet was already becoming a serious matter in the mid-1990s. As noted in the report "Child Pornography: An International Perspective," prepared for the World Congress against Commercial Sexual Exploitation of Children (held in Stockholm in 1996), "The development of home video equipment and computer technology has revolutionized the international production and distribution of child pornography. Rapidly expanding international access to increasingly inexpensive technology has transformed child pornography into a sophisticated cottage industry."[50] These abuses were obviously not limited to child pornography. Through the Internet reams of sexually exploitative images were being transmitted instantaneously across the globe. To deal with such a problem, international organizations were likewise indispensable. The just-mentioned conference in Stockholm was a good example. It brought together representatives of UNICEF, the government of Sweden, and several nongovernmental organizations to discuss ways to exchange information on child pornography and to urge nations to undertake legislation to control it. The protection of children, the previously mentioned paper asserted, "must become a global priority and nations must commit their resources accordingly."[51] The advancement in information technology was calling forth an international organizational response, a characteristic phenomenon of the age of globalization.

The positive consequences of the global spread of information were obvious. Thanks to the Internet, bringing together individuals sharing the same interests and concerns was now much easier. When, for instance, controversy arose in 1995 regarding a planned exhibit at the Smithsonian Institution of the *Enola Gay*, the U.S. aircraft that dropped the atomic bomb on Hiroshima, an ad hoc committee for the study of the history of the bombing was organized by American historians and journalists who were concerned over the tendency to remember such a past emotionally. Not just in the United States but also across nations, opinions were expressed through the Internet that were both critical and supportive of the atomic bombing. Both specialists and laypeople participated in the debate. Whether this new means of communication would serve to enhance international understanding was not yet clear, but there was no escaping that the instantaneous exchange of ideas, of whatever variety, was making the work of nongovernmental organizations all the more critical, for they were in a position to ensure that the global electronic networks would serve the cause of international cooperation and peace, not divisiveness and conflict.

Apart from electronic communication, the transnational exchange of information and ideas was also facilitated by the widespread use of such devices as the copying machine, the cassette tape recorder, and the facsimile (fax) transmission system. As one example of a successful, systematic attempt at collecting and distributing new information, the National Security Archive, a nongovernmental organization established in Washington in the 1980s, used the Freedom of Information Act to probe into U.S. archives to obtain material dealing with recent events such as the Polish Solidarity crisis and the Iran-Contra affair. The organization cooperated with others at home and abroad. For instance, it joined the

Mershon Center of Ohio State University, the Watson Institute of Brown University, the Ludwig Maximilian University in Munich, and the Gorbachev Foundation in Moscow to investigate the way the Cold War had been brought to an end. The Cold War International History Project at the Woodrow Wilson Center for International Scholars, as another example, energetically promoted efforts to obtain access to the archives of the former Soviet Union and of the People's Republic of China.

All these efforts entailed the networking of researchers across nations, a remarkable development that was further promoted during the 1980s and the 1990s by the holding of numerous international symposiums bringing together intellectuals from the former antagonists in the Cold War. Without the existence and initiatives of nongovernmental organizations, such gatherings would have been much more difficult to arrange. A 1987 Belagio conference, sponsored by the Rockefeller Foundation, brought together historians from China and the Soviet Union, as well as from the United States and other countries, to review the international history of the 1950s.[52] The conference was organized by the Committee on American–East Asian Relations, a scholarly organization on whose board scholars from various parts of the Pacific would come to be invited to sit. The International House of Japan sponsored highly successful international conferences in 1991 and 1995, the fiftieth anniversaries, respectively, of the coming and the ending of the Pacific War. Historians from a large number of countries in Asia, Europe, and North America came together to reexamine the past on the basis of newly acquired material.[53] By then, the participation of scholars from China and the former Soviet Union in such gatherings was becoming a common sight. The Japan Foundation's Center for Global Partnership — a public corporation and therefore not a nongovernmental organization, strictly defined, but functioning without governmental control — held a symposium in 1993 on some significant themes at the end of the twentieth century. (The themes discussed included the collapse of communism, migrations across borders, human rights, environmental issues, and the future of nationalism. No sustained discussion of non-governmental organizations took place, however, indicating that the awareness of their existence and growing importance was not yet shared even by some of the leading intellectuals of the time.)[54] The Japan Center for International Exchange periodically sponsored international conferences, and in 1995 it established a global "think-net," a network of think tanks throughout the world that could be called on to provide information, insights, and personnel for the discussion of urgent issues of the day. One such gathering, held in 1998, brought together over thirty participants from research organizations of eleven countries to explore the question of governance in the context of an increasingly globalizing world in which civil society was on the rise.

Even where the construction of civil society was met with a setback, as happened in China after 1989, when student organizations pushing for greater democracy were crushed at Tiananmen Square, the overall trend toward greater cross-national exchange remained. Prior to 1989, there had been an impressive outflow of Chinese students and scholars for study abroad. Between 1979 and 1989, some eighty thousand Chinese were issued student/scholar visas to visit the United States — almost three times the total number of Chinese students who had come to study during 1860–1960. By the end of the 1980s, nearly twenty-nine thousand Chinese were enrolled in American colleges and universities.[55] In return, several thousand American students, teachers, and scholars went to China, making the bilateral exchange one of the fastest growing in the world. But other countries also became part of the global network, and as more and more young Chinese acquired higher degrees in the United States, Britain, Japan, and elsewhere, a significant portion of them stayed in the host countries to teach and engage in research. To facilitate exchanges and organize conferences and joint projects, new organizations were set up, such as the Chinese Association of American Studies and the Beijing Society of Comparative International Studies.[56] Both these (and many other) organizations were created just prior to the Tiananmen incident, and they continued to function even after the event. While China's suppression of political freedom tended for a time to isolate the country in the international community, the educational and intellectual ties that had been built up were never severed. The development of electronic communication facilitated the process, but that was not the only reason. More fundamentally, it would be correct to say that exchange programs involving China were not significantly affected by the political crisis of 1989 because they were developing with their own momentum.

In a book published in 1997, I called this momentum "cultural internationalism."[57] The term expressed the view that cross-national cultural undertakings had been a significant aspect of twentieth-century history and that while it was tempting to see such activities as aspects of, or as minor footnotes to, geopolitical relations among states, they had never been completely identifiable with those relations. The exchange of ideas, cultures, and persons had served to develop an international community that was not interchangeable with the world order defined by military power and considerations of national interests. The further growth of educational and scholarly exchanges between China and other countries demonstrated that power and culture were not entirely identical, that power did not always determine culture, and that culture did not necessarily seek the support of power. That was so, in the framework of this volume, because cultural activities were almost always embedded in institutions that ensured their longevity irrespective of what was happening at the formal governmental level. Of course, institutional contexts could change, as happened when the United States government decided to bring the United States Information Agency into the State Department in 1999; henceforth, the informational and exchange programs the former had undertaken would become a more integral part of the foreign policies determined by the latter. But it could just as plausibly be argued that United States foreign policy, too, would change now that educational programs were becoming part of it. Besides, these changes were taking place within the governmental bureaucracy and did not affect cultural agendas and activities undertaken by private organizations. If anything, their role would become even more conspicuous because of the abolition of the USIA as an independent entity.

A significant feature of international exchange programs in the last decades of the century was the mushrooming of grassroots organizations undertaking such activities. Ranging from sister-city arrangements to visits by amateur musical groups, from home-stay programs for school-children to concerts by popular singers, mass-level cultural contact expanded throughout the 1980s and the 1990s. When the Japan Foundation's Center for Global Partnership advertised grants for grass-roots exchanges for the first time in 1991, it immediately received nearly eighty applications from local organizations in the United States and Japan. The proposals included such topics as "lectures and demonstrations by Japanese and American performers," "a symposium to be attended by representatives of Japanese and U.S. transport industries, transportation and environmental agencies," "a delegation of women to travel to the United States to conduct a grass-roots study of various measures designed to deal with the growing percentage of senior citizens in society," and "a seminar to promote mutual understanding between American and Japanese labor unions."[58] Such topics were undoubtedly being discussed among various organizations in other parts of the world as well.

Were all these activities, added together, creating a global community? The answer would depend on how one defines "global community." If the term means the establishment of networks of communication through intergovernmental organizations and international nongovern-mental organizations, that was clearly evident, as seen in the accelerating pace of interchanges and cooperative activities on the part of those orga-nizations, their increased funding, and the way real-time communication was becoming possible. That, however, did not mean that the emerging global community was creating a homogeneous world civilization. The sociologist Mike Featherstone wrote in 1995, "One paradoxical conse-quence of the process of globalization . . . is not to produce homogeneity but to familiarize us with greater diversity, the extensive range of local cultures."[59] That did not mean, however, that globalization amounted to fragmentation. Rather, even as "goods, capital, people, knowledge, images, communications, as well as crime, culture, pollutants, drugs, fashions and beliefs, readily [flew] across territorial boundaries," as David Held and Anthony McGrew observed in 1993, an awareness of differences among peoples, cultures, and regions of the world also grew — to such an extent that in the same year, Samuel Huntington published a widely read essay on "the clash of civilizations."[60] The seemingly contradictory statements may be reconciled if we emphasize the crucial roles international organizations have played in recent history. They have served to link different parts of the world closer together, and in doing so, diversity as well as homogeneity have, hardly surprisingly, emerged as central themes. It would be a major task facing international organizations to try to solidify forces for a global community in which both themes would thrive and serve the welfare of all people. If left to the states, it might be more difficult to do so, given their political agendas and parochial interests. International organizations, on the other hand, have proved quite successful in reconciling differences because their only weapons are ideas, a sense of commitment, and voluntary service. They have not spent billions on arms, nor have they engaged in mass killing. They are civilized societies, and so they have a mission to turn the world into a civilized community.

Conclusion

At the end of the twentieth century and the beginning of the twenty-first, few phenomena attracted more attention, and at the same time aroused more controversy, than globalization. The twentieth century, Ralf Dahrendorf wrote in 1998, "has been largely . . . determined by divisions which led to wars, hot and cold, but which also provided sources of identity." All that had changed. Globalization had come to "dominate people's lives, hopes, and fears," and people everywhere had "to think globally to respond to an increasingly global reality."[1]

In the rapid advancement in information technology, in the development of a global financial market, and in the spread of the English language and other manifestations of American popular culture, human affairs were unmistakably globalizing or becoming globalized. At the same time, debate ensued as to the direction and desirability of the phenomenon. Was the world going to continue the process of globalization, or would the pace eventually slow down or even be replaced by other developments? Would the people and countries of the world be better or worse off when they were more globalized? What tasks should individual states and such traditional institutions as families, local governments, churches, and schools perform in the age of globalization? Such questioning suggested the fascination with the possible role of globalization in defining future history. Just as earlier generations speculated on the implications of industrialization for nations and individuals, now there was much interest in the impact globalization would have on the shape of the world to come.

A look at the notes to this book indicates that an increasing number of scholarly books and articles with titles that included the word "global" or "globalization" began to appear in the 1990s, especially during the second half of the decade, suggesting that the term that mass media were widely using was also gaining intellectual respectability. By then, globalization had generally come to mean not just technological innovations and economic forces linking different parts of the world, but something even more extensive; as James H. Mittelman wrote in 1997, "globalization is a coalescence of varied transnational processes and domestic structures, allowing the economy, politics, culture, and ideology of one country to penetrate another."[2] Political scientists, sociologists, anthropologists, and economists debated whether such a seemingly inexorable process should be left to develop with its own momentum, or if it could somehow be controlled or steered in a desirable direction. In the latter case, should the state be the key to the future direction of globalization, or would some other agency emerge to take its place? If globalization became too "predatory," to use Richard Falk's word, what institutions could tame such a tendency?[3] Such debate would undoubtedly continue and be joined by intellectuals in all parts of the world; this itself would be an aspect of globalization. As yet few historians were involved in the debate, perhaps because they had not yet come to reconceptualize history in the framework of globalization.

This book has sought to provide a historical context for the phenomenon of globalization by pointing to the growth of international organizations. This phenomenon has not been systematically examined in the literature on globalization, but there seems little doubt that international organizations have served to turn the world's attention to global issues — humanitarian relief, development, human rights, the environment, cross-national understanding — when geopolitics and military strategy have divided nations against one another. Awareness of transnational problems — in other words, global consciousness — is not the same thing as globalization. One could develop a sense of transnational interconnectedness and at the same time question aspects of globalization, such as environmental hazards resulting from foreign investment in developing countries or the use of child and female labor in degrading circumstances by manufacturers interested in competitive advantages. The 1999 meeting in Seattle of the World Trade Organization, an intergovernmental organization, drew world attention because many nongovernmental organizations staged demonstrations to protest against what they took to be the trade organization's connivance at the destruction of the natural environment and the employment of "slave labor" as it sought further to deregulate international trade. A Washington meeting in the spring of 2000 of the International Monetary Fund drew a similar protest from various private associations and groups. These incidents gave the impression that nongovernmental organizations were opposed to globalization, whereas intergovernmental organizations were pushing for it, but that was missing the point. Both were becoming active participants in the worldwide debate on the nature and the possible future direction of globalization and were thus very much part of the emerging global community. Besides, the protesting organizations were all making use of the Internet, a crucial means for spreading information and coalescing individuals and groups for specific objectives.[4]

Most supporters and opponents of globalization alike assumed that there had to be some universal, global standards, in financial, accounting, environmental, human rights, and other matters. Standardization in some of these areas would be extremely difficult to achieve, but the idea itself would be very much part of the phenomenon of globalization. The debate in Seattle or Washington was not so much about globalization as about the specific fields (labor, environmental protection) in which global standards should be applied. To deny the very idea of universal standards was, of course, possible, but the majority of the protesters in Seattle or Washington were not doing so; they accepted the notion of transnational interconnectedness. They were keenly aware of the global issues, and their activities revealed not so much forces opposed to globalization as those that recognized the transnational nature of contemporary issues. Even those opposed to globalization in the business sphere considered themselves members of a global community, committed to supporting "poor people in representing their own interests in global decision making," as a statement by the American Friends Service Committee pointed out.[5] In this sense, the organizations that staged demonstrations in Seattle and Washington were no different from the large number of international organizations that had, over the decades, been constructing transnational networks.

And those organizations were more active than ever before. Underneath the headline-grabbing incidents in these cities, various types of nongovernmental organizations were quietly carrying on their tasks, suggesting that their growth had not been affected, nor had their activities been discouraged, by occasional incidents and disturbances. It was symbolic that the Seattle demonstrations coincided with the awarding of the Nobel Peace Prize to Doctors without Borders for its humanitarian activities. Accepting the prize, the organization's director, James Orbinski, stated, "We don't know for sure whether words save lives, but we know for sure that silence kills."[6] Two years later, in December 2001, representatives of Doctors without Borders joined those of the International Committee of the Red Cross, Amnesty International, the Office of the United Nations High Commissioner for Refugees, the American Friends Service Committee, the International Campaign to Ban Landmines, International Physicians for the Prevention of Nuclear War, and other organizations in a ceremony held in Oslo to commemorate the hundredth anniversary of the Nobel Prizes. These organizations were all recipients of the Nobel Peace Prize, and by participating in the ceremony along with such individual recipients of the prize as Mikhail Gorbachev, the Dalai Lama, and Shimon Peres, they were demonstrating that international organizations had played just as significant roles as states and statesmen in promoting peace throughout the twentieth century.[7]

In August 2001, Moral Rearmament, a nongovernmental organization established in 1938 by Protestant clergymen in the United States, changed its name to Initiatives of Change. The idea, according to its new director, Cornelio Sommaruga, who had served as president of the International Committee of the Red Cross for eighteen years, was to work for "globalization of responsibility." Ethical and spiritual values, which Moral Rearmament had emphasized over the years, would form the basis of the organization's new initiatives.[8] The transformation of an organization that at the height of the Cold War had been closely identified with the free world into a broader global movement — only one-fourth of its twenty thousand members was now Protestant — was symbolic of the changing international circumstances at the beginning of the new century. Likewise, in December 1999, as President Kim Dae Jung of South Korea, whose personal and political life had been deeply involved in the vicissitudes of the Cold War, welcomed a gathering of representatives of nongovernmental organizations from over one hundred countries who assembled in Seoul, he told them that in the coming century democratic government, the market, and civil society would constitute the three pillars of national and international development. In all these three, nongovernmental organizations play crucial roles. At this meeting, some members of Chinese, Korean, and Japanese organizations conferred among themselves and decided to launch a regional forum of nongovernmental organizations to which delegates from North Korea would also be invited. Korean and Japanese nongovernmental organizations, in the meantime, were collaborating in such diverse fields as humanitarian relief of North Korea, environmental protection, access to information, joint inquiry into the past, and assistance to Korean victims of atomic bombings.[9]

These were typical examples. Throughout the world, nongovernmental organizations were continuing to expand in the number and scope of their activities. On one hand, many small, local organizations were being built. Their agendas were often parochial, such as planning for a park, proposing regulations to restrict automobile traffic, or building a community center.[10] Others were national in scope, such as the Community Technology Center Network, established in the United States to teach how to use Internet-accessed information to those too poor to afford computers.[11] Regardless of scope, however, most such organizations were invariably establishing ties with one another, not just within a country but across nations. When, for instance, in 1995 a faculty member at Peking University opened a small office, renting an inexpensive room at a local inn, to serve the needs of women suffering from domestic violence, job discrimination, and other problems, it quickly established itself as one of the first nongovernmental organizations in China concerned with women's issues. When President Bill Clinton made an official visit to China in June 1998, his wife included the organization in her itinerary. Nongovernmental organizations from South Korea, Thailand, and India contacted the Beijing office so as to form an Asian network. Women's groups in Europe and North America also came in touch with it through its Internet home pages.[12] That this and many other private associations were created in China in the wake of the 1995 Beijing conference on women suggests the cumulative effect of such events. Whereas few Chinese had ever heard of nongovernmental organizations, by the end of the 1990s over two hundred thousand of them were said to have come into being.[13]

Examples can be multiplied. Nongovernmental organizations had grown to such an extent that Lester Salamon, one of the leading scholars of the subject, was calling it a "revolution," comparable in its impact on world affairs to the emergence of the nation state in the nineteenth century. His research group conducted a survey of nonprofit organizations in twenty-two countries (thirteen from Europe, five from Latin America, and Japan, Australia, Israel, and the United States) in the late 1990s and found that altogether they employed nineteen million individuals, or 4.9 percent of their combined workforce. In some countries the ratio was much higher: in the Netherlands, 12.4 percent of workers were employed by nonprofit organizations, and in the United States 7.8 percent. All these organizations, according to Salamon, produced goods and services amounting to $1.1 trillion, a figure that exceeded the gross domestic products of most countries, including Russia, Brazil, or Spain.[14] Although his "nonprofit organizations" may not be wholly interchangeable with the nongovernmental organizations that this book has discussed, it is clear that no matter what they are called and whatever their definition, something unprecedented was taking place. Moreover, while Salamon's study included national as well as international non-profit organizations, the distinction between the two was often blurred, as some of the previous examples suggest. Here was a phenomenon that demanded attention, a development that had to be incorporated into any discussion of national and international affairs at the turn of the new century.[15]

A century earlier, some astute observers were noting a new trend in the world that, they were convinced, would profoundly alter human life. Some called it "internationalism," others "international life." Many had no precise word to describe what they saw. J. A. Hobson referred to the "great world forces" that were creating "bonds of interests which band us together irrespective of the natural limits of the country to which we belong and in which we were born."[16] H. G. Wells predicted the emer-gence of "a new kind of people" as a result of these forces who would come to constitute a "floating population . . . , developing, no doubt, customs and habits of its own, a morality of its own, a philosophy of its own."[17] These observers were certain that the new phenomenon, which would in time be called "globalization," would fundamentally alter the nature of both national and international affairs.

From the perspective of 2001, it is, of course, possible to argue that these prophets a hundred years ago were to be proven wrong, that the forces of globalization, or whatever term they preferred to use, did not really transform how nations behaved, either domestically or toward one another. After all, imperialism, or control by one state over another, was a powerful force at that time and would remain so for several more decades. Part of the phenomenon of globalization was undoubtedly attributable to imperialism, involving the breaking down of national and ethnic boundaries and the penetration of "uncivilized" parts of the world by forces of "civilization." To say that globalization was imperialism by another name, however, would be to ignore that forces of globalization continued to strengthen themselves, while empires came and went — and they were conspicuous by their rarity at the end of the twentieth century. Anti-imperialism as much as imperialism proved to be a key theme of the century, and the former, if anything, was a more global phenomenon than the latter. Many of the postcolonial states were to be just as concerned with their self-interests as had the colonial powers, and the state, new or old, still remained the key unit of human association in most parts of the world.

Conceptually, therefore, one could write a history of twentieth-century international affairs as a story of interstate interactions without introducing extraneous themes like globalization. This book has argued, however, that to do so would be a gross oversimplification and that underneath the geopolitical realities defined by sovereign states, the century witnessed a steady growth of another reality — the global (and globalizing) activities by international organizations. Hobson, Wells, and others may have too hastily concluded that the geopolitical realities would soon be transformed by newer forces of globalization. These geopolitical realities continued to shape international relations at one level, but these thinkers were justified in believing that cross-national movements of men, their ideas, and their organizations would sooner or later come to revolutionize the way in which people and nations dealt with one another. They would feel vindicated if they came back to life today and saw the activities by thousands of transnational organizations.

Will the alleged "revolution" in today's world, evidenced in the growth of international organizations, be shown to have been an exaggeration, if not a misperception, a century hence? Will those organizations, no matter how numerous and how extensive, remain largely confined to their own spheres of activity and have little impact on the nature of national and international affairs? Or will they come to alter fundamentally how states deal with their own people and with other states? Instead of these two extreme possibilities, will a situation develop in which states and nonstate actors come to cooperate more closely than in the past and in that process define yet another world order?

Any response to those questions must remain tentative and speculative. But even before speculation is attempted, it is important to pay attention to many issues that have arisen because of the very growth of international organizations, especially of the nongovernmental variety. For one thing, such a variety of organizations has emerged that different, often clashing, orientations and agendas among them have become virtually inevitable. Even in the earlier years, divergent objectives were sometimes pursued by organizations allegedly sharing a common goal, such as the conservation of nature or the promotion of women's rights. Among intergovernmental organizations, the United Nations' Economic and Social Council has often been at odds with its other agencies such as the Human Rights Commission or the International Labor Organization. With a rapid increase in international organizations, it is not unimaginable that anarchy instead of order might come to characterize their relationships with one another, just as it has characterized interstate relations. An example of this took place in April 1999 when the Armed Forces Communications and Electronics Association, a nongovernmental organization founded in the United States in 1946 to sponsor exhibitions and conferences all over the world on military communications, electronics, and intelligence systems, ran into opposition to its plans for holding a European fair in Brno, the Czech Republic. A founder of the Doctors without Borders in Belgium vehemently sought to stop the event on antimilitaristic grounds. Even among humanitarian agencies, there is not always agreement as to how they should aid victims of earthquakes or volcanic eruptions, and sometime they work at cross-purposes. For instance, the nongovernmental organizations that sent rescue missions to Colombia when it was devastated by an earthquake in January 1999 followed their respective agendas and failed to coordinate their activities, so there was no systematic distribution of food and medical goods sent from overseas.

To cope with such problems, many individuals and groups have agreed that it would be necessary to establish a minimum of guidelines or common standards to govern the conduct of nongovernmental organizations. Already in 1994, the International Red Cross, Oxfam, and other agencies came together to draft basic principles to guide humanitarian activities, and the document was accepted by over 150 nongovernmental organizations from forty-three countries. Then in late 1998, the United Nations as well as other intergovernmental organizations and nongovernmental groups adopted a list of "minimum standards" for such matters as nourishment, water quality, and toilet facilities in areas where relief work was to be carried out.[18] These guidelines amount to international protocols, akin to treaties and agreements among states, and provide some order amid the seeming disorder created by the establishment of so many international organizations.

Would it be possible to draft similar standards for international organizations engaged in other than humanitarian work? In the area of environmental protection, international standards have already been promulgated in such matters as the preservation of the whale, the prohibition of trade in ivory, and restrictions on the emission of carbon dioxide. The relative success at arriving at international environmental standards owes itself to a great extent to cooperation among intergovernmental organizations, nongovernmental organizations, and national governments. On the other hand, establishing global standards in human rights would be more difficult. Although such standards exist on paper, thanks to the work of the United Nations Human Rights Commission and many nongovernmental organizations, activities by these organizations have frequently been uncoordinated. When human rights concern political affairs, domestic and international organizations have been able to work together quite well in such matters as the observation of a local election, but applying uniform standards to the treatment accorded women or prison inmates has been more difficult.[19] Nevertheless, the growth of civil society throughout the world may make it possible to apply certain standards of democratization and human rights to all countries. The establishment in 2000 of the International Court of Criminal Justice is a good case in point. It is seen as a custodian of human rights everywhere in the world, a reflection of shared consciences that transcend national boundaries.

Some such institutional framework for coping with transnational issues has become more urgent than ever because of the increasing number of migrant workers, expatriates, and others who are not confined to a given territorial state, as well as the growth of transnational issues that need the attention of the electorate of more than one country. As David Held has observed, because "[national] boundaries have traditionally demarcated the basis on which individuals were included and excluded from participation in decisions affecting their lives," the questions of representation, legitimacy, and democratic governance might have to be recast in a globalizing world.[20] In this connection, the fact that some government officials and thinkers in Europe have developed an idea of "European citizenship" is interesting and may possibly be a harbinger of things to come. A conception of citizenship that transcends national units is congruent with such other notions as "hybridization" and "syncretism" that have begun to appear in the literature. They all challenge traditional definitions of space, territory, and nationality and raise the question of just what it is that binds people together, what it is that constructs a human community.[21]Although no consensus yet exists as to who would be included in, and who excluded from, European citizenship, the vision seems to indicate the awareness that transnational society is here to stay, even if it is still vaguely understood.

With regard to the work of international organizational activities in the field of developmental assistance, some serious problems have also arisen. Here, the issue of interorganizational coordination has been bound up with the very important question of accountability. The previous chapter illustrated some of the difficulties international relief organizations faced in administering their aid because of complex local political problems and divergent perspectives between such organizations and the United Nations as well as some of the nations providing peacekeeping forces. Economic assistance programs were even more complicated because they were designed as long-term projects. The more numerous such programs became, the more varied grew their approaches, and above all, the question of how to keep track of their activities inevitably arose. Were they using their funds wisely? To whom were they reporting? Who was keeping records? Were those records available for inspection by governmental officials and private groups?

These problems have always existed, but in recent years they have come to command much public and scholarly attention because of the very fact that aid projects have come to cover the entire globe. (The number of developmental nongovernmental organizations registered with the Organization of Economic Cooperation and Development had neared three thousand by the early 1990s, and their total spending approximated $6 billion.[22]) In a widely read article published in the *Economist* in January 2000, the writer chided some nongovernmental aid workers for bringing in "western living standards, personnel and purchasing power which can transform local markets and generate great local resentment." The discrepancy between "expatriate staff" and "impoverished local officials trying to do the same work" was a source of "deep antipathy."[23] Already in 1988, a scholar was warning that "the corruption of NGOs will be the political game in the years ahead."[24] Scholarly specialists have been raising serious questions about the conduct of aid workers and the organizations they represented. As just one example, in a book entitled *Non-Governmental Organisations: Performance and Accountability* (1995), one of the first serious attempts at examining the issue of accountability, the editors noted, "Performing effectively and accounting transparently are essential components of responsible practice, on which the legitimacy of development intervention ultimately depends."[25] And yet most of the case studies contained in this volume pointed out that there had been no standardized system for measuring accountability of nongovernmental organizations. In some instances pertinent data were missing, while in others data were there, but the organizations were reluctant to divulge them for fear of political or ideological intermeddling with their affairs. Because donor agencies, whether governmental or nongovernmental, would want the receiving organizations to account for the funds they received, financial accountability was often a condition of such grants. But the staff involved in developmental programs found bookkeeping time-consuming and thought their time could better be spent in more constructive ways. For all organizations, a writer noted, "*who* defines accountability, *for whom* and *why*, are questions" that required careful analysis.[26]

The question of accountability has grown in seriousness in recent years because of the tendency on the part of a large number of development-oriented organizations to receive funding from public agencies. Michael Edwards and David Hulme note that already in the mid-1990s, nongovernmental organizations "which are *not* dependent on official aid for the majority of their budgets are now the exception rather than the rule."[27] In such a situation, it is not surprising that governments would insist on budgetary oversight of aid programs. But that in turn raises the question of the proper relationship between governmental and nongovernmental organizations. The latter, according to the *Economist*, had become "the most important constituency for the activities of development aid agencies."[28] The symbiotic relationship between the state and nonstate actors inevitably leads to the question of the latter's autonomy. Are they becoming an arm of the state, doing for the latter more informally and cheaply what it wants to be accomplished? With so much funding coming from public sources, accompanied with the need for more strict accountability for how the money is used, would nongovernmental organizations be able to remain "nongovernment"? Could their staff, who are not accountable to the electorate, be counted on to serve the public interest? Conversely, to the extent that private organizations work in collaboration with government bureaucracies, how would the latter be required to share policy deliberations with them or give them access to official information, however confidential? Should nongovernmental organizations be allowed to have an input into official decision making?

Similar questions may be raised regarding the relationship between nongovernmental organizations and business enterprises. Both are non-state actors, but they have traditionally been distinguished because only the latter are profit-seeking. The relationship between the two has more often than not been adversarial. According to a survey of 140 international nongovernmental organizations, 41 percent of them expressed such an attitude toward multinational corporations, and 47 percent said they had had little to do with them. Some, such as Greenpeace, have organized a worldwide boycott of certain firms suspected of causing damage to the natural environment, while others, such as Transparency International — established in 1992 to respond to the worldwide "corruption eruption" — have periodically published reports on cases of bribery involved in local negotiations for establishing plants.[29] The Seattle demonstrations in December 1999 against multinational businesses were but the tip of the iceberg; global networks connected by the Internet spread information on corporate practices that appear to violate the principles for which the nongovernmental organizations stand.[30]

The situation, however, may be changing, just like the relationship between state and nonstate actors. The line between business enterprises and nongovernmental organizations is becoming blurred as some business organizations sponsor humanitarian work abroad while individuals with extensive experiences with relief, aid, or environmental activities are hired by manufacturing or marketing firms.[31] Moreover, some multinational corporations have begun soliciting the views of nongovernmental organizations on the impact of their business activities on local environmental and labor conditions. These instances suggest that some sort of collaborative relationship may develop between profit-seeking and nonprofit organizations. In the past, regulation of businesses was largely in the hands of the state, whether national or local. This may be changing as nongovernmental organizations are steadily gaining in visibility and self-confidence. In particular, international nongovernmental organizations, as well as intergovernmental organizations, may develop a new definition of their relationship with multinational corporations. If that happens, it will mean that even the notions of profit and nonprofit may change. For that matter, the distinction between state and nonstate actors, state and society, public and private, may also undergo reformulation. A realization may emerge that all organizations—the state, business enterprises, international organizations, and nongovernmental associations—will form what Kofi Annan, secretary general of the United Nations, has called a "strategic partnership" in the service of all people as the world becomes ever more globalized.[32]

That is a grand vision, far grander than the image of global community that has been proposed by any international organization. Whereas most ideas of international society, global community, and "planet earth" have supposed an interdependence of nations and peoples, none has yet developed a view of the world's organizations that interact with one another and promote the common welfare of humankind. That would be too much to expect at this stage of global history. The global community that international organizations have been seeking for decades will be a good beginning. That community has tended to develop with its own momentum, on a separate level of existence from the international system defined by sovereign states or from the business world. If these separate communities were to come closer together, then there would truly emerge a human community that would consist of various complementing organizations sharing the same concerns and seeking to solve them through cooperative endeavors. Whether such a situation will ever arrive is far from clear, but to the extent that it is now possible even to speculate on such a possibility, credit should be given to international organizations, especially nongovernmental organizations, for having led the way.

NOTES

PREFACE

1. These quotes are taken from Thomas Jefferson, *Political Writings*, edited by Joyce Appleby and Terence Ball (Cambridge, Mass., 1999), 552, 555; and Bradford Perkins, *The Creation of a Republican Empire, 1776–1865* (New York, 1993), 47. For Jefferson's pastoral vision, see Carl J. Richard, *The Founders and the Classics: Greece, Rome, and the American Enlightenment* (Cambridge, Mass., 1994). The best-known account of Jefferson as an agrarian isolationist is Charles A. Beard, *The Idea of National Interest: An Analytical Study in American Foreign Policy* (New York, 1934).

INTRODUCTION

1. Lyman Cromwell White, *International Non-Governmental Organizations: Their Purposes, Methods, and Accomplishments* (New Brunswick, 1951), ix. Among the standard works on international organizations, particularly useful are D. Mittrany, *The Progress of International Government* (London, 1933); and Robert O. Keohane and Joseph S. Nye, *Power and Interdependence*, 2nd ed. (London, 1989).

2. See Thomas G. Weiss and Leon Gordenker, eds., *NGOs, the UN, and Global Governance* (Boulder, 1996). The editors state that they are excluding from their study of international nongovernmental organizations "profit-making corporations and banks, criminal elements (both organised crime and terrorists),

insurgents, churches in their strictly religious function, transnational political parties and the mass communication media" (19). This way of limiting the scope of study corresponds to that adopted in the book.

3. The exact number of international nongovernmental organizations at a given moment is difficult to obtain; various studies and reports give conflicting estimates because of their different definitions. A United Nations report in 1995 mentioned the figure of twenty-nine thousand, and several observers suggest that the number reached thirty thousand by the end of the 1990s. See the *Economist*, January 29, 2000, 25.

4. Harold Jacobson, *Networks of Interdependence: International Organizations and the Global Political System*, 2nd ed. (New York, 1984).

5. Evan Luard, *International Agencies: The Emerging Framework of Interdependence* (London, 1977).

6. White, *International Non-Governmental Organizations*.

7. Lester M. Salamon and Helmut K. Anheier, *Defining the Nonprofit Sector: A Cross-National Analysis* (Manchester, 1997). Curiously, neither the book by White nor the one by Salamon and Anheier treats environmental protection as a separate category for international nongovernmental organizations, although the latter does recognize it as one of the twelve activity groups for domestic nonprofit organizations.

8. To give a few examples, among the widely read histories of the twentieth century are Michael Howard and Wm. Roger Louis, eds., *The Oxford History of the Twentieth Century* (Oxford, 1998); J. A. S. Grenville, *A History of the World in the Twentieth Century* (Cambridge, Mass., 1994); William Keylor, *The Twentieth-Century World: An International History*, 2nd ed. (New York, 1992); C. J. Bartlett, *The Global Conflict, 1880–1970: The International Rivalry of the Great Powers* (London, 1984); and Eric Hobsbawm, *The Age of Extremes: A History of the World, 1914–1991* (New York, 1994). None of these books, excellent in many respects, treats international organizations extensively. A recent and superb history of the second half of the century, David Reynolds's *One World Divisible: A Global History since 1945* (New York, 2000), likewise is silent on such organizations, with a few exceptions such as the United Nations.

9. A list of useful and insightful works by political scientists includes Luard, *International Agencies*; Jacobson, *Networks of Interdependence*; Johan Galtung, *The True Worlds: A Transnational Perspective* (New York, 1980); Paul. F. Diehl, ed., *The Politics of Global Governance: International Organizations in an Interdependent World* (Boulder, 1997); Brian Smith, *More Than Altruism* (Princeton, 1998); and

Margaret E. Keck and Kathryn Sikkink, eds., *Activists beyond Borders: Advocacy Networks in International Politics* (Ithaca, 1998). Although they are sociologists, not political scientists, John Boli and George M. Thomas have edited an extremely important collection of essays on the subject: *Constructing World Culture: International Nongovernmental Organizations since 1875* (Stanford, 1999).

10. Henry Kissinger, *Diplomacy* (New York, 1994); Paul Kennedy, *The Rise and Fall of the Great Powers* (New York, 1985); Michael Howard, *The Causes of Wars, and Other Essays* (London, 1983); James Joll, *The Origins of the First World War* (London, 1984); Akira Iriye, *The Origins of the Second World War in Asia and the Pacific* (London, 1987).

11. Among the exceptions that present a broader approach is Andre Gunder Frank, *ReOrient: Global Economy in the Asian Age* (Berkeley, 1998).

12. On the idea of "anarchical society," see Hedley Bull, *The Anarchical Society: A Study of Order in World Politics*, 2nd ed. (New York, 1995).

13. I have used these terms myself in my other works, including *After Imperialism: the Search for a New Order in the Far East, 1921–1931* (Cambridge, Mass., 1965); *The Cold War in Asia* (Englewood Cliffs, N.J., 1974); and *The Globalizing of America* (New York, 1993).

14. See Akira Iriye, "Culture and Power: International Relations as Intercultural Relations," *Diplomatic History* 3, no. 2 (spring 1979): 115–28; and "Cultural Relations and Policies," in Alexander DeConde, ed., *The Encyclopedia of American Foreign Policy*, 2nd ed. (forthcoming).

15. To cite a few examples in each of these categories, among the most innovative recent works in bringing gender and international affairs closer together are Harriet Hyman Alonso, *Peace as a Women's Issue: A History of the U.S. Movement for World Peace and Women's Rights* (Syracuse, 1993); and Kristin L. Hoganson, *Fighting for American Manhood: How Gender Politics Provoked the Spanish-American and Philippine-American Wars* (New Haven, 1998). An example of a study that seeks to establish a connection between a nation's social classes and foreign policy is Christian G. Appy, *Working-Class War: America's Combat Soldiers and Vietnam* (Chapel Hill, 1993). One of the first systematic attempts at examining the relationship between ethnic and international relations is Alexander DeConde, *Ethnicity, Race, and American Foreign Policy: A History* (Boston, 1992). The best example of a study that points to ideological foundations of foreign policy is Frank Ninkovich, *Modernity and Power: A History of the Domino Theory in the Twentieth Century* (Chicago, 1994). See also Ninkovich's *The Wilsonian Century: U.S. Foreign Policy since 1900* (Chicago, 1999), and *The United*

States and Imperialism (Malden, Mass., 2001). Emily Rosenberg's *Spreading the American Dream: American Economic and Cultural Expansion, 1890–1945* (New York, 1982), is a splendid study of the ideology of liberal capitalist internationalism underlying the nation's domestic and overseas affairs. For an excellent analysis of the making of public memory, see John Bodnar, *Remaking America: Public Memory, Commemoration, and Patriotism in the Twentieth Century* (Princeton, 1992). A notably successful study of cultural foreign policy is Jessica C. E. Gienow-Hecht, *Transmission Impossible: American Journalism as Cultural Diplomacy in Postwar Germany, 1945–1955* (Baton Rouge, 1999).

16. For examples, see Jane Hunter, *The Gospel of Gentility: American Women Missionaries in Turn-of-the-Century China* (New Haven, 1984), a study of American missionary activities in China; and Bruce Kuklick, *Puritans in Babylon: The Ancient Near East and American Intellectual Life, 1880–1930* (Princeton, 1996), an examination of American travelers and explorers in the Ottoman empire.

17. See Bull, *Anarchical Society;* Thomas Risse-Knappen, ed., *Bringing Transnational Relations Back In: Non-State Actors, Domestic Structures, and International Institutions* (Cambridge, U.K., 1995); Keck and Sikkink, *Activists beyond Borders;* and Miranda A. Schreurs and Elizabeth C. Economy, eds., *The Internationalization of Environmental Protection* (Cambridge, U.K., 1997).

18. Boli and Thomas, *Constructing World Culture;* Salamon and Anheier, eds., *Defining the Nonprofit Sector* (Manchester, 1997); Lester Salamon and Helmut K. Anheier, eds., *The Emerging Nonprofit Sector: An Overview* (Manchester, 1997).

19. Among other recent writings on globalization, see Rolland Robertson, *Globalization: Social Theory and Global Culture* (London, 1992); Mike Featherstone, Scott Lash, and Roland Robertson, eds., *Global Modernities* (London, 1995); James H. Mittelman, ed., *Globalization: Critical Reflections* (Boulder, 1997); Benjamin R. Barber, *Jihad vs. McWorld: How Globalism and Tribalism Are Reshaping the World* (New York, 1995); Thomas L. Friedman, *The Lexus and the Olive Tree: Understanding Globalization* (New York, 1999); Ulrich Beck, *What Is Globalization?* (Cambridge, U.K., 2000); John Tomlinson, *Globalization and Culture* (Chicago, 1999); Michael Beaud et al., *Mondialisation: Les mots et les choses* (Paris, 1999); J. Adda, *La mondialisation de l'économie* (Paris, 1998); and G. Lafay, *Comprendre la mondialisation* (Paris, 1999).

20. Beaud et al., *Mondialisation,* 7.

21. Mike Featherstone, ed., *Global Culture: Nationalism, Globalization, and Modernity* (London, 1990).

22. An excellent recent work (by nonhistorians) traces the historical development of forces of global transformation: David Held, Anthony McGrew, David Goldblatt, and Jonathan Perraton, *Global Transformations: Politics, Economics, and Culture* (Stanford, 1999).

CHAPTER I

1. Hedley Bull, *The Anarchical Society: A Study of Order in World Politics*, 2nd ed. (New York, 1995), 13.

2. The best treatment of these early instances of international cooperation is H. L. S. Lyons, *Internationalism in Europe* (Leiden, 1963). For an excellent study of the development of international law reflective of the new internationalism, see Hatsue Shinohara, "Forgotten Crusade: The Quest for a New International Law," Ph.D. diss., University of Chicago, 1996.

3. A good summary of the histories of some of these organizations is presented in Shiroyama Hideaki, *Kokusai gyōsei no kōzō* (The structure of international administration; Tokyo, 1997).

4. Saul H. Mendlovitz, ed., *On the Creation of a Just World Order* (New York, 1975), 161.

5. Paul Weindling, ed., *International Health Organisations and Movements, 1918–1939* (Cambridge, U.K., 1995), 5.

6. See Paul Schroeder, *The Transformation of European Politics, 1763–1848* (Oxford, 1994), 578.

7. John Boli and George M. Thomas, eds., *Constructing World Culture: International Nongovernmental Organizations since 1875* (Stanford, 1999), 22.

8. There is a growing body of literature on the origins and development of nongovernmental organizations in various countries. On the United States, where these organizations have probably had a longer history than anywhere else, see, for instance, the excellent anthology edited by David C. Hammack: *Making the Nonprofit Sector in the United States: A Reader* (Bloomington, Ind., 1998).

9. Irie Keishirō and Ōhata Tokushirō, *Gaikōshi teiyō* (An outline of diplomatic history; Tokyo, 1967), 27.

10. Ibid., 146–48.

11. John F. Hutchinson, "Disasters and the International Order: Earth-

quakes, Humanitarians, and the Ciraolo Project," *International History Review* 22, no. 1 (March 2000): 9.

12. Akira Iriye, *Cultural Internationalism and World Order* (Baltimore, 1997), 31.

13. Boli and Thomas, *Constructing World Culture*, 134–37.

14. Leila J. Rupp, *Worlds of Women: The Making of an International Women's Movement* (Princeton, 1997), 15, 51, 76.

15. See Barbara Keys, "Dictatorship of Sport," Ph.D. diss., Harvard University, 2001.

16. Kristin Hoganson, *Fighting for American Manhood: How Gender Politics Provoked the Spanish-American and Philippine-American Wars* (New Haven, 1998).

17. Lyman Cromwell White, *International Non-Governmental Organizations: Their Purposes, Methods, and Accomplishments* (New Brunswick, 1951), 147.

18. *La vie internationale* 1 (1912): 5.

19. David Held, Anthony McGrew, David Goldblatt, and Jonathan Perraton, *Global Transformations: Politics, Economics, and Culture* (Stanford, 1999), 155–57.

20. Ibid., 41.

21. Leonard S. Woolf, *International Government* (London, 1916), 149, 150.

22. Quoted in Akira Iriye, *Cultural Internationalism and World Order* (Baltimore, 1997), 15.

23. Ibid., 6.

24. M. P. Follett, *The New State: Group Organization the Solution of Popular Government* (London, 1918), 350–54.

25. Mendlovitz, *On the Creation*, 161.

26. Follett, *New State*, 344.

27. Weindling, *International Health Organisations*, 61.

28. Ibid., 6.

29. Iriye, *Cultural Internationalism*, 61.

30. Osborne Mance, *International Air Travel* (London, 1944), 1.

31. Shiroyama, *Kokusai*, 119–26.

32. Ibid., 114–17.

33. Hutchinson, "Disasters and the International Order," 1–36.

34. Mance, *International Air Travel*, 22.

35. Shiroyama, *Kokusai*, 154.

36. Sherman Strong Hayden, *The International Protection of Wild Life* (New York, 1942), 148–55.

37. Lynton Keith Caldwell, *International Environmental Policy from the Twentieth to the Twenty-First Century*, 3rd ed. (Durham, 1996), 145.

38. White, *International Non-Governmental Organizations*, 124–30.

39. Lyman Cromwell White, *The Structure of Private International Organizations* (Philadelphia, 1933), 273–75.

40. Weindling, *International Health Organisations*, 181.

41. Ibid., 183.

42. Information taken from the Internet: www.ines.gn.apc.org/ines/sci/h-origins.html, August 1999.

43. Ronald E. Stenning, *Church World Service: Fifty Years of Help and Hope* (New York, 1996), 2.

44. White, *International Non-Governmental Organizations*, 174–75.

45. The best study of the founding of the Institute is Tomoko Akami, "Experimenting with a New Order in the Pacific: The Institute of Pacific Relations in the U.S., Japan, and Australia, 1919–1945," Ph.D. diss., Australian National University, 1998. See especially 106–32.

46. Ibid., 236.

47. White, *Structure of Private International Organizations*, 11, 15.

48. Ibid., 15.

49. Boli and Thomas, *Constructing World Culture*, 50–51.

50. Rupp, *Worlds*, 16–18.

51. Quoted in ibid., 151.

52. Boli and Thomas, *Constructing World Culture*, 219.

53. Victor Klemperer, *I Will Bear Witness: A Diary of Nazi Years, 1933–1941* (New York, 1998), 120.

54. Weindling, *International Health Organisations*, 186.

55. Michael Sherry, *In the Shadow of War: The United States since the 1930s* (New Haven, 1995).

56. The best study of the Mexican cultural revolution during the 1930s is Mary Kay Vaughan, *Cultural Politics in Revolution: Teachers, Peasants, and Schools in Mexico, 1930–1940* (Tucson, 1997).

57. Erik J. Zürcher, *Turkey: A Modern History* (New York, 1998), 203–4.

58. Iriye, *Cultural Internationalism*, 103–8.

59. Ōshima Masanori, one of the Japanese delegates, published a report after the cruise. See *Teiyū rinri kōenshū* (Lectures on ethics), December 1939, 82–104.

60. White, *International Non-Governmental Organizations*, 167, 177, 187.

61. Keys, "Dictatorship of Sport," chap. 4.

62. Klemperer, *I Will Bear Witness*, 182.

63. White, *Structure of Private International Organizations*, 160; White, *International Non-Governmental Organizations*, 200.

64. In the economic sphere, we may have to add that the multinational trade policy being pursued by the United States government, under the direction of Secretary of State Cordell Hull, was one instance where a state took the initiative to revive the spirit of internationalism. On Hull's tariff revision proposals and policies, see Alfred E. Eckes Jr., *Opening America's Market: U.S. Foreign Trade Policy since 1776* (Chapel Hill, 1995).

65. White, *International Non-governmental Organizations*, 6–7.

CHAPTER 2

1. Leonard Woolf, *The War for Peace* (London, 1940), 36–37.

2. For the best treatment of the "long peace," see John Lewis Gaddis, *The Long Peace: Inquiries into the History of the Cold War* (New York, 1987). See also Campbell Craig, *Destroying the Village: Eisenhower and Thermonuclear War* (New York, 1998).

3. Elizabeth Clark Reiss, *American Council of Voluntary Agencies for Foreign Service* (New York, 1985), "The Organization," 1–10.

4. On the consumer revolution, see David Reynolds, *One World Divisible: A Global History since 1945* (New York, 2000), 122–23.

5. See Alfred E. Eckes Jr., *Opening America's Market: U.S. Foreign Trade Policy since 1776* (Chapel Hill, 1995).

6. Craig, *Destroying the Village*, p. 30.

7. The Brookings Seminar on Problems of American Foreign Policy (mimeographed; Washington, 1947), 1, 20.

8. Ibid., 18.

9. Henry R. Luce, "The American Century," reprinted in *Diplomatic History* 23, no. 2 (spring 1999): 159–71.

10. Wendell Willkie, *One World* (New York, 1943).

11. Lyman Cromwell White, *International Non-Governmental Organizations: Their Purposes, Methods, and Accomplishments* (New Brunswick, 1951), 305–11.

12. Zimmern memorandum, n.d., FO924/294/LC106, Foreign Office Archives, Public Record Office.

13. John G. Winant to Anthony Eden, memorandum, August 18, 1944, FO924/20/LC768, Foreign Office Archives, Public Record Office.

14. The best survey of the founding and the early activities of UNESCO is still Walter H. C. Laves and Charles A. Thomson, *UNESCO: Purpose, Progress, Prospects* (Bloomington, Ind., 1957). See also Charles A. Thomson and Walter H. C. Laves, *Cultural Relations and U.S. Foreign Policy* (Bloomington, Ind., 1963).

15. For the Salzburg seminar, see Oliver Schmidt, "Empire by Co-Optation," Ph.D. diss., Harvard University, 2000.

16. F. O. Matthieson, *From the Heart of Europe* (New York, 1948), 13–14.

17. *Asahi*, international ed., August 2, 1997, 20.

18. Tomoko Akami, "Experimenting with a New Order in the Pacific: The Institute of Pacific Relations in the U.S., Japan, and Australia, 1919–1945," Ph.D. diss., Australian National University, 1998.

19. Shiroyama Hideaki, *Kokusai gyōsei no kōzō* (The structure of international administration; Tokyo, 1997), 136–37.

20. See World Jewish Congress, *40 Years in Action: A Record of the World Jewish Congress, 1936–1976* (New York, 1976). This organization had a specific agenda — to provide support to Jews everywhere — and might not be comparable with other, more broadly conceived humanitarian agencies. Nevertheless, it was given consultative status by the United Nations Economic and Social Council as well as by UNESCO and was one of the most active international nongovernmental organizations in the early postwar era.

21. Maggie Black, *The Children and the Nations: Growing Up Together in the Postwar World* (New York, 1987), 16, 20.

22. Ronald E. Stenning, *Church World Service: Fifty Years of Help and Hope* (New York, 1996), 3–7. See also information available on the Internet: www.churchworldservice.org/history.html, February 2001.

23. John W. Bachman, *Together in Hope: 50 Years of Lutheran World Relief* (New York, 1995), 16.

24. Wallace J. Campbell, *The Story of CARE: A Personal Account* (New York, 1990), 110.

25. Ibid., 31–32.

26. Walter L. Hixon, *Parting the Curtain: Propaganda, Culture, and the Cold War, 1945–1961* (New York, 1997), 10.

27. For an excellent discussion of governmental involvement in international cultural affairs, see Frank Ninkovich, *The Diplomacy of Ideas: U.S. Foreign Policy and Cultural Relations, 1938–1950* (New York, 1978).

28. Volker Berghahn, "Philanthropy and Diplomacy in the 'American Cen-

tury'," *Diplomatic History* 23, no. 3 (summer 1999): 393–419. See also the same author's *America and the Intellectual Cold Wars in Europe: Shepard Stone between Philanthropy, Academy, and Diplomacy* (Princeton, 2001).

29. White, *International Non-Governmental Organizations*, viii, 287.

30. Dexter Masters and Katharine Way, eds., *One World or None* (London, 1946), 59, 154.

31. Lawrence S. Wittner, *One World or None: A History of the World Nuclear Disarmament Movement through 1945* (Stanford, 1993); Paul Boyer, *By the Bomb's Early Light: American Thought and Culture at the Dawn of the Atomic Age* (New York, 1985); Charles DeBenedetti, *The Peace Movement in American History* (Bloomington, Ind., 1980).

32. American Friends Service Committee, *American-Russian Relations: Some Constructive Considerations* (New Haven, 1950).

33. Saul H. Mendlovitz, *On the Creation of a Just World Order: Preferred Worlds for the 1990s* (New York, 1975), 161.

34. United Nations, *Yearbook on Human Rights for 1947* (New York, 1949), 449.

35. Jack Donnelly, *International Human Rights*, 2nd ed. (Boulder, 1998), 6.

36. See the annual volumes of the United Nations' *Yearbook on Human Rights* for texts of these constitutions.

37. Lynton Keith Caldwell, *International Environmental Policy: From the Twentieth Century to the Twenty-First Century*, 3rd ed. (Durham, N.C., 1996), 43, 50–51.

38. Evan Luard, *International Agencies: The Emerging Framework of Interdependence* (London, 1977), 242–43.

39. Brookings Seminar, 47–48.

40. For a systematic discussion of the evolution of the concept of development, see Michael Cowen and R. W. Shenton, *Doctrines of Development* (London, 1996).

CHAPTER 3

1. This paragraph is a simplified distillation of the vast literature on the Cold War. Among the most recent studies focusing on the Cold War, particularly impressive are John L. Gaddis, *We Now Know: Rethinking Cold War History* (New York, 1997); and Melvyn P. Leffler, *A Preponderance of Power: National Security, the Truman Administration, and the Cold War* (Stanford, 1992).

2. See, for instance, Daniel Yergin, *The Shattered Peace: Origins of the Cold War*, rev. ed. (New York, 1990), and Michael Sherry, *In the Shadow of War: The United States since the 1930s* (New Haven, 1995).

3. For a good discussion of this term, see Sherry, *In the Shadow*.

4. There is a vast literature on Cold War culture. Among the most recent works, see, for instance, Stephen J. Whitfield, *The Culture of the Cold War* (Baltimore, 1991); Elaine Tyler May, *Homeward Bound: American Families in the Cold War Era* (New York, 1988); and Bruce Cumings, *Parallax Visions: Making Sense of American–East Asian Relations at the End of the Century* (Durham, N.C., 1999).

5. A recent book by Aaron L. Friedberg, *In the Shadow of the Garrison State: America's Anti-Statism and Its Cold War Grand Strategy* (Princeton, 2000), stresses that civil society's "anti-statism" remained quite vigorous during the Cold War. Even so, the author readily admits that there were forces moving in the opposite direction, toward the establishment of a "garrison state."

6. The most recent, full treatment of the origins and development of European integration is Jeffrey William Vanke, "Europeanism and the European Economic Community, 1954–1966," Ph.D. diss., Harvard University, 1999. For an excellent discussion of Charles de Gaulle's conception of the European Economic Community that stresses nongeopolitical themes (agriculture, trade, economic modernization), see Andrew Moravcsik, "De Gaulle between Grain and *Grandeur*: The Political Economy of French EC Policy, 1958–1970," *Journal of Cold War Studies* 2, no. 2 (spring 2000): 3–43; and *Journal of Cold War Studies* 2, no. 3 (fall 2000): 4–68.

7. For an interesting discussion of the relationship between industrialization, geopolitics, and international organization, see Craig N. Murphy, *International Organization and Industrial Change: Global Governance since 1850* (New York, 1994).

8. For a good recent study of the Bandung conference, see Miyagi Taizō, *Bandung kaigi to Nihon no Ajia fukki* (The Bandung conference and Japan's return to Asia; Tokyo, 2001).

9. Evan Luard, *International Agencies: The Emerging Framework of Interdependence* (London, 1977), 123.

10. Ibid., 122–23.

11. Ibid., 80–81.

12. Lawrence S. Wittner, *One World or None: A History of the World Nuclear Disarmament Movement through 1953* (Stanford, 1993), 157–59.

13. Michael Schaller, *Altered States: The United States and Japan since the Occupation* (New York, 1997), 72–74.

14. Matthew Evangelista, *The Transnational Movement to End the Cold War* (Ithaca, 1999), 3.

15. Susan Lynn, *Progressive Women in Conservative Times: Racial Justice, Peace, and Feminism, 1945 to the 1960s* (New Brunswick, 1992), 97.

16. Harriet Human Alonso, *Peace as a Women's Issue: A History of the U.S. Movement for World Peace and Women's Rights* (Syracuse, 1993), 205.

17. Micael Brown and John May, *The Greenpeace Story* (London, 1989), 8.

18. Milton S. Katz, *Ban the Bomb: A History of SANE, the Committee for a Sane Nuclear Policy* (New York, 1987), 27.

19. Walter L. Hixson, *Parting the Curtain: Propaganda, Culture, and the Cold War, 1945–1961* (New York, 1997).

20. On the "people-to-people program," the best study is still John E. Juergensmeyer, *The President, the Foundations, and the People-to-People Program* (Indianapolis, 1965).

21. Quoted in Tina Klein, "Sentimental Education: Winning American Minds for the Cold War in Asia," unpublished paper, 2000, 66.

22. Ibid., 161.

23. Charles A. Thomson and Walter H. C. Laves, *Cultural Relations and U.S. Foreign Policy* (Indianapolis, 1963), 128.

24. American Friends Service Committee, *American-Russian Relations: Some Constructive Considerations* (New Haven, 1950).

25. American Friends Service Committee, *Meeting the Russians: American Quakers Visit the Soviet Union* (Philadelphia, 1956), 12, 43, 91.

26. Stephen Castles and Mark J. Miller, *The Age of Migration: International Population Movements in the Modern World*, 2nd ed. (London, 1998), 73.

27. Paul F. Basch, *Textbook of International Health*, 2nd ed. (New York, 1999), 61–62.

28. Luard, *International Agencies*, 155; Kohayagawa Takatoshi, ed., *Kokusai hoken iryō kyōryoku nyūmon* (Guide to cooperation in the international health field; Tokyo, 1998), 154–55.

29. Information obtained through the Internet: www.ines.gn.apc.org/ines/sci/welcome.html, August 1999.

30. Information obtained through the Internet: www.brothersbrother.com/founder.html, February 2001.

31. Charles Condamines, *L'aide humanitaire entre la politique et les affaires* (Paris, 1989), 23.

32. Akiie Henry Ninomiya, *Ajia no shōgaisha to kokusai NGO* (Asia's disabled and the international nongovernmental organizations; Tokyo, 1999), 18.

33. Luard, *International Agencies*, 244–45.

34. The relationship between developmental assistance and the Cold War is a complex issue that is attracting the attention of an increasing number of historians. For a recent scholarly assessment, see Nick Cullather, "Development? It's History," *Diplomatic History* 24, no. 4 (fall 2000): 641–53. The article contains a valuable critique of the vast literature on modernization and development, but its Cold War–centered perspective differs from the approach adopted by this book.

35. Miyagi, *Bandung kaigi*, 144–46.

36. Society for International Development home page: sidint.org/about/ 40yearsI.htm, August 1999.

37. Oliver Schmidt, "Empire by Co-Optation," Ph.D. diss., Harvard University, 1999, chap. 5, 14, 30.

38. Brian Smith, *More than Altruism: The Politics of Private Foreign Aid* (Princeton, 1990), 53.

39. Ibid., 4, 58.

40. For a critical view of modernization theory, see Bruce Cumings, *Parallax Visions*; and Shinobu Takashi, ed., *Kankyō to kaihatsu no kokusai seiji* (The problems of the environment and development in international politics; Tokyo, 1999), 20–21.

41. Daniel Lerner, "Modernization," *International Encyclopedia of the Social Sciences* (New York, 1968), vol. 10, 386.

42. See Joseph S. Tulchin, *Argentina and the United States: A Conflicted Relationship* (Boston, 1990), 118.

43. Walter Johnson and Francis J. Colligan, *The Fulbright Program: A History* (Chicago, 1965), 345.

44. Ibid., 97–103.

45. This is the argument of Schmidt, "Empire by Co-optation."

46. David Lodge, *Out of the Shelter* (London, 1970), 152.

47. Neal Rosendorf has documented the flourishing tourist industry that brought thousands of Americans to Spain during and subsequent to the 1950s. Although that country was still ruled by Francisco Franco, this tourism served to

redefine U.S.-Spanish relations in ways that more formal ties, such as Spain's joining the North Atlantic Treaty Organization, could not have. See Rosendorf, "Hollywood in Madrid," Ph.D. diss., Harvard University, 2000.

48. Johnson and Colligan, *Fulbright Program,* 344.

49. See "Seikei–St. Paul's, 1949–1999," publication of Seikei High School (Tokyo, 1999).

50. See Asada Sadao's essay on the origins of the Grew Foundation appended to the Japanese translation of Waldo Heinrics, *American Ambassador: Joseph C. Grew and the Development of the United States Diplomatic Tradition* (Tokyo, 1999).

51. On textbook revision in Europe, see John E. Farquharson and Stephen C. Holt, *Europe from Below: An Assessment of Franco-German Popular Contacts* (London, 1975), 65–66, 169.

52. On UNESCO's activities in this period, see Walter H. C. Laves and Charles A. Thomson, *UNESCO: Purposes, Progress, Prospects* (Bloomington, 1957).

53. Miyagi, *Bandung kaigi,* 151.

54. Uno Shigeaki et al., eds., *Gendai Chūgoku no rekishi, 1949–1985* (A history of contemporary China, 1949–1985; Tokyo, 1986), 140–46; Uno Shigeaki and Amako Satoshi, eds., *20 seiki no Chūgoku* (China in the twentieth century; Tokyo, 1994), 349–50.

55. Leila J. Rupp, *Worlds of Women: The Making of an International Women's Movement* (Princeton, 1997), 15.

56. World Jewish Congress, memorandum, October 5, 1951, UN Commission on Human Rights papers.

57. John Boli and George M. Thomas, eds., *Constructing World Culture: International Nongovernmental Organizations since 1875* (Stanford, 1999), 119.

58. Minutes of meetings of working group, April 26–27, 1951, Human Rights Commission papers.

59. Daniele Archibugi, David Held, and Martin Kohler, eds., *Re-imagining Political Community: Studies in Cosmopolitan Democracy* (Stanford, 1998), 314.

60. Minutes of subcommittee meeting, October 3, 1952, Human Rights Commission papers.

61. Margaret E. Keck and Kathryn Sikkink, *Activists beyond Borders: Advocacy Networks in International Politics* (Ithaca, 1998), 11.

62. Lynton Keith Caldwell, *International Environmental Policy: From the Twentieth to the Twenty-First Century,* 3rd ed. (Durham, 1996), 144.

63. Ibid., 54.

CHAPTER 4

1. Union of International Associations, *International Organization: Abbreviations and Addresses, 1984–85* (Munich, 1985), 508.

2. I am indebted to Alicia Ingalls's unpublished paper, "American Friends Service Committee and VISA" (2001), for information concerning VISA's activities in South Vietnam.

3. Atlee and Winifred Beechy, *Vietnam: Who Cares?* (Scottdale, Pa., 1968), 10; Mary Sue Rosenberger, *Harmless as Doves: Witnessing for Peace in Vietnam* (Elgin, Ill., 1988), 3.

4. Beechy, *Vietnam*, 19–20. The authors mention a number of church groups and other nongovernmental organizations that were then involved in volunteer work in Vietnam: the Christian and Missionary Alliance, the Southern Baptists, the Seventh-Day Adventists, the East Asia Christian Conference, the Quakers, the Catholic Church, the Eastern Mennonite Board of Missions and Charities, Project Concern, World Vision, Christian Children's Fund, Christian Children's Federation, Foster Parents, CARE, International Voluntary Service, and International Social Service.

5. Rosenberger, *Harmless as Doves*, 6.

6. Information taken from the Internet: www.ines.gn.ape.org/ines/sci/welcome, August 1999.

7. Elizabeth Clark Reiss, *The American Council of Voluntary Agencies for Foreign Service* (New York, 1985), "IV. Committee on Development Assistance," 72.

8. Elizabeth Cobbs Hoffman, *All You Need Is Love: The Peace Corps and the Spirit of the 1960s* (Cambridge, Mass., 1998), 5, 25.

9. Information obtained from the Internet: www.anera.org/index2.shtml, February 2001.

10. Charles Condamines, *L'aide humanitaire entre la politique et les affaires* (Paris, 1989), 23–24.

11. Ibid., 24.

12. Shinobu Takashi, ed., *Kankyō to kaihatsu no kokusai seiji* (Problems of the environment and development in international politics; Tokyo, 1999), 70.

13. Evan Luard, *International Agencies: The Emerging Framework of Interdependence* (London, 1977), 247.

14. Ibid., 245.

15. Takeda Isami, *Imin nanmin enjo no seijigaku* (The politics of immigration, refugees, and aid; Tokyo, 1991), 132–37.

16. For information on Japan's nongovernmental organizations, see Japan NGO Center for International Cooperation, *NGO Directory '98* (Tokyo, 1998).

17. See Carlos R. S. Milani's essay in Michael Beaud et al., eds., *Mondialisation: Les mots et les choses* (Paris, 1999), 175.

18. Information obtained from the Internet: www.sidint.org/about/40yearsI, August 1999.

19. *International Organizations,* 508.

20. Hoffman, *All You Need,* 149–50.

21. Reiss, *American Council,* "IV. Committee on Development Assistance," 87.

22. Brian Smith, *More Than Altruism: The Politics of Private Foreign Aid* (Princeton, 1990), 62.

23. Harold K. Jacobson, *Networks of Interdependence: International Organizations and the Global Political System* (New York, 1984), 317.

24. Amnesty International, *Report 1997* (New York, 1997), opposite title page.

25. See Mike Featherstone, ed., *Global Culture: Nationalism, Globalization and Modernity* (London, 1990), 27.

26. Lisa McGirr, *Suburban Warriors: The Origins of the New American Right* (Princeton, 2001).

27. Statement quoted from course syllabus, University of Chicago, 1988.

28. Michael Brown and John May, *The Greenpeace Story* (London, 1989), 12–14.

29. Matthew Evangelista, *Unarmed Forces: The Transnational Movement to End the Cold War* (Ithaca, 1999), chap. 4.

30. Luard, *International Agencies,* 125–27.

31. Robert Lamb, *Promising the Earth* (London, 1996), 23.

32. Margaret Keck and Cathryn Sikkink, *Activists beyond Borders: Advocacy Networks in International Politics* (Ithaca, 1998), 11.

33. Lynton Keith Caldwell, *International Environmental Policy from the Twentieth to the Twenty-First Century,* 3rd ed. (Durham, 1996), 40.

34. Ibid., 123.

35. Robert G. Darst, "The Internationalization of Environmental Protection in the U.S.S.R. and Its Successor States," in *The Internationalization of Environmental Protection,* ed. Miranda A. Schreurs and Elizabeth C. Economy (Cambridge, U.K., 1997), 104–5.

36. Philip H. Coombs, *The Fourth Dimension of Foreign Policy: Educational and Cultural Affairs* (New York, 1964), 92–93.

37. Ibid., 94.

38. UNESCO, *Appraisal of the Major Project on Mutual Appreciation of Eastern and Western Cultural Values, 1957–1966* (Paris, 1968), 5, 9, 49–57, 81, 98, 101, 102.

39. David Held, Anthony McGrew, David Goldblatt, and Jonathan Perraton, *Global Transformations: Politics, Economics, and Culture* (Stanford, 1999), 361.

40. See A. W. Coats, ed., *The Post-1945 Internationalization of Economics* (Durham, 1997).

41. Ibid., 123–24, 132.

42. The papers presented at the conference were subsequently published as *Pearl Harbor as History*, ed. Dorothy Borg and Shumpei Okamoto (New York, 1976).

43. Joan Scruton, *Stoke Mandeville Road to the Paralympics* (Aylesbury, 1998), 308, 12.

44. Matsumura Masayoshi, *Kokusai kōryūshi* (A history of international exchanges; Tokyo, 1996), 389.

CHAPTER 5

1. Eric Hobsbawm, *The Age of Extremes: A History of the World, 1914–1991* (New York, 1994).

2. Union of International Associations, ed., *International Organizations: Abbreviations and Addresses, 1984–1985* (Munich, 1985), 508.

3. Hobsbawm, *Age of Extremes*, 277.

4. See, for instance, Helen Milner, *Resisting Protectionism: Global Industries and the Politics of International Trade* (Princeton, 1988).

5. Michel Beaud et al., *Mondialisation: Les mots et les choses* (Paris, 1999), 176–77.

6. See Leszek Kolakowski, "The Search for Community," in *Experiencing the Twentieth Century*, ed. Nobutoshi Hagihara et al. (Tokyo, 1985), 155–67.

7. David Held, Anthony McGrew, David Goldblatt, and Jonathan Perraton, *Global Transformations: Politics, Economics, and Culture* (Stanford, 1999), 301.

8. For a good example, see a study of a community organization in Bombay in *Non-Governmental Organizations: Performance and Accountability*, ed. Michael Edwards and David Hulme (London, 1995), 83–93.

9. For an excellent overview of the emerging civil society in Asia and the Pacific, see Tadashi Yamamoto, ed., *Emerging Civil Society in the Asia Pacific Community* (Tokyo, 1996).

10. *International Organizations*, 548.

11. See Johan Galtung's essay in *On the Creation of a Just World Order: Preferred Worlds for the 1990s*, ed. Saul H. Mendlovitz (New York, 1975), 151–88.

12. Evan Luard, *International Agencies: The Emerging Framework of Interdependence* (London, 1977).

13. Harold K. Jacobson, *Networks of Interdependence: International Organizations and the Global Political System* (New York, 1979), viii.

14. Margaret E. Keck and Kathryn Sikkink, *Activists beyond Borders: Advocacy Networks in International Politics* (Ithaca, 1998), 11.

15. Harriet Alonso, *Peace as a Women's Issue: A History of the U.S. Movement for World Peace and Women's Rights* (Syracuse, 1993), 227.

16. Keck and Sikkink, *Activists beyond Borders*, 175.

17. Human Rights Watch, information obtained from www.hrw.org/annual-report/1998/20years2.html, August 1999.

18. Henry Akiie Ninomiya, *Ajia no shōgaisha to kokusai NGO* (Asia's disabled and international NGOs; Tokyo, 1999), 19–24.

19. Joan Scruton, *Stoke Mandeville Road to the Paralympics* (Aylesbury, 1998), 159.

20. Amnesty International, *Report 1997* (New York, 1997), 378.

21. Keck and Sikkink, *Activists beyond Borders*, 96–98.

22. Luard, *International Agencies*, 181.

23. Information taken from the Internet: www.africare.org/about/history/history.html, February 2001.

24. Information taken from the Internet: www.fh.org/learn/aboutus.shtml, February 2001.

25. Kohayagawa Takatoshi, ed., *Kokusai hoken iryō kyōryoku nyūmon* (Introduction to international cooperation in health care; Tokyo, 1998), 87–88.

26. Information obtained from the Internet: www.msf.org/intweb99/library/history.html, August 1999.

27. Charles Condamines, *L'aide humanitaire entre la politique et les affaires* (Paris, 1989), 21–27.

28. Ibid., 25.

29. Information taken from the Internet: www.cgiar.org/history.html, August 1999.

30. Information taken from the Internet: www.sidint.org/about/40yearsII.html, August 1999.

31. Lynton Keith Caldwell, *International Environmental Policy from the Twentieth to the Twenty-First Century*, 3rd ed. (Durham, 1996), 64.

32. Ibid., 81.

33. Jonathan Hewitt, ed., *European Environmental Almanac* (London, 1995), 20–23.

34. Robert Lamb, *Promising the Earth* (London, 1996), 22–23.

35. Keck and Sikkink, *Activists beyond Borders*, 11.

36. Information taken from the Internet: www.asoc.org/general/1998.html, August 1999.

37. Lamb, *Promising the Earth*, 68–70.

38. Caldwell, *International Environmental Policy*, 304.

39. Shinobu Takashi, ed., *Kankyō to kaihatsu no kokusai seiji* (The international politics of environmentalism and development; Tokyo, 1999), 162–63.

40. Nikolai Sivachev and Nikolai Yakovlev, *The Soviet Union and the United States* (Chicago, 1977).

41. The information in this and the following paragraphs is taken from J. M. Mitchell, *International Cultural Relations* (London, 1986), 116–27.

42. Ibid., 169.

43. Ibid., 127.

44. Information taken from the Internet: www.afs.org/efil/introduction.html, August 1999.

45. The information on these organizations is taken from Alliance for International Educational and Cultural Exchange, ed., *International Exchange Locator* (Washington, 1994).

46. Mitchell, *International Cultural Relations*, 64.

CHAPTER 6

1. See, for instance, William R. Keylor, *The Twentieth-Century World: An International History*, 3rd ed. (New York, 1996). Chapter 12 is titled "The Resurgence of East-West Tension (1975–1985)."

2. Johan Galtung, *The True Worlds: A Transnational Perspective* (New York, 1980).

3. To cite a few examples from the books published during the 1980s, Trygve

Mathisen, *Sharing Destiny: A Study of Global Integration* (Oslo, 1984), and Christer Jónson, *International Aviation and the Politics of Regime Change* (London, 1987), examined intergovernmental organizations, while J. M. Mitchell, *International Cultural Relations* (London, 1986), and Jack Donnelly, *Universal Human Rights in Theory and Practice* (Ithaca, 1989), dealt with transnational phenomena.

4. See, for instance, Roland Robertson, *Globalization: Social Theory and Global Culture* (London, 1992); Mike Featherstone, *Undoing Culture: Globalization, Postmodernism, and Identity* (London, 1995); Arjun Appadurai, *Modernity at Large: Cultural Dimensions of Globalization* (Minneapolis, 1998); James H. Mittelman, ed., *Globalization: Critical Reflections* (Boulder, 1997); John Tomlinson, *Globalization and Culture* (Chicago, 1999); Peter Stalker, *Workers without Frontiers: The Impact of Globalization on International Migration* (Boulder, 2000); Will Hutton and Anthony Giddens, eds., *On the Edge: Living with Global Capitalism* (London, 2000); and Richard Rorty, *Achieving Our Country* (Cambridge, Mass., 1998). One of the most comprehensive accounts of globalization is David Held, Anthony McGrew, David Goldblatt, and Jonathan Perraton, *Global Transformations: Politics, Economics, and Culture* (Stanford, 1999). One historian who has written on both geopolitical developments and globalization at the end of the century is Jean Heffer. See his *La fin de Xxe siècle: De 1973 à nos jours* (Paris, 2000).

5. Kenneth Boulding, *Three Faces of Power* (Newbury Park, Calif., 1989), 244.

6. Michael King, *Death of the Rainbow Warrior* (Auckland, 1986), 48.

7. Harriet Hyman Alonso, *Peace as a Women's Issue: A History of the U.S. Movement for World Peace and Women's Rights* (Syracuse, 1993), 249.

8. On the impact of the Pugwash movement on the ending of the Cold War, see Matthew Evangelista, *Unarmed Forces: The Transnational Movement to End the Cold War* (Ithaca, 1999).

9. Ibid., 255.

10. The role of nongovernmental organizations in Arab-Israeli relations awaits systematic study. I am basing my general statements on personal observations made while in Israel in 1994.

11. See Motoko Mekata's essay in *The Third Force: The Rise of Transnational Civil Society*, ed. Ann M. Florini (Tokyo, 2000), 142–76.

12. Information taken from the Internet: www.healthnet.org/cihc, February 2001.

13. Stephen Castles and Mark J. Miller, *The Age of Migration: International Population Movements in the Modern World*, 2nd ed. (London, 1993), 87.

14. *Amnesty International Report 1997* (New York, 1997), 5–6.

15. SVA, ed., *Ajia, kyōsei, NGO* (Asia, coexistence, NGOs; Tokyo, 1996), describes the activities by a volunteer organization established by the Sōdō sect of Buddhism.

16. Médecins sans Frontières, *Faces aux crises* (Paris, 1994), chapter 1.

17. Ibid., chap. 10.

18. For information concerning Japanese nongovernmental organizations, I am indebted to various data collected by the Japan Center for International Exchange and by the Center for Global Partnership of the Japan Foundation.

19. Laurie Garrett, "Calling for a Global Solution: AIDS Fund Poses Worldwide Challenge," *Newsday*, June 17, 2001. Available through the Internet: www.aegis.com/news/newsday/2001/ND10607.html.

20. Akiie Henry Ninomiya, *Ajia no shōgaisha to kokusai NGO* (Asia's disabled and international NGOs; Tokyo, 1999), 24–25.

21. Joan Scruton, *Stoke Mandeville Road to the Paralympics: Fifty Years of History* (Aylesbury, 1998), 332–33.

22. Ibid., 347.

23. Ninomiya, *Ajia*, 111–17.

24. Held et al., *Global Transformations*, 202–3.

25. Ibid., 213.

26. I am indebted to Lee Hampton's senior thesis, Harvard University, 2001, for information concerning UNICEF's involvement in polio eradication programs.

27. J. P. Deler, Y. A. Fauré, A. Pveteau, and P. J. Roca, eds., *ONG et développement: Société, économie, politique* (Paris, 1998).

28. Information obtained from the Internet: www.jsi.com/idr/IS.html, February 2001.

29. M. Holt Ruffian and Daniel Waugh, eds., *Civil Society in Central Asia* (Seattle, 1999), 58–60.

30. Michael Edwards and David Hulme, eds., *Non-Governmental Organisations: Performance and Accountability* (London, 1995), 65.

31. Florini, *Third Force*, 83–84.

32. Lynton Keith Caldwell, *International Environmental Policy: From the Twentieth to the Twenty-First Century*, 3rd ed. (Durham, 1996), 243.

33. Information taken from the Internet: www.cgiar.org/history.html, February 2001.

34. Margaret E. Keck and Kathryn Sikkink, *Activists beyond Borders: Advocacy Networks in International Politics* (Ithaca, 1998), 11.

35. Jonathan Hewett, ed., *European Environmental Almanac* (London, 1995), 24.

36. Thomas G. Weiss and Leon Gordenker, eds., *NGOs, the UN, and Global Governance* (Boulder, 1996), 111.

37. Hewett, *European Environmental Almanac*, 11.

38. Ibid., 13.

39. Caldwell, *International Environmental Policy*, 164.

40. Yamamura Tsunetoshi, *Kankyō NGO* (Environmental NGOs; Tokyo, 1998), 40.

41. Ibid., 72–79.

42. Ibid., 257–83.

43. Thomas Risse-Kappen, ed., *Bringing Transnational Relations Back In: Non-State Actors, Domestic Structures, and International Institutions* (Cambridge, U.K., 1995), 246.

44. Shinobu Takashi, ed., *Kankyō to kaihatsu no kokusai seiji* (International politics of environment and development; Tokyo, 1999), 169–72.

45. Caldwell, *International Environmental Policy*, 320.

46. Weiss and Gordenker, *NGOs*, 141.

47. Ibid., 149–50.

48. Ibid., 17.

49. Keck and Sikkink, *Activists beyond Borders*, 180.

50. "Child Pornography: An International Perspective" (paper presented at the World Congress against Commercial Sexual Exploitation of Children, Stockholm, 1996), 2.

51. Ibid., 22.

52. See Warren I. Cohen and Akira Iriye, eds., *The Great Powers in East Asia, 1953–1960* (New York, 1990).

53. Unfortunately, the papers presented at these conference have been collected and published together only in Japanese: Hosoya Chihiro et al., eds., *Taiheiyō sensō* (The Pacific war; Tokyo, 1993); and Hosoya Chihiro et al., eds., *Taiheiyō sensō no shūketsu* (The ending of the Pacific war; Tokyo, 1997).

54. See Japan Foundation, ed., *The End of the Century: The Future in the Past* (Tokyo, 1995).

55. Caroline Reeves, "An Overview: Sino-American Academic Exchange since Tiananmen," unpublished paper, 1990, 3–4.

56. Tadashi Yamamoto, ed., *Emerging Civil Society in the Asia Pacific Community* (Tokyo, 1995), 102–6.

57. Akira Iriye, *Cultural Internationalism and World Order* (Baltimore, 1997).

58. Center for Global Partnership, "Information Packet" for Third Advisory Committee Meeting, May 1992.

59. Mike Featherstone's essay is in *Globalization*, ed. Roland Robertson; see also Featherstone's introductory essay in *Global Culture: Nationalism, Globalization, and Modernity*, ed. Mike Featherstone (London, 1990).

60. Held and McGrew, cited in James Mayall, "Globalization and the Future of Nationalism," in Japan Foundation, *End of the Century*, 441; Samuel P. Huntington, "The Clash of Civilizations," *Foreign Affairs* (summer 1993): 2–26.

CONCLUSION

1. Michael Howard and Wm. Roger Louis, eds., *The Oxford History of the Twentieth Century* (Oxford, 1998), 334–35. It would be interesting to investigate the extent to which the concept of globalization has penetrated school textbooks. A cursory look at some high school history texts in the United States indicates that as yet, few, if any, of them use the term. See, for instance, one of the most widely read world history textbooks that has been used as the basis for international baccalaureate examinations: R. R. Palmer and Joel Colton, *A History of the Modern World*, 8th ed. (New York, 1995). The book chronicles international developments during the 1990s in its last chapter, using the words "global" and "globally" frequently, but globalization as such is nowhere discussed.

2. James H. Mittelman, ed., *Globalization: Critical Reflections* (Boulder, 1997), 3. Of course, such a definition of globalization may be applied to global developments since the nineteenth century, even including imperialism. This is an example where a historical perspective becomes crucial.

3. Richard Falk, *Predatory Globalization: A Critique* (Cambridge, U.K., 1999).

4. When Jubilee 2000, a nongovernmental organization dedicated to persuading the richer nations to forgive their loans to poorer countries, opened its Web site, four thousand individuals from Europe, the Western Hemisphere, Asia, and Africa signed on, each of whom would in turn spread information by e-mail to many others. Of course, some areas in the world were not thus "wired," and in such cases it was imperative that local nongovernmental organizations should exist and be willing to spread the message. See *Asahi*, April 30, 2000, 1.

5. American Friends Service Committee, *Quaker Service Bulletin* 81, no. 1 (spring 2000): 1, 3.

6. Doctors without Borders, in a fund-raising appeal, 2000.

7. Norwegian Nobel Committee to author, May 8, 2001.

8. *Le Monde*, August 19–20, 2001, 1.

9. *Asahi shinbun*, international ed., April 19, 2000, 18.

10. *Asahi shinbun*, international ed., October 16, 1999, 6.

11. *Nihon keizai shinbun*, October 26, 1999, 17.

12. *Asahi shinbun*, October 29, 1999, 2.

13. *Asahi shinbun*, international ed., April 7, 1999, 3.

14. *Asahi shinbun*, international ed., January 1, 1999, 13.

15. For Salamon's basic methodology and definitions, see Lester M. Salamon and Helmut K. Anheier, *The Emerging Nonprofit Sector: An Overview* (Manchester, 1996); and the same authors' *Defining the Nonprofit Sector: A Cross-National Analysis* (Manchester, 1997).

16. J. A. Hobson, "The Ethics of Internationalism," *International Journal of Ethics* 17, no. 1 (October 1906): 19–21, quoted in Hugh McNeal, "Imagining Globalization," unpublished paper, 2000, 1.

17. H. G. Wells, *An Englishman Looks at the World* (London, 1914), 19–20.

18. *Asahi shinbun*, international ed., February 24, 1999, 4.

19. On the internationalization of human rights, see Jack Donnelly, *International Human Rights*, 2nd ed. (Boulder, 1998).

20. Daniele Archibugi, David Held, and Martin Köhler, eds., *Re-Imagining Political Community* (Stanford, 1998), 22.

21. An extremely insightful essay on these and related questions is offered by Klaus Eder and Bernhard Giesen, German sociologists: "Citizenship and the Making of a European Society" (paper presented at Harvard University, February 2001).

22. Michael Edwards and David Hulme, eds., *Non-Governmental Organisations: Performance and Accountability* (London, 1995), 3.

23. "NGOs: Sins of the Secular Missionaries," *Economist*, January 29, 2000, 27.

24. Edwards and Hulme, *Non-Governmental Organisations*, 5.

25. Ibid., 6.

26. Ibid., 117.

27. Ibid., 5.

28. *Economist*, January 29, 2000, 25.

29. On Transparency International, see Fredrik Galtung's essay in *The Third*

Force: The Rise of Transnational Civil Society, ed. Ann M. Florini (Tokyo, 2000), 17–48.

30. *Nihon keizai shinbun*, December 8, 1999, 29.

31. For examples, see *Nihon keizai shinbun*, January 12, 2000, 1.

32. *Yomiuri shinbun*, January 24, 2000, evening ed., 6.

INDEX

European Economic Community, 62–63

European Federation for Intercultural Learning, 155

European integration, 39, 62–63, 86, 205, 221n6

Evangelista, Matthew, 69, 116

Falk, Richard, 92, 196

Fanon, Franz, 154

Featherstone, Mike, 192

Federation of Atomic Scientists, 53–54

Florence Nightingale International Foundation, 34–35

Follett, Mary P., 20–21

Food for the Hungry International, 139

Ford Foundation, 53, 79–80, 82, 138

Fourth World Conference on Women (Beijing, 1995), 185

Franco, Francisco, 33

French-American Foundation, 155

Frères des Hommes, 102

Friendship Force, 155

Friends of the Animals, 181

Friends of the Earth, 146–47

Friends' World Committee for Consultation, 43

Fulbright Association, 155

Fulbright program, 46, 83, 85

Gaither, H. Rowan, 80

Galtung, Johan, 133, 159

Geopolitical focus. *See* Conflict paradigm

German Historical Institute, 155

Global community, defined, 8, 192–93

Global consciousness. *See* Globalization; Internationalism

Global Forum, 178–79

Globalization, defined, 7–8, 12, 196–97, 201–2, 233n2. *See also* Internationalism

Global Transformations (Held), 172

Gordenker, Leon, 185

Greenpeace, 70, 116, 161, 178, 181–82, 208

Grew, Joseph C., 85

Handicap International, 162

Haverford College, 79

Health care, 15, 43–44, 74–76, 139–41, 173

Held, David, 172, 193, 205

Helsinki Accord (1975), 136, 150

Helsinki Watch, 136

Hideki, Yukawa, 68

Hingson, Robert Andrew, 76

Hiroshima conference (1955), 68–69

Historic and heritage preservation, 148, 152

Hixson, Walter, 71

Hobsbawn, Eric, 126–27

Hobson, J. A., 201

Hoffman, Elizabeth Cobbs, 101

Hoganson, Kristin, 16

Hulme, David, 206–7

Humane Society, 181

Humanitarian relief work, 14, 26–27, 32, 38–40, 48–52, 74–77, 98–102, 138–41, 163–66

Human rights advocacy, 56–57, 77, 89–93, 111–13, 134–41, 163, 166, 204–5

Human Rights Watch, 162

Hunger Corps, 139

Huntington, Samuel, 193

Hutchinson, John F., 14, 23–24

Huxley, Julian, 118

Imperialism, 18, 201–2

Industrial Development Organization, 104

Institute for Development Research, 174

Institute of Pacific Relations, 27–28, 47

Intellectual Cooperation Organization, 44

Intelstat, 119

InterAction, 174

International Frequency Registration
Board, 48
International Government (Woolf), 18
International House of Japan, 189
International Institute for Intellectual
Cooperation, 22, 34
Internationalism, 9–12, 18–20, 36,
113–16, 127–29, 133–34, 149, 186,
201; cultural, 25, 44–47, 83–89,
152–53, 156, 191; defined, 9–10;
non-western, 11, 22, 29–30, 64, 98,
131–32, 181. *See also* Globalization;
Third World perspective
International Labor Organization, 21,
34, 43, 91, 169
International League for the Rights of
Man, 90
International Medical Assistance, 102
International Migration Service, 34
International Monetary Fund, 123,
173, 197
International nongovernmental
organizations: accountability of, 110,
206–7; defined, 2–3, 211–12n2;
early examples of, 25–28; numbers
of, 3, 11, 20–21, 28, 42–43, 55, 97–
98, 118, 129, 133, 174, 177–78, 200,
212n3; relationship to states, 13–16,
52–53, 80, 109–10, 174–75, 182,
203, 207
International Olympic Committee, 16,
35, 125
International organizations: funding
of, 12, 53, 80, 82, 107, 110, 138, 167;
and globalization, 5–8, 30–33, 196–
97; relations among, 23–24, 43–44,
108, 138, 200–209; types of, 1–4.
See also Intergovernmental organizations; International nongovernmental organizations
International Red Cross, 13–14, 24, 52
International Refugee Organization, 49
International Relief Union, 23–24
International Research Council, 25
International Sanitary Council, 10

International Shipping Conference, 24
International Student Exchange
Program, 155
International Telegraph Union, 10, 22
International Union for Child
Welfare, 90
International Union for Conservation
of Nature and Natural Resources,
57, 118, 147, 178, 182
International Union for the Protection
of Nature, 93
International Voluntary Service, 76
International Whaling Commission,
57
International Women's Health
Coalition, 184

Jacobson, Harold K., 3, 133–34
Japan Center for International
Exchange, 189
Japan Committee against Atomic and
Hydrogen Bombs, 69
Japan Foundation, 155, 189, 192
Jubilee 2000, 233n4
Jung, Kim Dae, 199

Keck, Margaret, 118, 134, 177
Kemal, Mustafa, 33
Kennedy, John F., 100, 105, 106–7
Kennedy, Paul, 158
Keys, Barbara, 35
Khagram, Sanjeev, 175–76
Khrushchev, Nikita, 60
Kissinger, Henry, 158
Klemperer, Victor, 32, 35
Korean War, 66
Kyoto global warming conference
(1997), 180

Labor and Socialist International, 29
Landmines, 162
League of Nations, 21–22, 24–25, 30,
34, 42, 44, 56
League of Nations Health
Organization, 21, 34

Compositor: BookMatters, Berkeley
Text: 10/15 Janson
Display: Janson
Printer and Binder: Maple-Vail Book Manufacturing Group